The Memphis Cookbook

Contains over 700 tasted and tested old
southern family recipes.

JUNIOR LEAGUE
OF MEMPHIS

The Junior League of Memphis, Inc. is an organization of
women committed to promoting voluntarism and improving
the community through the effective action and leadership of
trained volunteers. Its purpose is exclusively educational and
charitable.

Suggested Retail Price $9.95

Copies of THE MEMPHIS COOKBOOK may be obtained by addressing Memphis Junior League Publications, 2711 Union Avenue, Extended, Memphis, Tennessee, 38112. Price $9.95, plus $1.75 each postage and handling. Tenn. residents add 77¢ sales tax.

These prices are subject to change without notice.

Printed in the United States of America by
S. C. TOOF & CO.
670 S. COOPER ST.
MEMPHIS TN 38104

TABLE OF CONTENTS

FOREWORD

Since Forewords are usually wordy, seldom-read epistles, we have decided to dispense with it here. In its place is printed something more entertaining (if not entirely respectful), yet pertinent to the subject at hand. It is taken from a cook book of the 1800's and appreciatively dedicated to the long-suffering men in our lives who have tested, tasted and typed with us, until a lowly peanut butter sandwich is King's Fare to them, if they can just eat in peace and tranquility from an uncluttered table.

How To Cook A Husband

A good many husbands are utterly spoiled by mismanagement in cooking and so are not tender and good. Some women keep them constantly in hot water; others let them freeze by their carelessness and indifference. Some keep them in a stew with irritating ways and words. Some wives keep them pickled, while others waste them shamefully. It cannot be supposed that any husband will be tender and good when so managed, but they are really delicious when prepared properly.

In selecting a husband, you should not be guided by the silvery appearance as in buying a mackerel; nor by the golden tint as if you wanted salmon. Do not go to the market for him as the best ones are always brought to the door. Be sure to select him yourself as tastes differ. It is far better to have none unless you will patiently learn how to cook him.

Of course, a preserving kettle of the finest porcelain is best, but if you have nothing better than an earthenware pipkin, it will do—with care. Like crabs and lobsters, husbands are cooked alive. They sometimes fly out of the kettle and so become burned and crusty on the edges, so it is wise to secure him in the kettle with a strong silken cord called Comfort, as the one called Duty is apt to be weak. Make a clear, steady flame of love, warmth and cheerfulness. Set him as near this as seems to agree with him.

If he sputters, do not be anxious, for some husbands do this until they are quite done. Add a little sugar in the form of what confectioners call kisses, but use no pepper or vinegar on any account. Season to taste with spices, good humor and gaiety preferred, but seasoning must always be used with great discretion and caution. Avoid sharpness in testing him for tenderness. Stir him gently, lest he lie too flat and close to the kettle and so become useless. You cannot fail to know when he is done. If so treated, you will find him very digestible, agreeing with you perfectly; and he will keep as long as you choose unless you become careless and allow the home fires to grow cold. Thus prepared, he will serve a lifetime of Happiness.

THE ORIGINAL
COOKBOOK COMMITTEE

EDITOR
Mrs. Archibald McClure

CO-EDITORS
Mrs. Charles B. Dudley, Jr.—Mrs. Nancy B. Cook

Committee Chairmen

Mrs. Paul Gillespie—Publicity

Mrs. George S. Miles–Selection & Testing

Mrs. Marcus J. Stewart—Distribution

Mrs. Howard Willey, Jr.—Promotion

Mrs. John McDonough—Composition

Mrs. John Coulter Wycoff, II—Typist

30 YEARS OF SERVICE

ACKNOWLEDGMENTS

The Junior League of Memphis wishes to thank the contributors to the original cover and illustrations which helped to make THE MEMPHIS COOKBOOK the classic it is today.

Edward O. Bailey, Jr.—Memphis Art Academy

Joe Bennett, student—Memphis Art Academy

Richard S. Guenther—Bluff City Engraving

Bill Edge, Jr.—Standard Printing

The Counsel of Wade Bros.

Mrs. Cooper Y. Robinson—Illustrations

Mrs. J. Seddon Allen, Jr.—Illustrations

Any resemblance between the recipes contained in this book and good things to eat and drink is purely intentional. Every such recipe has been tasted and tested by a member of the copyright owner. Some acknowledgment should be given to the sacrifice of figures which this entailed!

The Cookbook Committee is grateful for the help and interest shown by the hundreds of recipe donors. We recognize, too, the endless hours of time spent by the Members of the Junior League in typing, testing, and editing these recipes.

The Junior League is an organization of women who are trained for effective participation in the community and dedicated to the belief that volunteer service is an essential part of responsible citizenship.

Founded in 1922, the Junior League of Memphis is part of an international women's organization of 270 Junior Leagues in the United States, Canada, Mexico, and England.

Some of the projects founded and cofounded by the Junior League of Memphis with proceeds from the sale of this book include:

1953 Visiting Nurses Association	1977 Sunset Symphony/Memphis in May
1955 WKNO - Public Television	1980 *A Man's Taste Cookbook*
1959 Youth Museum	1980 Community Calendar
1961 Memphis Arts Council	1980 Community Education Program
1966 Community Day Care Association	1980 Community Board Institute
1966 *Memphis Guide to Architectural Barriers for the Handicapped Handbook*	1983 Visitors' Information Center
	1983 *Good Abode*, Illustrated History
1971 Memphis House	1984 Memphis Alcohol and Drug Council
1971 *Party Potpourri Cookbook*	1984 Senior Citizens' Crafts Fair
1972 Changing Exhibit Area/$100,000 to Memphis Pink Palace Museum	1985 Parenting Center of Memphis
	1986 Memphis/Shelby County Council of Family Violence
1975 The Volunteer Center	

**MEMPHIS IN MAY
INTERNATIONAL
FESTIVAL, INC.™**

Memphis blooms in Spring. This yearly reawakening does not become the exclusive privilege of nature. Memphians too are caught up in an annual celebration. Memphis in May is a unique festival whose purpose is to promote the city locally, nationally, and internationally by honoring a foreign country. This annual festival benefits the Memphis community and the honored country economically, culturally, and educationally. The festival provides a vehicle through which Memphis can celebrate her own traditions and unique flavor with the joint purpose of developing camaraderie among the residents and increasing tourism in Memphis. Imagine an entire month of celebration! Memphis in May includes honored country celebrations, a Children's Festival, educational projects for Memphis school children, Fine Arts Exhibits throughout the city, and a Sunset Symphony on the bluff overlooking the Mississippi River. It is an incredible month of fun and fellowship.

The Junior League of Memphis has been an active supporter and participant of the Memphis in May International Festival from the beginning. In recognition of the League's support, *The Memphis Cookbook* has been designated the official cookbook of the Memphis in May International Festival. As we reflect upon our support of Memphis in May, the Junior League of Memphis dedicates this cookbook to the festival and to all our future celebrations.

THE MAYOR'S RECIPES

When the Honorable Richard C. Hackett, Mayor of Memphis, proclaimed the MEMPHIS COOKBOOK the "Official City of Memphis Cookbook," he graciously agreed to loan us the following recipes for our collection.

POTATOES A LA PARMESAN

5 lbs. red potatoes
2 sticks butter (no substitute)
12 oz. grated Parmesan cheese
2 large white onions (sliced)
Salt

Black Pepper
Paprika
Tabasco Sauce
1 c. fresh parsley (chopped)

Peel and boil potatoes until nearly done (not mushy, but very firm). Drain and when cool enough to handle, slice as you would for scalloped potatoes. Sauté the sliced onions in 1 stick of butter until translucent. In a bowl mix parsley, onions, potatoes, 1 stick of butter (cut in pats), salt and pepper to taste, several dashes of Tabasco Sauce, and about two-thirds of the Parmesan cheese. Mix well. Place in large casserole dish or several small ones. Sprinkle with remaining Parmesan cheese and paprika. Bake in 300° - 350° oven for 45 minutes. Serves 24.

LASAGNE

1 lb. ground chuck *or* Italian sausage
1 clove garlic, minced
1 ½ T. salt
10 oz. lasagne noodles
½ c. Parmesan *or* Romano cheese
2 eggs, beaten
½ t. black pepper

1 16 oz. can tomatoes
2 6 oz. cans tomato paste
3 c. Ricotta *or* cottage cheese
2 T. parsley flakes
2 t. salt
1 lb. Mozzarella cheese, grated

Preheat oven to 375°. Brown meat slowly, spooning off excess fat. Add garlic, tomatoes, tomato paste and 2 teaspoons salt. Simmer, uncovered, for 30 minutes, stirring occasionally. Cook noodles, in salted water, according to package directions; drain and rinse. Combine remaining ingredients, except Mozzarella cheese, in another bowl. Place half the noodles in a 13x9x2-inch baking dish. Spread with the cottage cheese mixture; add half the meat sauce and half the Mozzarella cheese. Repeat layers. Bake for 30 minutes.

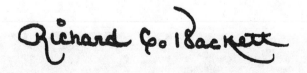

Appetizers and Canapes

It's the little things in life that count. And so it is with those delectable bits called "Canapés," designed to tantalize the taste buds and served with a Cup of Good Fellowship in the living room or on the terrace before dinner.

These savory morsels, both hot and cold, lend a delightful air of informality to any gathering. They should whet the appetite rather than satisfy it, but their failing in life is that they are such tasty tidbits that each guest would like to make an entire meal of them.

The ingredients can be simple or elaborate as you please. From the tiny round of tongue-teasing toast to the jar of imported caviar, let your imagination be your guide. Serve the hot ones hot and the cold ones cold, and remember the sage words of Lewis Carroll:

"And if you strew them sparsely,
They whet the appetite;
But if you lay them on too thick
They spoil the matter quite."

— 1952

Quick Appetizers

1. Almonds, roasted and crushed, and mixed with anchovy paste.

2. Caviar flavored with lemon and onion juice.

3. Crabmeat or lobster moistened with lemon juice and mayonnaise.

4. Cream cheese with chopped dill pickle.

5. Cream cheese, can of deviled ham, prepared mustard and dash of Angostura bitters.

6. Cream cheese, chopped watercress, touch of horseradish.

7. Cream cheese with finely chopped chutney and one-half teaspoon curry powder.

8. Cream cheese and horseradish.

9. Cream cheese, Russian imported caviar, and onion juice.

10. Cream cheese with chives and dash of Worcestershire sauce.

11. Cream cheese and anchovy paste and touch of grated onion.

12. Goose livers minced and moistened with mayonnaise.

13. Kippered herring mashed in its own juice with a dash of Tabasco sauce and a dash of vinegar.

14. Liverwurst with pistachio nuts.

15. Minced eggs and sardines, or anchovies.

16. Minced ham and olives moistened with mayonnaise and Worcestershire sauce.

17. Minced sardines or anchovies with chopped olives.

18. Minced shrimp moistened with French dressing.

19. Minced shrimp with onion juice and mayonnaise.

20. Onions (pickled) chopped very fine with Spanish olives, and mixed with deviled ham.

21. Peanut butter and bacon toasted on brown bread.

22. Creamed pimento cheese and horseradish.

23. Roquefort cheese, or Stilton cheese, moistened with Port wine.

24. Sardines, anchovies or caviar paste.

The above should be served with potato chips, crackers, melba toast, thin sliced toasted bread and such.

See Table of Equivalents (p. 240) for sugar and cream references.

ALMOND-CHICKEN LOAF

| 6 whole chicken breasts | 5 hard-boiled eggs |
| or 1 whole hen | ¾ c. almonds |

Boil chicken breasts. Put meat through smallest meat grinder. Chop almonds and grate eggs. Season with salt and pepper and enough mayonnaise to hold it together. Rinse loaf pan in cold water; shake water out but do not dry. Put chicken mixture in loaf pan and chill overnight. Run spatula around edges to remove from pan. Serve on plate with crackers. Serves 25.

Mrs. Thomas R. Price

CHICKEN LIVER LOAF IN ASPIC

¾ pound yellow chicken livers (regular livers are perfectly satisfactory). Put them through a grinder with a small piece of onion and then through a sieve.

4 whole eggs	Pinch of pepper
1 pt. XX cream	Chopped parsley
Pinch of salt	

Mix 2 whole eggs and 2 egg yolks, cream, salt, pepper, parsley, and livers. Now beat the whites of the two remaining eggs stiff and add to the mixture. Pour into a 9-inch bread pan that has been greased with sweet butter. Place this in a pan of boiling water and cook 1 hour in 350° oven. Remove and cool.

ASPIC FOR CHICKEN LIVER LOAF

| 2 pkg. of salad gelatin aspic | ¾ c. cold water |
| Add ¾ c. boiling water | Juice of 1 lemon |

Take another 9-inch bread pan and grease it. Mix aspic ingredients. Add about 1 inch of aspic to pan and put in icebox to cool. When cool, but not too stiff, take liverloaf from pan and place over aspic, then pour the rest of the aspic on top of the liver loaf. (If you cannot get the salad aspic, use 2 cans of consommé and add lemon juice and 1 envelope of plain gelatin to make aspic.) Serves 6 to 8.

Mr. A. Arthur Halle, Cordova, Tenn.

ALLUMETTES

Take some anchovies, wipe free from oil. Cut each into long strips. Have some plain pastry (p. 188) rolled very thin ready. Spread with anchovy butter. Envelop each strip of anchovy in the pastry and fry in very hot lard until crisp and yellow. Serve "Log House" fashion and put fried parsley in the corners. Serve very hot. May also be made with sardines.

Mrs. McKay Van Vleet

ANCHOVY AND EGG HOR D'OEUVRES

Fry small rounds of toast in butter. Place 2 anchovy filets on rounds, sprinkle with grated hard-boiled egg and top with a sliced olive.

MRS. EDWARD W. COOK

BACON AND OYSTERS

12 fresh or canned oysters   12 thin slices bacon

Drain and wrap each oyster in slice of bacon, using wooden toothpicks as skewers. Place in pan, put in 350° oven and bake until bacon is done. Place on toast and serve.

BACON WRAPS

Use rectangular soda crackers, separated into sections. Starting diagonally, wrap a thin, wide strip of bacon around each cracker, being sure to completely cover cracker. Secure with toothpick and cut off any left over piece of bacon. Bake in 350° preheated oven, in shallow pan, until golden brown. Serve hot.

These can be made ahead and kept in refrigerator. Have bacon soft, it's easier to handle. Very good, as grease makes cracker almost like pastry.

MRS. DAVID T. GILDART, JR.

OLIVE BACON FRIES

Wrap pimento-stuffed olives in thin slices of bacon, secure with toothpick, and fry in hot fat until bacon is crisp. Drain and serve hot.

COCKTAIL HAM BISCUITS

⅔ c. flour   2 to 3 T. milk
6 T. grated cheese   Deviled ham or marble size,
½ t. salt   cooked sausage balls
2 T. butter

Mix flour, cheese, and salt; chop in butter and add enough milk to form a stiff dough. Roll very thin and cut with a small round cutter. Moisten edges with slightly beaten egg. Spread half the rounds with ham or sausage ball. Cover with remaining rounds and press edges together. Brush with melted butter and bake 12 to 15 minutes in hot oven 400°. Makes approximately 40 small biscuits.

This can be made ahead of time and put in deep freeze. Also one box of pastry mix can be substituted for dough.

MRS. JOHN MCDONOUGH

PIGS IN BLANKET

1 lb. little pig sausage   1 recipe pie crust (p. 188)

Make pie crust, then fry sausages until done. Roll crust very thin and cut in strips. Cut each sausage in half and roll in pie crust. Cook in 500° oven until brown. Can be reheated by putting in 250° oven.

CHEESE BOXES

½ lb. butter   ½ t. salt
½ lb. sharp yellow cheese   1 unbeaten egg white
1 T. cream   Tabasco

Cream cheese and butter until smooth, add unbeaten egg white, cream, salt and Tabasco to taste. Chill until mixture can be easily spread. Remove crusts from one loaf of unsliced bread and cut in one inch cubes. Spread five sides with cheese mixture. Place sixth side down on cookie tin and bake 15 minutes or until golden brown in a pre-heated 375° oven.

These are very good kept in a freezer until ready to bake.

MRS. W. L. DEAN FORD

HAM AND CHEESE BALLS

¼ lb. cooked ham (ground   ⅛ t. pepper
    very fine)   1 t. lemon juice
¼ lb. cream cheese   Chopped chives
2 t. Worcestershire sauce   Salt to taste
1 T. catsup

Blend ingredients thoroughly and form into tiny balls. Roll in chopped chives. Serve speared on toothpicks. Makes about 30 balls.

MRS. JAMES K. DOBBS, JR.

MOCK PATE DE FOIS GRAS

4 lbs. chicken livers   ½ c. mayonnaise
2 T. chow-chow pickle   1 c. celery, chopped fine
1 t. Tabasco   ¼ grated onion
1 T. Worcestershire sauce   Salt and pepper

Broil chicken livers in butter and put through grinder or sieve. Mix all ingredients and make into mold. Put in icebox. This amount serves 50 or more people. Quartered will serve 16.

ADELE BRAKE (CATERESS)

SALMON CANAPE

Slice smoked salmon very thin. Place on buttered pumpernickel bread with a dash of black pepper and lemon juice.

Capers and olive oil make a good variation.

RED-DEVIL BALLS

Several hours ahead: Blend 1 8-oz. pkg. of soft cream cheese and 1 4½-oz. can deviled ham. Refrigerate until easy to handle; then shape into 30 small balls. Roll in 1 cup chopped pecans or walnuts. Refrigerate just long enough to firm up again.

At serving time: Serve balls on toothpicks, alone or with olives or crackers. Makes 30.

MRS. WILLIAM G. PHILLIPS, JR.

CUCUMBER CANAPE

2 T. Roquefort or Bleu cheese
2 T. butter
1 t. lemon juice
Salt to taste

1 T. chopped parsley
20 slices cucumber, soaked in salted ice water

Cream butter, cheese and lemon juice. Spread on toasted bread rounds and cover with a slice of cucumber. Sprinkle with salt and parsley. Serves 20.

Good also for a tea or luncheon sandwich.

CHICKEN CUCUMBER SPREAD

½ c. minced chicken
¼ c. minced cucumber

Mayonnaise to soften
Salt and pepper to taste

Combine all ingredients and serve cold as a spread, or hot on toast rounds run in the oven and heated through at the last minute.

CHEESE-OLIVE SPREAD

2 pkg. cream cheese
Small bottle stuffed olives

Tarragon vinegar to taste
Pinch of dried tarragon leaves

Soften cream cheese, chop olives fine and add to cheese, then add vinegar and tarragon leaves to taste. Serve in a bowl, surrounded by crackers or potato chips.

CRABMEAT PATTY

1 pkg. cream cheese
1 small can of crabmeat
½ t. salt

A little grated onion
1 t. Worcestershire sauce

Mix ingredients well. Put slices of tomato on toast rounds. Cover with crabmeat mixture. Place thin slices of Velveeta cheese on top. Bake 20 minutes in 250° oven.

MRS. BLISS ROGERS

CREAM CHEESE AND CRABMEAT

1 c. crabmeat
1 can tomato soup
(undiluted)

1 pkg. cream cheese
¼ t. salt
Pepper to taste

Heat soup and add crabmeat. Mash cream cheese and add to mixture, stirring constantly. Do not let boil. Add salt and pepper and serve on toast, rye is good. Serves 4.

This is easy to fix and good for lunch or Sunday night, as well as for an appetizer.

MRS. CHARLES L. PIPLAR

CRAB NEWBURG APPETIZERS

1 can or 1 lb. fresh crabmeat
4 hard-boiled eggs
Salt
½ lb. Wisconsin cheese
1 onion, juiced

Cayenne pepper
2 T. butter
1 heaping t. flour
2 c. milk

Clean all shells out of crabmeat. Add grated eggs, onion juice, salt and cayenne. Melt and blend in flour. When smooth, add milk and cook until thick. Add cheese, then crabmeat. Serve from a chafing dish on melba toast. Serves 6.

MRS. DUNBAR ABSTON, GERMANTOWN, TENN.

SHRIMP AND ONION

2½ lbs. uncooked shrimp
½ c. celery tops
3 t. salt
¼ c. mixed pickling spices
2 c. thin sliced onions
7 or 8 bay leaves

1¼ c. salad oil
¾ c. white vinegar
1½ t. salt
2½ t. celery seed
2½ T. capers and juice
Dash of Tabasco

Cover shrimp with boiling water. Add celery tops, salt and pickling spices. Cook shrimp 10-12 minutes. Clean shrimp and alternate shrimp with sliced onions in a shallow dish. Add bay leaves. Combine in separate dish salad oil, vinegar, salt, celery seed, capers and juice, and Tabasco. Mix well and pour over shrimp. Cover and store for 24 hours in icebox. When ready to serve, place toothpicks on table or tray, so guests may spear shrimp and eat. Serves 10.

MRS. EDWARD W. COOK

CHUTNEY BALLS

1 bottle imported chutney   1 doz. egg yolks, hard-boiled
½ lb. bacon

Drain juice off chutney and chop fine. Add enough mashed hard-boiled egg yolks to make a paste. Roll into balls, wrap in bacon, hold together with toothpicks, and put in 350° oven until bacon is cooked. Serves 10.

MRS. HUBERT K. REESE

CURRIED CREAM CHEESE AND CHUTNEY SPREAD

1 pkg. cream cheese   Few drops garlic juice
2 T. cream   4 T. finely chopped chutney
1 t. curry powder   1 t. Worcestershire sauce
Salt   Dash Tabasco

Blend cheese and cream until smooth. Add curry powder, garlic juice, Worcestershire sauce, Tabasco, Chutney and a little salt. Stir until smooth. Serve on crackers or shape into mold and let your guests serve themselves. Serves 6.

MRS. JAMES K. DOBBS, JR.

MEXICAN APPETIZER

1 pkg. cream cheese   1 T. carraway seed
½ stick butter   1 T. prepared mustard
1 T. onion, grated   1 T. paprika
1 T. chopped capers   1 T. anchovy paste

Mix above ingredients well, and serve on crackers or shape into mold and let your guests serve themselves. Serves 4 to 6.

MRS. JOHN P. K. CAVENDER

CREAM CHIVE CHEESE SPREAD

2 3-oz. pkg. chive cheese   Dash of Tabasco
½ c. creamed cottage cheese   Salt to taste
2 T. onion juice   1 t. lemon juice
1 T. Worcestershire sauce   ½ c. mayonnaise

Cream chive cheese, cottage cheese and mayonnaise; then add above seasoning. Let stand at least 2 hours before serving, for seasoning to permeate. Serve with potato chips or pretzels. Serves 6 to 8.

Good for a tea, sherry party or cocktail party.

MRS. BEN C. ADAMS, JR.

FRIED CHEESE BALLS

4 T. butter	Cayenne pepper
Cracker crumbs	½ c. flour
1 c. milk	1 egg
1 c. grated N. Y. State cheese	Salt and pepper

Melt butter, blend in flour. Add milk and cook until smooth and thick. Season with salt and pepper to taste. Add 1 cup grated cheese to ½ cup thick white sauce. Season with salt and pinch cayenne. Put mixture in ice box to get thoroughly cold. When cold, shape into small balls, roll in fine cracker crumbs, dip in slightly beaten egg, roll in crumbs again. Fry in hot salad oil or fat 390° until brown. They must brown quickly or they will split. Yield: 2 dozen cheese balls.

MRS. CAREY G. BRINGLE

CHEESE BALLS

¼ lb. Roquefort cheese	1 c. chopped pecans
3 pkg. (small) cream cheese	Worcestershire sauce to taste
½ lb. sharp cheese	Garlic or onion juice
1 c. chopped parsley	Red pepper

Let cheeses soften in bowl and blend thoroughly. Add ½ cup nuts and ½ cup parsley plus other seasonings and mix well. Mix the remaining nuts and parsley together on bread board. Mold cheese into ball and roll over and over in nuts and parsley until all adhere. Put in covered bowl and chill until firm. Serves 15.

This can be made into marble sized balls and rolled in parsley and nuts. It will keep two weeks.

MRS. KEITH M. SPURRIER, JR.

ONION AND CHEESE CANAPES

With a biscuit cutter, cut white sandwich bread into rounds 1½-2 inches in diameter. Spread with cream cheese, highly seasoned. Place thin slice of white onion, which has been soaked in ice water, on top of cheese on the bread rounds. Cover with Hellman's Mayonnaise (no other will brown) generously and brown on a cookie sheet under the flame in a 400° oven.

MRS. MERRILL PARRISH HUDSON

CHEESE TOAST

2 c. grated Cheddar cheese	½ t. Worcestershire sauce
2 T. butter, melted	Dash Tabasco
1 egg	½ t. dry mustard
2 T. cream	Salt and pepper to taste

Grate cheese, beat in egg, butter, cream (add a few bread crumbs if desired), Tabasco, Worcestershire, salt, pepper and mustard. Spread on small buttered toast rounds and run in 400° oven until golden brown. Serves 40 to 50.

This mixture keeps several days in refrigerator.

MRS. GEORGE S. MILES

AUDREY'S CHEESE STRAWS

1 stick butter (½ cup)   ½ t. red pepper
2 cups sifted flour   1 t. salt
1 lb. New York State Cheese, grated

Cream butter well. Sift dry ingredients together, add to butter, then add cheese. Press with cookie press, place in greased tin, bake at 400° for ten minutes. They may be rolled on floured board and cut in strips for cheese straws, or rolled out in round thin biscuits with a nut in center of each one. Yield 36 straws.

MRS. W. L. TAYLOR

CHEESE COCKTAIL SPREAD

1½ large pkg. cream cheese   Red pepper to taste
⅔ large pkg. Velveeta cheese   Salt to taste
2 cucumbers grated   2 T. chili powder
Grated onion to taste   ½ lb. pecans

Mix cheeses, cucumbers, onion, pepper and salt. Mold on oil paper in pan, chill. Take out of pan, removing to serving dish. Top with coarsely chopped pecans and chili powder. Serves about 40-50.

This may be served with crackers and is also excellent for sandwiches.

MRS. J. HAL PATTON

CHEESE PUFFS

1 c. bread flour   ½ c. butter
¼ t. salt   1 pkg. (3 oz.) cream cheese

Blend butter and cheese; mix with flour and salt. Chill. Roll very thin and cut with 2-inch cookie cutter. Spread with anchovy paste, deviled ham, chutney, sardines or whatever filling desired. Fold over and bake in 400° oven, for 10 minutes. Serve hot. Serves 20.

Wonderful with a drink before dinner.

MRS. GEORGE S. MILES

ROQUEFORT STUFFED CELERY

Cream together 1 package cream cheese and 1 package Roquefort Cheese. Soften slightly with cream and fill celery ribs.

GARLIC CHEESE

1 small clove garlic
1 roll Smoky cheese
1 pkg. cream cheese
1 drop Tabasco

Few drops Worcestershire
  sauce
Paprika

Put garlic through meat grinder, followed by Smoky cheese. Mix with cream cheese until thoroughly blended, adding Tabasco, Worcestershire sauce to taste. When smooth, form in roll, sprinkle with paprika, wrap in wax paper and put in refrigerator until firm. Can also be put in small bowl, covered with paprika to be served with crackers around it. Serves 12.

Delicious if you like the flavor of garlic.

MRS. GEORGE S. MILES

CHEESE DREAMS

1 lb. Old English cheese,
  grated
Dash of Tabasco sauce

Dash of Worcestershire sauce
Dash of paprika
½ c. cream

Mix ingredients well. Cut very thin slices of light bread. Remove crusts. Spread a thin layer of mixture on slices, sprinkle with paprika, roll into blanket roll, brush with melted butter, and sprinkle with paprika. Run in 400° oven for a few minutes to brown lightly. Serves 30.

This has been served for years at the Memphis Country Club.

MRS. ALLIE STARKE PATTESON

CAVIAR MOUSSE

2 T. gelatin
2 T. cold water
½ cup boiling water
1 T. lemon juice
1 T. Worcestershire

4 T. Mayonnaise
½ pt. XX cream
4 cans caviar (1⅛ oz. size)
Dry mustard to taste

Soak gelatin in cold water, add hot water. Mix all ingredients and place in large mold or individual molds. Chill six hours. When served as a salad, thin mayonnaise with a little cream to which has been added pieces of fresh boiled lobster and small amount of grated onion. Note: For an appetizer, serve with crackers.

MRS. W. L. DEAN FORD

MUSHROOM APPETIZERS

½ lb. mushrooms
1 3½-oz. can pimentos
1 small onion
2 T. butter

2 T. flour
¾ t. salt
Cayenne pepper

Chop mushrooms, pimentos and onion. Cook in melted butter in saucepan over low heat for about 5 minutes, stir occasionally. Sprinkle the flour over the mushroom mixture and stir until thick. Season with salt and pepper, then cool. Spread slices of lightly buttered bread with mushroom mixture. Put together in pairs and toast. Cut into strips and serve hot. Makes 2 dozen small sandwiches.

MRS. HUBERT K. REESE

STUFFED MUSHROOMS

Select small mushrooms, peel and remove centers from the mushroom caps. Make small balls of well seasoned sausage and stuff the mushroom caps with it. Arrange in pan, surround with a small quantity of water. Put under broiler and broil until sausage is done.

WATERCRESS DIP

Chopped watercress
Chopped chives
Mayonnaise

Cucumber strips
2 cloves garlic
½ t. celery salt

Blend finely chopped watercress and chives with mayonnaise to make a paste. Serve cold in a bowl, surrounded with cucumber strips, which have been soaked in ice water containing garlic and celery salt.

TOASTED CHEESE SNAPS

Spread snappy cheese on rounds of bread. Run under broiler until cheese is melted and slightly browned.

PECAN CANAPE

Use very large pecans. Make filling of cream cheese, Roquefort cheese and mayonnaise. Squeeze in a few drops of lemon juice. Mix well. Put between pecans. Let stay in refrigerator to harden.

STUFFED CELERY

Wash celery (scrape if necessary). Fill hollows with soft pimento or cream cheese, seasoned with paprika, pimentos, olives, chopped nuts and mayonnaise to soften. Smooth off even with a knife. Place in ice box several hours before serving. Before serving, cut in slices about 1 inch thick. Stick each with a toothpick and serve as appetizers.

Soups

Of soup and love the first is best — or so saith Thomas
Fuller. Perhaps that is true in a small measure, since love has
its age, and soup is completely ageless. For only soup so well
nourishes the young, yet stokes the fires of manhood, then com-
forts the old.

The versatility of soup is infinite. There are bouillons and
broths, then consommés, and hearty soups that satisfy, and
each one can be varied a hundredfold, yet be a new adventure
in eating every time.

Here you will find them all — plain and hearty, hot and
cold, exotic, clear and creamed. In other words, there are soups
aplenty, and all of them better than love — almost!

— 1952

See Table of Equivalents (p. 240) for sugar and cream references.

WHITE VELVET SOUP—(Auntie Mitchell's)

1 large hen	1 c. almonds, chopped fine
2 qt. water	2 c. fine white bread crumbs
1 clove	A little grated nutmeg
2 T. onion	Red pepper
2 bunches celery, cut up	Salt to taste
2 sprigs parsley	1 pt. XX cream

Cover hen with water. Cover, let simmer. While simmering add cloves, onions, celery and parsley. When hen is tender (about 2 hours) remove from stock. Remove breast meat from hen, chop fine. Measure 1 cupful. Strain stock, add finely chopped breast, almonds, bread crumbs, nutmeg, red pepper, cream and salt to taste. Let it boil up once. Serve with toasted crackers or thin white bread, buttered. Serves 8.

Mrs. James E. Stark

CREAM OF CORN AND CRAB SOUP

1 lb. crabmeat, flaked	Salt and pepper to taste
1 qt. good chicken stock	Few dashes of Maggi seasoning
1 qt. X cream	Few drops of Tabasco
1 can (No. 2) cream style corn	½ c. melted butter
	½ c. sifted flour
1 medium onion, sliced	

Put chicken stock, corn and sliced onion in top of double boiler and cook over boiling water until onion is soft. Press all this through a sieve (all the corn husk won't go through). Put in top of double boiler, add cream and flaked crabmeat. Heat over boiling water. Add blended flour and butter, stirring until creamy. Add seasonings. If desired, 1 or 2 teaspoons sugar may be added. Serve hot. Serves 8.

Miss Mary Robinson

CREAM OF CRAB SOUP

1 qt. milk or cream, or half and half	2 hard-boiled eggs
2 T. butter	1 grated lemon peel
1 T. flour	1 t. Worcestershire sauce
1½ lb. crabmeat	½ c. sherry
	Salt and pepper to taste

Blend butter and flour in a double boiler. Add eggs which have been mashed, lemon peel and milk or cream. Stir until it thickens. Add the crabmeat, cut into chunks. Let simmer for 5 minutes. Add seasonings. Stir in sherry, heat thoroughly. Serves 6 to 8.

Mrs. William A. Leatherman, Robinsonville, Miss.

FRESH SHRIMP SOUP

1½ lbs. shrimp
3 or 4 peppercorns
1 small onion, chopped fine
1 stick butter

3 c. hot milk
1 c. XX cream
Salt and pepper to taste
⅓ c. sherry

Cook shrimp in boiling, salted water containing peppercorns. Simmer gently for 15 minutes. Drain shrimp, saving broth. Shell and clean, put in bowl and cover with broth. Sauté onion in butter without browning. Drain the shrimp and put through chopper (medium knife). Add to onion and butter and place over hot water. Add plenty of freshly ground pepper, cook together for 5 minutes. Add hot milk gradually, cooking for a few minutes longer. Add cream slowly, salt to taste, then add sherry. Serve with oyster crackers. Serves 6 to 8.

MRS. ELIZABETH DANTZLER GRAYSON, BILOXI, MISS.

OYSTER STEW

4 small carrots
2 turnips
4 small white onions
4 hearts of celery
Parsley
2 heaping T. flour

6 T. butter
2 doz. oysters
2 c. scalded milk
1 pt. X cream
Salt and pepper

Chop parsley, onions, celery, carrots and turnips. Put 2 tablespoons butter in frying pan, add vegetables and sauté until a golden brown. Make a cream sauce in a double boiler by melting 2 tablespoons butter, 2 heaping tablespoons flour and 2 cups scalded milk. Keep warm. Place oysters and juice in an enamel pan, with 2 tablespoons butter, freshly ground pepper and a little salt. When ready to serve, heat oysters until the edges curl. Add chopped vegetables to the cream sauce, then add heated cream, and then the oysters with a little of their juice. Omit parsley from vegetable mixture if desired, and sprinkle on top.

This is a meal in itself and should be used as such.

MRS. HUBERT K. REESE

CREAM OF CORN SOUP

2 c. chicken broth
2 c. cream style corn
½ c. chopped celery
1 T. chopped onion

2 T. butter
2 T. flour
2 c. X cream

Simmer above ingredients for 15 minutes. Strain and mash through strainer. Make a thin cream sauce with 2 T. flour, 2 T. butter and 2 cups X cream. Add the corn mixture and season with salt and pepper. Heat to boiling point and serve with chopped parsley.

MRS. ROBERT HUSSEY

BLACK BEAN SOUP

1 lb. black beans
3 onions, chopped
2 bay leaves
½ t. soda
3 buttons garlic, chopped

1 T. vinegar
¼ c. olive oil
½ bell pepper, chopped
4 strips bacon, chopped
Salt and pepper

Add soda to the water and soak beans overnight. Wash beans well, place in 2 quarts of water and boil slowly. Heat olive oil in skillet, add all other ingredients and fry until a light brown. Add to beans. Simmer until done, then put through sieve. Season to taste. Reheat to serve. Serves 4 if used as main dish; 6 to 8 if used as soup course.

This dish improves if allowed to stand several hours before serving.

MRS. WILLIAM A. LEATHERMAN, ROBINSONVILLE, MISS.

FRENCH ONION SOUP

8 medium onions
1 pt. boiling water
4 T. flour
1½ T. butter
1 qt. seasoned meat stock

Salt
Freshly ground pepper
Parmesan cheese
Toast squares

Peel, slice and separate onions. Cook in butter until golden brown. Add hot water and simmer until tender. Add stock, reserving 4 tablespoons to blend with flour when cool. Add and stir into mixture. Season with salt and freshly ground pepper and cook only a few minutes. Pour into soup bowls. Place squares of toast in center, sprinkle with cheese, run under broiler to slightly brown cheese. Serves 6-8.

White Rose Madrilene or chicken soup may be used for stock.

MRS. FERD HECKLE, JR.

CHICKEN OKRA GUMBO

2½ or 3 lb. chicken
1 qt. canned tomatoes (or
equal amount of fresh
tomatoes)
1 large onion

1 qt. canned okra (or 1½ lb.
fresh okra)
1 small cheese cloth bag filled
with bay leaves

Cut chicken as for frying. Fry until half done. Chop onion and make a roux with flour and the grease from the chicken. Cook chicken in 3 quarts of boiling water until well done. Cut into small pieces, removing all bones. Put into pot and add the tomatoes and okra, cut into small pieces. Add roux and small bag of bay leaves for seasoning. Cook gumbo slowly so that all ingredients will be well done. Usually half a day is necessary to make a good gumbo. Just before serving, season with salt and pepper and remove bay leaves. Gumbo should be served with dry cooked rice. Crabmeat may be added a short time before serving, if desired. Serves 6 to 8 for large portions. Serves 10 for small portions.

MRS. McKAY VAN VLEET

CREAM OF ONION SOUP

4 medium yellow onions   2 c. of X cream
2 T. butter   2 c. milk
1 T. flour

Sauté onions in butter. First blend flour in a little warm milk. Heat remaining milk and pour over onions then add flour paste, blending well. Add cream and sprinkle Parmesan cheese over mixture. Serve with croutons. Serves 6.

MRS. EVERETT R. COOK, GERMANTOWN, TENN.

GUMBO

1 bay leaf   1 T. file powder
1 t. Worcestershire   1 can crabmeat
2 c. cooked shrimp   1 piece bacon (3 oz.)
16 okra pods (canned or fresh) 1 t. bacon fat
1 large onion   1 clove garlic
1 small green pepper   2 T. flour
1 stalk (bunch) celery   3 c. stock—consomme
½ c. canned tomatoes   ½ t. thyme

Cut bacon in small pieces. Put in kettle with fat. Fry 2 minutes. Add okra, sliced onion, and chopped green pepper. Cook 5 minutes over low fire. Add garlic and flour and stir. Add consomme, chopped celery, tomatoes, thyme, bay leaf, Worcestershire, salt, pepper to taste. Simmer 1 hour covered, then add shrimp and crab. Cook 2 minutes, then add file powder.

MRS. G. DUGAN MITCHELL

HOT VEGETABLE BOUILLON

3 cans mixed vegetable juice   4 whole cloves
  (V-8 may be used)   4 peppercorns
2 small onions, sliced   ¼ t. salt
Celery leaves   Sprig of parsley

Heat vegetable juice in a saucepan. Add onions, few celery leaves, sprig of parsley, cloves, peppercorns and salt. Simmer 10-15 minutes. Strain and serve very hot with a spoonful of Bleu Cheese Garnish. Serves 6.

BLEU CHEESE GARNISH

Mix ¼ cup sieved Bleu or Roquefort cheese with ½ cup sour cream. Serves 6.

MRS. HARRY S. MOORE, CLARKSDALE, MISS.

TOMATO SOUP

1 large onion	1 T. flour
2 T. butter	2 T. sugar
1 large can tomatoes	

Fry chopped onion in butter; add tomatoes, salt and pepper to taste. Cook 20 minutes and strain. Melt 1 tablespoon butter in another pan, add flour and sugar, then slowly add and stir in the tomato mixture. Float cream, whipped or plain, if desired. Serves 6.

Mrs. Caruthers Ewing

SEVEN CAN SOUP

1 3-oz. can B in B Chopped Mushrooms	1 pkg. frozen mixed vegetables
4 T. butter	1 can chicken broth
1 onion, chopped	1 can chicken gumbo
2 T. bacon fat	1 can beef bouillon
1 c. solid pack canned tomatoes	1 herb bunch
½ No. 2 can small whole peeled potatoes, sliced	2 T. chopped parsley
	Salt and pepper to taste
	Sliced French bread
1 lb. chicken breasts	

Put chicken broth, chicken gumbo, beef bouillon, herb bunch and parsley into large soup kettle and simmer slowly. Cook mixed vegetables and add to mixture. Cook ¼ of a chicken breast in butter in skillet. When done, chop up and add to soup. Broil mushrooms, with juice. When cooked, add ingredients and butter to soup. Now broil onions in butter only, until golden and transparent. Add tomatoes and cook slowly for a few minutes, then add to soup. Lastly, fry potatoes in bacon fat for 5-10 minutes and add to soup. Let soup simmer for 30-40 minutes. Meanwhile, broil rest of chicken breasts in butter. Put slices of French bread, buttered and toasted, in bottom of soup plates, place chicken on top, pour soup over all and serve. Serves 6 to 8.

Mrs. Hubert K. Reese

BOULA SOUP

1 can green pea soup	Whipped cream
1 can green turtle soup	Parmesan cheese
Sherry wine to taste	

Place soup mixture in casserole. Spread a layer of whipped cream about 1 inch thick on top. Sprinkle generously with cheese. Place in 350° oven for 30 or 40 minutes, until soup is thoroughly hot and whipped cream is crusty with cheese. Serve from casserole. Serves 6.

Mrs. Edward W. Cook

CREAM SENEGALES SOUP—"21" IN NEW YORK

2 apples, peeled and chopped
2 stalks celery, chopped
2 onions, chopped
6 T. curry powder

2 T. flour
1 pt. X cream
Chopped chicken
2 qt. chicken or beef broth

In order to make soup, curry sauce must be made first. Brown apples, celery and onions in butter. Add curry powder, and simmer for 15 minutes. Add flour and simmer for 5 more minutes. Add about 2 quarts chicken or beef broth (p. 26). Cook for ½ hour. Strain. When cold, add 1 pint of light cream, some finely chopped chicken and salt to taste. Serve hot or cold. Whipped cream may be added if desired. If served cold, add chopped chives. Serves 10-12 if used as soup course, and 6-8 if used as main dish.

MRS. EVERETT R. COOK, GERMANTOWN, TENN.

EASY MUSHROOM SOUP

2 c. chicken broth
1 c. chopped mushrooms
Salt and pepper to taste

2 onions
1 c. cream
1 hard-boiled egg

Heat chicken broth. Season well. Add chopped sautéed mushrooms and onions, sliced and fried until transparent. Add cup of hot cream, and at the last moment, shredded egg. Serves 4.

MRS. HUBERT K. REESE

BASIC BEEF BROTH

1 lb. veal knuckle
1½ lb. lean brisket
1 beef knuckle
4 chicken feet (cleaned and skinned)
2 leeks

1 large onion stuck with 2 cloves
2 stalks celery with leaves
3 sprigs parsley
6 peppercorns
2 t. salt

Put ingredients into large soup kettle. Add 3 quarts of cold water and bring slowly to a boil, removing scum as it accumulates. Simmer for 1 hour. Add salt and simmer for another hour, or until meat is tender. Season to taste with more salt and pepper if necessary. Strain through fine sieve. Clarify if necessary (p. 242). Cool, remove fat and store in refrigerator.

BASIC CHICKEN BROTH

4 lb. chicken
1 veal knuckle
4 chicken feet (cleaned and skinned)
2 t. salt
6 peppercorns
1 pinch of thyme

3 small leeks
2 carrots
1 onion stuck with cloves
2 stalks celery
1 clove garlic
½ bay leaf

Put chicken in large soup kettle with 3 quarts of water. Add veal, chicken feet, salt and peppercorns. Bring to boil slowly and simmer for 1 hour, skimming surface frequently. Add leeks, carrots, onion and celery, all cut in small pieces. Add garlic, bay leaf and thyme and continue to simmer for another hour. Add more seasoning if necessary. Strain through fine sieve and cool. Remove fat and store in refrigerator.

VICHYSSOISE

6 onions (leeks preferably, or half and half)
2 c. thinly sliced potatoes
4 c. chicken stock (or chicken bouillon)

1 c. heavy cream
Salt and white pepper to taste
Minced parsley or chives
⅓ c. butter

Melt butter in large saucepan, add sliced onions and sauté 5 minutes over low heat. Add potatoes and stock, cooking until potatoes are tender. Mash through fine sieve and add cream. Season to taste. Serve hot or cold, garnished with parsley or chives. If served cold, both soup and soup cups must be thoroughly chilled.

Variation: Add 1 cup tomato juice to 3 cups vichyssoise, to be served hot or cold.

Mrs. Gus Morgan

WIMAN SOUP

1 can of mushroom soup, 1 can of green turtle soup, a little cream and 2 teaspoons gelatin to make the chilled result quiver slightly. Add thick cream to top to serve. Serves 8.

Mrs. Hubert K. Reese

JELLIED CLEAR GREEN TURTLE SOUP

1 can turtle soup
2 whole cloves
Strip of lemon peel (1-inch)

Salt to taste
½ cup of madeira or sherry wine

Pour strained contents of can of turtle soup in a saucepan. Put turtle meat aside. Add cloves, lemon peel and a little salt. Boil 2 minutes, remove from fire; add ½ cup of madeira or sherry wine, and strain. Cool and place in ice-box. Serve cold with quartered pieces of lemon and garnish with thin slices of turtle meat. Serves 2.

Mrs. Hubert K. Reese

WINE SOUP

4 c. claret wine
2 c. water
1 lemon, sliced thin
1 T. broken cinnamon

1 T. sugar
1 T. sage leaves
2 egg yolks

Cook sage in 1 cup of boiling water until tender. As water evaporates add more. In another vessel put wine, 2 cups water, lemon, cinnamon and sugar, let boil 18 minutes or until well blended, add cooked sage, let boil up and pour, boiling hot, gradually over the well-beaten yolks. Strain, serve ice cold, in well chilled cups. Serves 8-10.

ANDALUSIAN SOUP, COLD

1 qt. canned tomatoes
1 small cucumber
3 hard-boiled eggs
1½ t. Worcestershire sauce
1 medium onion, chopped fine
1 t. dry mustard

1 lime or lemon sliced thin
1 pinch finely chopped garlic
1 t. lime or lemon juice
2 T. olive oil
1 dash of Tabasco
1 green pepper

Work yolk of eggs and olive oil into smooth paste in wooden bowl. Add garlic, seasoning and lime or lemon juice. Work in tomato pulp, cucumber and green pepper. Stir briskly, and chill on ice for 3 hours. Cut egg white into strips, put on bottom of bowl with strips of green pepper, add thin slice of lime or lemon. Serves 6.

This may be made the day before.

LOBSTER BISQUE

1 onion, sliced
1 leek, chopped
1 carrot, sliced
1 stalk celery, chopped
½ t. thyme
1 bay leaf
1 t. salt

Meat 2 small lobsters
½ c. cognac
2 c. white wine or hot water
1 cup cooked rice
2 T. butter
3 T. cream
2 egg yolks, beaten

Heat 2 tablespoons butter in 2-quart kettle. Add onion, leek, carrot, and celery and brown lightly 3 minutes. Add herbs, seasoning, and lobster meat. Stir lightly over heat 5 minutes. Add ¼ cup cognac and the wine or water. Cover. Cook over low heat 15 minutes. Remove lobster meat, put through grinder, using finest knife, and return to kettle. Add rice; mix. Cover and boil 5 minutes. Strain mixture, then cook over low heat about 45 minutes until thick. Add butter, cream, egg yolks, and remaining cognac. Do not boil. Serves 4.

MRS. WILLIAM LEIGH SMITH

TOMATO AND COTTAGE CHEESE SOUP

Sprig parsley
Sour cream
1 can condensed tomato soup
1 pt. thin cream
1 t. lemon juice

½ c. creamed cottage cheese
¼ c. chopped green onions
1 t. horseradish
Few drops Tabasco
Salt and pepper to taste

Put everything but onion and cottage cheese into bowl. Beat with rotary egg beater until well mixed. Season with salt and pepper, add onion and cottage cheese. Stir until well mixed. Chill and serve in very cold bowls. Top with sour cream and a sprig of parsley. Serves 4 if used as main dish with salad, or 6 if used as soup course.

It must be a hot day for this one!

MRS. CHARLES B. DUDLEY, JR.

FROSTED TOMATOES

2 peeled small onions	1 t. curry powder
8 peeled large tomatoes	2 t. salt
6 T. mayonnaise	Pepper to taste
2 T. minced parsley	

Chop onion and tomatoes in wooden bowl. Add salt and pepper. Mix with chopper. Turn into freezing tray. Freeze until ice crystals start to form. Mix mayonnaise and parsley, then add curry powder. Arrange frosty tomato mixture in chilled bouillon cups. Top with mound of curry mayonnaise. Serves 8.

Mrs. Adgate Ellis Hill, St. Louis, Mo.

QUICK JELLIED BOUILLON

2 cans bouillon	Small piece celery
1 small can tomatoes	1 bay leaf
8 whole cloves	Red and black pepper
3 onions	1 t. salt
1 envelope gelatin	1 c. water (more if needed)

Simmer tomatoes, onions and seasonings for ½ hour. Strain through cheese cloth. Add bouillon. If necessary, clarify with white of an egg. To gelatin which has been softening for ½ hour in a little cold water, add hot soup. Add enough hot water to make 1 quart and 1 cup of liquid. When cool, place in refrigerator to congeal. Serve in bouillon cups with slices of lemon. Serves 6.

Mrs. Lemmon Buckingham

CLAM CHOWDER

2 to 3 doz. fresh clams	1 bay leaf, crumbled
½ c. boiling water	1 clove garlic, chopped
2 or 3 stalks celery, diced	6 medium-size potatoes,
3 medium-size onions, sliced	peeled
4 green peppers, sliced thin	2 qts. chicken broth
4 slices salt pork, cubed	1 t. salt
⅔ c. flour	¼ t. pepper
3 lbs. ripe tomatoes, peeled	3 T. minced parsley
1 t. minced thyme	

Scrub clams; rinse and drain; put in large kettle with ½ cup boiling water. Cover kettle; set it over heat until the steam opens the clams. Remove clams from shells; save all broth; chop clams. Sauté celery, onions, and peppers with salt pork until the fat is melted and browning; sprinkle flour over this and mix smoothly. Add broth from the clam kettle, tomatoes, thyme, bay leaf, garlic, and potatoes. Add chicken broth; stir. Cover and let simmer until vegetables are thoroughly cooked, 30 to 45 minutes. Season, add clams and parsley; stir and serve. Makes 2 quarts.

Mrs. William Leigh Smith

RULE FOR FREEZING SOUP

To conserve space, it is advisable to simmer stock until it is highly concentrated or ½ its original volume. Fat should be skimmed off. Soups having milk bases, such as certain chowders, do not freeze well because the milk is likely to curdle during the freezing-thawing process. Vegetable soups of cabbage, carrots, onions and other similar vegetables and lentil soups are excellent. Do not use potatoes in vegetable soup as they do not freeze well. To thaw a soup, place in the top of a double boiler. Add liquid if the soup is too concentrated.

Cheese and Eggs

An egg, if left to the mother hen,
Merely starts the old cycle over again.
But an egg snatched out of the mother's nest
Is a friend to all cooks, the worst and the best.
Once liberated from its shell
Its uses are legion, as these pages tell.
You'll find it in castles and also in huts
From breakfast to dinner, from soup to nuts.
One use in particular is certain to please,
Just combine this delight with your choice of cheese.
Some genius introduced them and called them soufflé,
And they've gone with each other since that very day.
Truly a marriage dedicated to taste,
Cheese and an egg and there's nothing to waste;
Or either alone, this fact you should peg
There's nothing better than cheese or an egg.

— 1952

See Table of Equivalents (p. 240) for sugar and cream references.

CHEESE CROQUETTES

1 c. bread crumbs	Salt and pepper to taste
2 T. butter	1 t. Worcestershire sauce
2 c. grated cheese	Paprika
2 eggs	Frying fat

Mix butter, crumbs, cheese, seasoning and well beaten eggs. Shape into balls and fry in deep fat. Drain on unglazed paper, sprinkle with paprika and serve piping hot. Serves 4.

These may be made ahead of time, chilled in refrigerator and fried just before serving.

Mrs. WILLIAM L. NICHOL

CHEESE GRITS

½ c. uncooked grits	½ lb. American cheese
1 egg	½ t. salt

Cook grits with 2½ cups water in double boiler for about half an hour (not too thick, just consistency to pour). Grate 2 tablespoons of cheese to sprinkle on top. Cut up remainder of cheese and stir into grits until melted. Salt to taste. Beat egg until very light and stir in. Grease casserole with a thick coating of butter and pour mixture in, sprinkling grated cheese on top. Set in pan of water and bake in 325° oven for 20 or 25 minutes. Serve immediately. Total cooking time, approximately 1 hour. Serves 6-8.

Mrs. DUNBAR ABSTON, GERMANTOWN, TENN.

CREOLE EGGS

½ stick butter	Salt
2 green peppers	Pepper
2 medium onions	Tabasco
3 stalks celery	6 eggs
1 large can tomatoes	Bread crumbs
1 c. medium white sauce	Almonds

Hard-boil the eggs. Melt butter in iron skillet and fry finely chopped peppers, onions and celery until well done, stirring frequently. Add tomatoes and cook until thick. Season highly with salt, pepper and Tabasco. Make medium white sauce (p. 129). In a baking dish place a layer of egg slices ¼ inch thick, layer of white sauce and a layer of creole sauce. Top with bread crumbs and almonds. Place casserole in pan of water in 350° oven. Heat well, do not bake. Total cooking time, approximately 45 minutes. Serves 4.

Mrs. JOHN PHILLIPS, III

COTTAGE CHEESE PUDDING

1 c. cottage cheese
2 T. melted butter
2 eggs
3 T. heavy cream
½ t. salt

Dash pepper
Dash paprika
2 T. blanched or chopped
almonds

Mix together cottage cheese and butter. Add and mix in beaten egg yolks, cream, salt, pepper and paprika. Fold in stiffly beaten egg whites. Turn into buttered glass baking dish. Set dish in pan of hot water and bake 25 minutes in 350° oven. When ready to serve cover the top with almonds. Makes a small pudding to serve 4.

Delicious served cold as a salad or hot as an entree for luncheon.

MRS. HENRY WETTER

CRUMBED EGGS

6 hard-boiled eggs
3½ t. mayonnaise
1 hard-boiled egg, chopped
fine

1 c. fine bread crumbs
1 egg, well beaten
1 t. water
¼ t. dry mustard

Cut hard-boiled eggs lengthwise. Remove yolks and mash well. Add mustard, mayonnaise and 1 hard-boiled egg, chopped fine. Stuff this mixture into egg whites and press halves together. Roll eggs gently in bread crumbs and then in well beaten egg to which 1 teaspoon of water has been added. Roll again in crumbs and place on greased baking sheet. Dot with butter and bake 20 minutes in 350° oven. Tomato sauce or white sauce made with chopped chives or parsley is good with these. Recipe serves 6. One egg is sufficient for one person.

May be made ahead of time and chilled until baking time.

DEVILED EGGS WITH MUSHROOMS

12 hard-boiled eggs
1 lb. mushrooms, chopped
and sautéed
1 t. salt
¼ t. pepper
¼ c. grated cheese

¼ t. paprika
½ t. curry powder (optional)
or 1 small can deviled ham
2 c. white sauce (p. 129)
½ c. buttered bread crumbs

Cut eggs in half lengthwise. Remove yolks and rub them through sieve. Add seasonings, some of the mushrooms and just enough white sauce to hold mixture together for easy handling. Refill egg whites with this mixture and press halves together. Place in casserole and cover with white sauce mixed with remaining mushrooms. Sprinkle with buttered crumbs mixed with cheese. Bake in 400° oven until thoroughly heated and browned, about 20 minutes. Serves 6 generously.

MRS. JOHN MCDONOUGH

BASIC SOUFFLE (CHEESE)

3 T. butter
3 T. flour
3 eggs (4 if small)
1⅓ c. milk

½ lb. packaged yellow cheese
(combined Parmesan and
yellow cheese may be used)
Mustard, onion salt, salt

Melt butter in top of double boiler. Stir in flour and salt. Add milk slowly. Lower flame and stir in chunks of cheese. When mixture is smooth, stir in beaten egg yolks. Add mustard, onion salt and salt. After cooling this mixture for 20 minutes, combine it with stiffly beaten egg whites. Fold together slowly and carefully until both become one mixture. Set casserole in pan of water and bake in 325° oven for about 1 hour. Serves 6.

CHICKEN, TURKEY OR HAM: Replace cheese with 2 cups of minced chicken or ground cooked ham or turkey. Substitute pepper, marjoram and ½ teaspoon curry powder for cheese soufflé seasoning. Serve with sauce made by heating 1 can of cream of mushroom soup with pieces of browned bacon, parsley and mushrooms.

FISH: Use 2 cups of flaked, canned or cooked fish instead of cheese. Add celery salt, pepper, fennel and ½ teaspoon chopped parsley. Squeeze lemon over top before baking. Serve with following sauce: 1 pint of sour cream heated in double boiler with ½ cup chopped cucumber that has been seeded and salted.

FRUIT: Use only 1 cup of milk. Substitute 2 small jars of puréed baby food fruit for cheese. Season with 2 teaspoons of sugar, add pinch of cinnamon, nutmeg and salt. Serve with fresh, crushed strawberries.

1 or 2 teaspoons of brandy gives it a marvelous flavor.

MRS. CHARLES M. KORTRECHT, COLLIERVILLE, TENN.

CHEESE SOUFFLE

4 thick slices bread
3 eggs
2 c. grated, aged Cheddar
cheese

2 c. milk
Salt
White pepper
Dash of Tabasco

Remove edges from bread. Cut in cubes and place in layers with cheese in baking dish. Beat whole eggs until light. Add milk and seasoning and pour over bread. Let stand 30 minutes or longer. Bake for 40 minutes in 350° oven. Serves 6.

MRS. HOLMES' CHEESE SOUFFLE

1 lb. N. Y. Cheddar cheese
1½ c. milk
8 saltine squares

3 eggs
Pinch of salt
Dash of Tabasco

Place crackers in bowl and cover with milk. Let stand about 1 hour, then mash thoroughly. Grate cheese and mix in. Add salt and Tabasco. Beat yolks and mix in. Fold in well beaten egg whites. Cook about 40 minutes in 325° oven. Serves 6.

MRS. GEORGE HOLMES, SHADOWHILL, HERNANDO, MISS

EGGS A LA MORGAN STEEP

4 rounds of bread
8 slices of bacon
4 tomato slices
4 eggs

4 T. butter
Minced onion
Minced green pepper
Chopped parsley

Prepare sauce first by adding onion, pepper and parsley to melted butter and simmering gently for a few minutes. Grease 4 individual baking dishes with butter. Cut ½ inch thick bread rounds with biscuit cutter. Broil bacon and then broil tomato slices in remaining bacon fat. Season with salt and pepper when done. Place a bread round in each baking dish and top with a slice of tomato. Place a slice of bacon on either side of tomato and carefully break a raw egg on tomato. Season again with salt and pepper and put in 375° oven to cook until whites are set. Pour the above sauce over just before serving. Serves 4.

EGG AND MUSHROOM CASSEROLE

2 c. medium white sauce
  (p. 129)
1½ c. grated N. Y. cheese

6 hard-boiled eggs
1 large can mushrooms
¾ c. bread crumbs

Stir cheese into white sauce until melted. Alternate layers of egg slices, sliced mushrooms, sauce and bread crumbs in a casserole. Cover with grated cheese and heat in 325° oven. Serves 4.

MRS. THOMAS R. PRICE

EGGS LA RUSSE

4 hard-boiled eggs
Caviar or anchovy paste
4 rounds buttered toast
4 thick tomato slices
1 can sardines
Mayonnaise
Parsley

Sauce:
½ chopped onion
1 c. chili sauce
1 c. tomato catsup
1 c. olive oil
½ lemon (juice)
Salt

Prepare the above sauce. Let stand overnight and strain. Cut off tops of hard-boiled eggs. Mix yolks with caviar or anchovy paste and stuff into whites. Place thick slice of tomato covered with sardines on each round of buttered toast. Top with stuffed egg and cover with previously prepared sauce. Place mayonnaise on top and garnish with parsley. Serves 4.

MRS. DUNBAR ABSTON, GERMANTOWN, TENN.

EGGS BENEDICT

Eggs (1 per serving)
Thick cream sauce (p. 129)
½ c. grated cheese
Salt and pepper

1 wine glass sherry (optional)
Buttered toast
Ham or Canadian bacon

Make thick cream sauce, adding cheese, salt and pepper to taste and sherry, if desired. Place rounds of buttered toast on platter and lay slices of ham or Canadian bacon on them. Put poached eggs on top and cover with sauce.

Variation: Broiled slices of tomatoes on top of ham. Also delicious served with hollandaise sauce (p. 129).

MRS. J. SEDDON ALLEN, JR.

EGGS BERCY

3 T. herb butter (p. 130)
½ lb. chicken livers
6 eggs
1 small onion, minced

¼ t. marjoram
¼ t. chervil
½ t. salt
½ t. fresh ground black pepper

Wash chicken livers, removing any skin or sinew, and lay on paper towel to dry. Melt herb butter in small skillet, add livers and minced onion. Toss livers about pan with 2 knives to chop them up while cooking to prevent loss of their juices. Cook 10 or 12 minutes. Add marjoram and chervil. Toss again to blend and set pan aside. Carefully break eggs into a well buttered baking dish and set dish on an asbestos pad over low flame to cook slowly for about 3 minutes (just long enough for eggs to set). Remove from heat and sprinkle with half the salt and pepper. Turn livers over eggs and season with remaining salt and pepper. Set dish in 300° oven for 10 minutes until livers are heated and eggs are cooked but not hard. Total cooking time about ½ hour. Serves 6.

MRS. HUBERT K. REESE

EGGS DE LUXE

2 oz. Roquefort cheese
1 doz. hard-boiled eggs
¼ c. finely chopped celery
¼ c. finely chopped onion
2 t. finely chopped parsley

½ t. salt
¼ c. water
1 raw egg
½ c. bread crumbs

Slice eggs lengthwise. Remove yolks and work in cheese, onion, celery and parsley. Fill whites and press halves together. Dip these into beaten raw egg to which 1 teaspoon water has been added. Roll them in bread crumbs and fry in deep fat until golden brown. Figuring 2 eggs per person, this recipe serves 6.

Good served with tomato sauce and garnished with stuffed olives, pepper rings and parsley.

MRS. EDWIN B. PHILLIPS

PETITS POTS DE CREME AU FROMAGE

1½ c. grated Swiss cheese   4 eggs
Salt and red pepper to taste   Pinch nutmeg
2 c. XX cream

Grate cheese. Beat whole eggs with fork, gradually adding cream. Add salt and red pepper to taste and pinch of nutmeg, if desired. Add 1 cup of cheese, stir well, and pour into 6 little custard cups. Be sure that part of cheese goes into each one. Place cups in pan of hot water and bake in 350° oven for about 30 minutes. Just before serving sprinkle rest of cheese over each one and serve at once. 6 portions.

MRS. HUBERT K. REESE

QUICHE LORRAINE

Line a pie plate with pastry that is not too thin. Brush with egg white to seal it.

1. Sprinkle 1 cup chopped cooked ham over pastry.

2. Sprinkle ½ onion which has been sliced and sautéed, over ham.

3. Slice and sauté in butter ½ box of fresh mushrooms or 1 small can of sliced mushrooms. Pour over ham.

4. Place six small balls of cooked spinach around edge of pie (about 1 T. each).

5. Use 1 package of Swiss sliced cheese (5 slices to pkg.). Cut cheese with scissors and sprinkle over the sliced mushrooms.

6. Make a custard of 2 cups of coffee cream and 4 whole eggs and beat well. Add dash nutmeg, salt and pepper and ½ clove of crushed garlic. Pour over pie and bake in hot oven at 450° for 12 minutes to set the pastry. Reduce oven to 300° and cook 35 to 50 minutes until custard is set. Serve hot.

MRS. R. FRANK JACKSON, JR.

FRIED CUSTARD

2-3 small cinnamon sticks   ½ c. sugar
1 pt. sweet milk   1 t. butter
2 T. cornstarch   3 egg whites
1 T. flour   Pinch salt
3 egg yolks   Cracker crumbs
½ t. vanilla

Boil cinnamon sticks in milk for 2 or 3 minutes. Remove cinnamon and take milk off stove. Mix in cornstarch, flour, sugar, butter, salt, egg yolks and vanilla. Cook and stir until very thick. Pour into greased pan and set in icebox for 24 hours. Cut in 2 inch cubes, roll in egg whites and cracker crumbs and fry in deep fat. Serves 6.

Delicious with fried chicken.

MRS. EDWARD W. COOK

GRITS SOUFFLE

½ c. grits
1 c. milk
1 c. water
2 T. butter
3 egg yolks

3 egg whites
3 T. grated yellow cheese
1½ t. salt
¼ t. paprika

Heat milk and water in top of double boiler. Add grits and cook and stir for 1 hour. Remove from fire and add well beaten egg yolks, butter, cheese, salt and paprika. Fold in stiffly beaten egg whites and pour into greased baking dish. Cook in 350° oven for 45 minutes. Serves 4.

MRS. JOHN A. STOUT

PALO EGGS

4 eggs
4 artichoke bottoms
4 pieces of toast

Hollandaise sauce (p. 129)
Benedictine
4 slices of bacon

Warm artichokes and place on toast with poached eggs (slightly runny) nestled on top of each artichoke. Pour a generous amount of Hollandaise flavored with a little Benedictine over each egg and top with crumbled, crisp bacon. Serves 4.

MRS. HUBERT K. REESE

SWISS CHEESE FONDUE

2 lbs. Gruyere cheese
2 wineglasses white wine
1 t. flour

1 T. water
2 jiggers Kirsch

Grate cheese and place in chafing dish over hot flame with warmed white wine. Bring mixture to slow boil, stirring constantly. When it begins to bubble, add flour mixed with warm water. Stir in warmed Kirsch. Keep mixture hot and serve with French bread. Very rich. Serves 8-10.

The Swiss cube their bread and, using a fork, dip it into the chafing dish.

MRS. ROBERT G. SNOWDEN

SPINACH AND EGGS IN CASSEROLE

2 lbs. fresh, or 2 boxes frozen,
    spinach
1 c. cream sauce (p. 129)
2 T. grated cheese

6 eggs
Salt
Pepper
Butter

Cook spinach and drain well. Chop fine and season with salt, pepper and butter. Put in baking dish and over it break eggs. Mix cream sauce and cheese together and pour over eggs. Cover with grated cheese and bake in 325° oven long enough to cook eggs as desired. Serves 6.

ONION CHEESE CUSTARD

6 eggs
1 qt. milk
8 oz. grated cheese (Old English)

½ c. finely chopped onion
Salt and pepper
1 t. Worcestershire sauce

Scald milk and stir in cheese until melted. Beat whole eggs with seasoning and onion (more onion may be used if desired) and add to cheese mixture. Put in a casserole in a pan of water and bake in 300° oven for about 1 hour. Serves 8 to 10.

CASA BLANCA, MONTEGO BAY, JAMAICA, B.W.I.

WELSH RAREBIT

1 lb. N.Y. State cheese, grated
2 T. butter
1 c. light beer, warmed
1 egg

Dash of cayenne
1 T. dry mustard
½ t. Worcestershire sauce
Dash of salt

Melt butter in blazer pan of chafing dish. Add cheese and melt very slowly. When it is melted add the warmed beer a little at a time. Stir constantly in the same direction, never letting the mixture bubble. Stop when it has reached the consistency of thick cream. Mix seasonings in a cup with a tablespoon of beer and the lightly beaten egg. Stir this slowly into the cheese mixture. Pour over toasted English muffins or Rusk. Cooking time about 40 minutes. Serves 4 to 6.

This creamy Rarebit is ideally made in a chafing dish, but a double boiler may be used. Pass a platter of sauteed chicken livers and crisp bacon surrounded by broiled tomatoes and mushrooms. Add a green salad and a fresh fruit bowl and there you have a dinner!

MRS. JACK S. GOLTMAN

EGG CHOPS

6 hard cooked eggs, chopped
½ c. butter
5 T. enriched flour
1 c. milk
2 t. salt
½ t. paprika

Dash nutmeg
1 T. chopped parsley
3 T. chopped canned pimento
1 T. chopped onion
½ t. celery salt

Make thick white sauce of butter, flour and seasonings. Add remaining ingredients; mix thoroughly. Spread 1 inch thick in greased shallow pan; chill thoroughly. Shape in form of chops. Dip in flour, then in slightly beaten eggs mixed with 2 tablespoons water; roll in cracker crumbs or crushed corn flakes. Fry in shallow fat 375° 5 to 7 minutes. Drain on absorbent paper. Serve with Mushroom Sauce (p. 63). Serves 6-8.

Seafood

A plate of seafood is a kaleidoscopic gumbo. It can take the diner to far climes and add poetic fragrance to the fruits of the sea. Is it shrimp? Then does your mind's ear catch the hoarse call of shrimpers answered by the shrill cry of gulls as the boats glide into a sunset-gold harbor? Oysters are the pearls from Neptune's casket. Do you envision gleaming divers combing the ocean's floors; or, in a more homely vein, do you see a small black boy pleading, ''I'se got a whole pail fulla eysters fo jus' fo' bits''? Crabs bring back long days spent sunning on a pier, lazily letting down nets to draw up crustacean treasure. Clams evoke a cold New England shore where the smell of burning driftwood mingles with the salt spray and the quick, stinging rain. Ah, yes, there's a Siren's song in the plate before you, to add Romance to the joy of good eating.

— 1952

See Table of Equivalents (p. 240) for sugar and cream references.

BOILED FISH SUPREME

1 large fish (any kind)
2 cloves garlic
2 bay leaves
Red pepper to taste

1 t. salt
Tabasco (optional)
Wine vinegar

Put all seasonings except vinegar in large kettle with enough water to cover fish. Boil 5 minutes, then add fish which has been wiped inside and out with vinegar and rolled in cloth for easy handling. Boil 10 minutes. Remove and drain. Serve hot or cold with Egg Sauce. Serves 4.

EGG SAUCE

1 c. white sauce
4 hard-boiled eggs (chopped)
½ c. celery (chopped)
¼ c. peppers

2 T. parsley
3 T. lime juice or wine vinegar
1 t. salt
1 T. soy sauce

Make thick white sauce (p. 129). Add vinegar and soy sauce, then the vegetables and seasonings. Fold eggs in lightly.

A grand luncheon dish served with hot buttered rye crisp or beaten biscuits and a tossed salad.

MISS FRANCES E. SHIELDS, COCOA, FLA.

CLAM FRITTERS

3 c. ground clams
2 c. milk
4 eggs, separated
6 t. baking powder
¾ c. clam liquor

1 t. salt
½ t. pepper
1 t. ginger
4 c. unsifted flour

Mix clams, milk and liquor. Sift dry ingredients together and add. Beat eggs separately. Stir in yolks. Fold in whites. Drop from tablespoon and fry in deep fat. Yield: 36 fritters.

Oysters or shrimp may be substituted. Canned or frozen products may be used if fresh are not available. Makes a delicious hors d'oeuvre if dropped from teaspoon, fried, and put on toothpick to serve hot.

MRS. CHARLES B. DUDLEY, JR.

CRABMEAT JUSTINE

1 c. fresh, lump crabmeat
1 hard boiled egg, grated
2 T. sherry
Generous dash Tabasco

½ stick butter
¼ T. lemon juice
1½ c. Hollandaise sauce
4 squares toast

Melt butter, add crabmeat, grated egg and seasonings. Heat thoroughly. Place squares of toast in individual casseroles. Cover with crabmeat mixture. Top with Hollandaise sauce (p. 129). Brown under broiler. Serve immediately. Serves 4.

MRS. DAYTON SMITH

CRABMEAT CASSEROLE

½ lb. crabmeat (flaked)
1 tomato, sliced
3 strips bacon
Buttered bread crumbs
½ T. butter
¼ c. water
½ clove garlic, chopped

½ c. grated sharp cheese
1 t. (heaping) flour
½ t. dry mustard
1 t. vinegar
¾ c. milk
½ t. salt
Red pepper

Combine butter, garlic, water and cheese in a double boiler and cook 10 minutes over hot water. Mix flour, mustard, vinegar and stir milk into this. Add salt and pepper. When mixed, add slowly to cheese mixture and cook until quite thick. Put crabmeat in a buttered baking dish. Pour cheese sauce over it and top with bread crumbs. Cover top with tomato slices and bacon. Cover and cook 35 minutes in 400° oven. Just before serving remove cover and brown bacon. Serves 4.

MRS. KEITH M. SPURRIER, JR.

DEVILED CRAB

4 c. crabmeat
1 c. milk
1½ c. cracker crumbs
¼ lb. butter
3 T. minced parsley
1½ T. grated onion
¾ t. salt

Dash pepper
Dash Tabasco
3 T. Worcestershire sauce
1 t. dry mustard
1 green pepper, cut fine
1 pimento, cut fine
2 hard-boiled eggs, grated

Cook all ingredients (except crabmeat and ½ cup cracker crumbs) 10 minutes, stirring. Add crabmeat. Cook 5 minutes. Fill crab shells. Top with cracker crumbs and brown in hot oven. Fills 6 shells.

FISH PUDDING REBECCA

2 lbs. red snapper
2 qt. water
2 bay leaves
6 or 8 whole black peppers
2 garlic cloves
½ t. oregano

2 t. salt
1½ c. bread crumbs
1½ sticks butter
6 eggs separated
3 c. milk
1 T. chopped parsley

Boil snapper 20 minutes in water seasoned with bay leaves, pepper, garlic, oregano and salt. Drain, shred and season with salt and pepper to taste. Add egg yolks beaten, melted butter, bread crumbs, milk and parsley. Fold in stiffly beaten egg whites and pour in large shallow greased baking dish. Place in pan of hot water and cook in 350° oven for 45 minutes. Take out. Sprinkle with bread crumbs, put back in oven until brown and firm (30 minutes). Serve with either sauce given below. Serves 8.

WHITE SAUCE: (p. 129), including hard-boiled eggs, capers and parsley. Or:
Place in saucepan: ½ cup India relish and 1 cup mayonnaise. When this begins to simmer add ½ cup sour cream, 4 tablespoons milk, 2 tablespoons chopped parsley, ¾ teaspoon salt and 2 tablespoons lemon juice. Cook slowly until thick. Serve hot.

MRS. HENRY H. HAIZLIP

FISH PUDDING (Calvary Church)

3 lbs. red snapper or 3 pkgs.
  frozen fish
1 T. chopped parsley
1 T. scraped onion
3 eggs
Salt to taste

½ c. cracker crumbs
1 lemon
1 c. milk
1 stick butter (melted)
Pepper
Sherry to taste

Fish should be baked with a little seasoning, boned and shredded. Then put in bowl, add eggs and beat in well. Add milk and ½ of butter, cracker crumbs, parsley, onion and lemon juice, salt and pepper. Put in baking dish and top with cracker crumbs and rest of butter. If mixture looks dry, add more milk. Set in pan of hot water and bake in 325° oven for 50 minutes. Serve with tartare sauce. Serves 8-10.

TARTARE SAUCE

Take 1 cup stiff mayonnaise, thin with a little cream. Add chopped parsley, chopped sour pickle and capers, if desired.

LOBSTER NEWBURG

4 lobsters (1½ lb. each)
2 t. salt
½ t. paprika
½ c. sherry or madeira

1½ c. cream
4 egg yolks beaten
1 T. cognac
4 T. butter

Cook lobsters in boiling salted water for 20 minutes. Remove meat from shells, cut into ½ inch slices and refrigerate until wanted.
Melt butter in top pan of a chafing dish or double boiler, add lobster meat and sauté over direct flame until outside membrane becomes a bright red. Sprinkle with paprika. Add wine and cook until wine is almost completely cooked away. Place over hot water, add cream blended with egg yolks and stir gently until thick. Add cognac. Keep hot until ready to serve on fresh toast with touch of lobster coral or paprika. Serves 6 generously.

Mrs. C. D. Smith, II

LOBSTER THERMIDOR

2 1½ or 2 lb. lobsters, boiled
¼ c. butter
½ t. paprika
½ c. sherry
2 T. flour

2 c. thin cream
2 egg yolks
1½ c. sliced mushrooms,
  sautéed
½ c. grated cheese

Split lobsters lengthwise of shell and remove all lobster meat. Clean shell and wash well. Cut meat into good size pieces. Melt butter in saucepan, add paprika, sherry and lobster meat. Cook for a minute or two, then sprinkle with flour and fold together. Add egg yolks to cream and beat together, then add to lobster mixture. Add 1 cup of the mushrooms and cook over low heat, folding over and over until well blended, thickened and smooth. Fill shells with mixture, top with mushrooms and cheese. Brown well under broiler in oven. Serves 4.

LOBSTER FARCI

1 c. chopped lobster meat
2 hard-boiled egg yolks
2 T. chopped parsley
1 c. thin white sauce

½ c. sherry
⅓ c. buttered crumbs
Salt to taste
Pepper

To cooked lobster meat add yolks of eggs rubbed to a paste. Add parsley, sauce and seasonings. Put in buttered baking dish, cover with crumbs and bake in 350° oven until brown. Serves 2-3.

MRS. W. LYTLE McKEE

OYSTERS A LA ELLIS

1 qt. oysters
2-3 shallots, minced
1 stick butter
1 box mushrooms, sautéed
1 t. lemon juice
Dash Worcestershire sauce

1 t. salt
Pepper
Sherry to taste
Hollandaise sauce
Brown roux

Drain oysters and pick out shells. Cut up and sauté mushrooms in butter. Add shallots and when they begin to cook, add oysters. Cook until oysters curl around edges. Add seasonings. Add Hollandaise sauce (p. 129) and ½ as much brown roux, made with flour, butter and moistened with beef stock. Squeeze in a little lemon juice and a dash of Worcestershire sauce. Season to taste with salt, pepper and sherry. Add to oyster mixture just before serving on thick toast. Serves 8.

MR. CASWELL P. ELLIS, NEW ORLEANS, LA.

OYSTERS "JOHNNY REB"

1 qt. select oysters
¾ stick of butter
1 t. lemon juice
¼ t. salt
1¼ c. cracker crumbs

¾ c. top milk
2 T. minced parsley
2 t. shallots, minced
Red pepper to taste

Butter shallow casserole, put layer of oysters in bottom. Sprinkle with parsley, shallots, salt, pepper, little lemon juice, cracker crumbs and dot with butter. Then make another layer of oysters and repeat. Cover top with cracker crumbs and dot with ample butter. Just before baking pour milk over all, letting milk mix in well with oysters. Bake in 325° oven for ½ hour. Serves 8.

MRS. MARY McKAY, VICKSBURG, MISS.

SCALLOPED OYSTERS

1 qt. oysters
2 T. butter
1 onion or 3 shallots, chopped
1 T. flour
2 t. dry mustard
2 t. lemon juice

½ t. vinegar
1½ t. Worcestershire sauce
Salt to taste
1 T. minced parsley
½ c. cream

Heat oysters slightly, drain and to this liquid add enough water to make 1 cup. Cook onion in butter, add flour and stir constantly. Add seasonings and cream. When very hot, pour over oysters and serve on toast or in patty shells. Serves 8.

MRS. H. G. THOMPSON

OYSTERS ROCKEFELLER

4 doz. oysters on half shell
8 strips crisp bacon
2 c. chopped spinach
3 T. minced parsley
½ can tomato paste
½ c. chopped celery and leaves
2 green onions and tops
½ t. salt

¼ t. pepper
¼ t. paprika
⅓ c. lemon juice
4 drops Anisette
1 T. white wine
1 stick butter, melted
Rock salt

Melt butter in saucepan. Put bacon, spinach, parsley, celery and onions through meat grinder. Add to butter with remaining ingredients except oysters. Cook 4 minutes to blend seasonings. Heat a layer of rock salt in pans until very hot. Place oysters in half shell on salt. Put a spoonful of sauce on each oyster. Cook in 475° oven for about 7 minutes or until oysters curl and sauce browns lightly. Serves 8 as appetizer, or 4 as main course.

For a Sunday night supper this makes a good main course served with a tossed salad and hot French bread.

Mrs. Gus Morgan

CHILLED SALMON

2 3-lb. salmon
1 c. diced carrots
1 c. chopped celery and leaves
⅓ c. chopped onion
⅓ c. chopped green pepper
4 T. butter

3 qt. cold water
1 bay leaf
4 sprigs parsley
¼ c. lemon juice
4 t. salt
¼ t. thyme

Sauté celery, onions, carrots and pepper in butter in a large pot. When soft add water and seasonings. Simmer for 30 minutes and strain. Wrap salmon in cheese cloth, place in pot and simmer in the clear broth until tender but not soft (about 12 minutes to the pound). Remove skin and let fish cool in broth. Chill for several hours or overnight. Serves 6-8.

Serve with sauce Verte (p. 137).

Mrs. Robertson G. Morrow

SALMON IN SHELLS

2 c. shredded salmon
2 c. white sauce (p. 129)
1 chopped pimento
1 chopped green pepper
1 t. chopped parsley

½ t. Worcestershire sauce
1 t. lemon juice
½ lb. yellow cheese
½ c. toasted bread crumbs

Combine above ingredients (except for cheese) in a buttered casserole. Cook 30 minutes in a 350° oven. Take out, cover with grated cheese and bread crumbs. Return to oven long enough to melt cheese. Serves 6.

Mrs. Lovick P. Miles, Jr.

SALMON SOUFFLE

3 T. butter
1 c. milk
1 c. flaked canned salmon,
drained
3 T. flour
1 t. salt

½ t. paprika
1 T. minced parsley
1 T. chives or grated onion
2 t. lemon juice
4 eggs, separated

Melt butter, blend in flour and add milk gradually. Add salmon and seasonings and last of all lemon juice. Beat egg yolks and add to first mixture. (This part may be done in morning and placed in refrigerator until 1½ hours before serving.) Beat egg whites until stiff but not dry and fold into salmon mixture. Bake 1½ hours at 300°, or at 425° for 25 minutes. Serves: 5-6.

Mrs. George S. Miles

JUSTINE'S SEAFOOD CASSEROLE

½ c. diced lobster
½ c. lump crabmeat
½ c. diced boiled shrimp
½ c. chopped fresh
mushrooms

½ stick butter
1 c. thin cream sauce
1 T. sherry
½ c. grated American cheese

Sauté mushrooms in butter. Mix seafood and cream sauce (p. 129). Pour in casserole. Top with grated cheese and bake 20 minutes at 350°. Serve with cheese sauce. Serves 4.

CHEESE SAUCE

1 egg yolk
1 c. cream
1 t. flour
Dash cayenne

Dash white pepper
¼ t. salt
¼ stick of butter
⅛ c. grated cheese

Put all ingredients except egg yolk in top of double boiler over medium flame and cook until slightly thickened. Remove sauce from fire and blend in beaten egg yolk.

Mrs. Dayton Smith

SHRIMP CREOLE

5 lb. cleaned raw shrimp
2 sticks butter
or ½ lb. salt pork diced
or ½ lb. diced bacon
3 green peppers, chopped fine
4 onions, chopped fine
2 cloves garlic, chopped fine
4 c. celery, chopped fine

½ c. parsley, minced
3 No. 3 cans tomatoes
½ t. black pepper
1 t. salt
1 t. curry powder
1 t. thyme
1 red pepper
or ½ t. cayenne

Sauté peppers, onions, garlic, celery, parsley in either salt pork, bacon or butter. Add tomatoes and seasonings and cook slowly 30 minutes. Add shrimp and cook 20 minutes more. Serve with rice (p. 105) in ring. Serves 8-10.

Mrs. E. Harrison Humphreys

FRENCH FRIED SHRIMP

1 c. flour
½ t. sugar
½ t. salt
2 T. Wesson oil

1 c. ice water
1 egg
2 lb. raw shrimp

Mix all but shrimp together. Clean and peel shrimp. Dip in batter and fry in very hot fat 350°, 8-10 at a time. Drain on absorbent paper. May be kept hot in oven, until all are prepared.

Mrs. Donald W. Lewis

CURRIED SHRIMP

1 c. butter or chicken fat
1 large onion, chopped
1 large apple, chopped
1 c. celery, chopped
2 t. curry powder
5 T. flour
1 T. lemon juice

1 c. X cream
½ t. salt
Dash black pepper
2 c. shrimp, cooked
½ c. seedless raisins
2 T. chutney
2¼ c. chicken broth

Melt butter in heavy skillet. Add apple, celery, onion, and cook gently for 5 minutes. Sprinkle curry and flour over mixture until blended. Remove from heat and gradually add chicken broth and lemon juice. Then add cream and mix well. Return to fire and cook until thick. Add salt and pepper. Add shrimp, raisins, and chutney and simmer for 15 minutes. Do not overcook. Serves 4 to 5.

Mrs. Donnell McCormack

SHRIMP NEWBURG

½ stick butter
2 T. flour
1 c. top milk
2 lb. cooked shrimp
1 c. X cream

Dash paprika
¼ t. salt
2 egg yolks, beaten
¼ c. sherry

Make white sauce using butter, flour and milk. Add seasonings, shrimp and cream. Remove from fire and stir in egg yolks and sherry. Serve with toast points. Serves 4.

Mrs. George A. Coors

SHRIMP PIQUANTE

2 lb. jumbo shrimp
Salt
Mace
Oregano
Cayenne

Paprika
Lemon juice
Onion juice or garlic
Butter
Olive oil

Peel and clean raw shrimp. Place in a flat pyrex baking dish or individual casseroles and season by sprinkling with seasonings. Then cover with slices of butter about ¼ inch thick and a tiny bit of olive oil. Place in 350° oven and cook 35-40 minutes. Allow 8-10 shrimp per serving.

These are good served in a chafing dish at a cocktail party. If used as a luncheon dish, French bread is excellent with it.

Mrs. Eric Babendreer

SEAFOOD CASSEROLE

1½ lb. shrimp
3 lobster tails
1 lb. fresh crabmeat
  or 1 large can mushrooms
½ lb. American cheese, grated
4 c. fish or chicken stock

3 T. butter
3 T. flour
2 pkg. frozen chopped spinach
Garlic salt
Salt to taste
Red pepper

Cook seafood in stock. Shell, breaking into bite size pieces. Make sauce using butter, flour and 3 cups of stock. Season to taste with salt and red pepper. Place spinach, thawed and seasoned with garlic salt, in bottom of large casserole. Pour seafood (mushrooms if used), and sauce mixed over this. Cook at 350° for 30 minutes. Then cover with cheese and cook 10 minutes more. Serves 8-10.

Seafood may be cooked day before. Canned shrimp may be used, but is not quite as good.

MRS. WALTER P. ARMSTRONG, JR.

SPICED SHRIMP

6 lb. shrimp
½ gal. water
1 T. caraway seed
1 T. pickling spice
1 T. whole pepper

4 t. salt
1 bay leaf
1 t. dry mustard
1 t. red pepper
Celery leaves

Put seasonings in water and boil 20 minutes. Add shrimp and boil 20 minutes more. Serve blistering hot.

BUTTER SAUCE:

2 lemons
1 T. tarragon vinegar
1 T. Worcestershire sauce
2 T. soy sauce

7 or 8 drops Tabasco
1 t. salt
½ lb. butter, melted

Combine and serve in bowls as dip for a "Peel your own" shrimp dinner. Serves 6-8.

MRS. STANFORD Y. SMITH

POMPANO DUCHESSE

4 sole or pompano filets
1 8¾-oz. can white unspiced
  grapes

½ c. cooking sauterne
½ stick butter
½ t. salt

Drain grapes and reserve juice. Cut grapes in half and soak 1 hour in sauterne. Broil filets under flame, turning once. When white side is up (last), baste with butter, salt and ⅛ juice from the can of grapes. Heat wine and grapes and baste filets with them 5 minutes before serving. Serve on hot platter with sauce and grapes poured over fish or in a sauce boat. Serves 4-6.

MRS. HENRY H. HAIZLIP

SHRIMP WITH CUCUMBER JELLY

6 or 8 cucumbers
Juice of 2 small onions, grated
4 t. salt
½ t. white pepper
Juice of 2 lemons

2 envelopes gelatin
¼ c. cold water
¾ c. boiling water
3 lb. cooked shrimp

Peel cucumbers. Score 2 of them with prongs of fork and slice very thin. Place in bowl of ice water (no salt), cover tightly and put in refrigerator to chill. Grate remaining cucumbers until you have 4 cups of pulp and juice. Add lemon juice and onion juice and salt and pepper. Soak gelatin in cold water; when softened add boiling water. Cool and add cucumber pulp. Mix well and pour in large (1½ to 2 quart) ring mold. Cover and place in refrigerator to set firm. To serve turn out on plate and garnish dish with well-drained crisp sliced cucumbers. Fill center of ring with shelled cold shrimp. Serve with Parsley Sauce.

PARSLEY SAUCE:

Chop the white of a hard-boiled egg with the leaves from a bunch of parsley, mash the yolk with 2 tablespoons olive oil, 1½ tablespoons lemon juice and 1 tablespoon of vinegar and beat the parsley mixture into it. Serves 6-8.

BOILED TROUT

5 lb. of trout
1 large stalk celery
3 carrots
2 large onions
1 lemon, sliced

2-3 T. vinegar
2 T. salt
2 t. mixed spices
4 c. cold water
2 green olives

Place trout in small roaster, leave head and tail on but remove eyes. Cut celery, carrots and onions very fine. Put in roaster with other seasonings. (Remove red peppers from mixed spices.) Add cold water, cover and let come to boil. Turn down heat and simmer for 30 minutes. Remove to platter, skin. Place carrot in mouth and olives in eyes. Pour Hollandaise sauce (p. 129) over all and serve. Serves 3-4.

MRS. J. WARFIELD RODGERS

TROUT MARGUERY

1 trout
3 T. butter or olive oil
6 young onions, sliced
12 shrimp, chopped
¼ lb. mushrooms, minced

2 truffles, sliced
   or few olives, chopped
1 recipe Hollandaise sauce
   (p. 129)

Put butter or olive oil in baking pan. Salt and pepper fish inside and out. Split, dip in flour and place in pan. Bake in hot oven ½ hour, basting often. Fry onions in small amount of butter until yellow. Add shrimp, mushrooms, truffles or olives and sauté for 5 minutes, stirring constantly. Fold this into Hollandaise sauce and pour over trout. Serves 2.

MRS. MILLARD M. BOSWORTH

CURRIED TUNA

1 7-oz. can tuna
1½ c. medium white sauce
2 T. onion, minced
2 T. celery, minced
2 T. green peppers, minced

½ c. ripe olives, chopped
2 hard-boiled eggs, chopped
1½ t. curry powder
3-4 c. cooked rice (p. 105)

Heat tuna in white sauce (p. 129). Add other ingredients. Blend in curry powder. Serve hot over rice. Serves 4-6.

Mrs. Walter P. Armstrong

JELLIED TUNA

1 T. lemon juice
1 T. parsley, chopped
1 c. celery, chopped
½ t. salt
⅛ t. pepper

2 c. flaked tuna
1 T. gelatin
¼ c. cold water
1 c. boiled salad dressing
  (p. 115).

Moisten gelatin in cold water, dissolve in hot boiled salad dressing. Add other ingredients. Mold and chill. Serves 8-10.

Mrs. Dunbar Abston, Germantown, Tenn.

TUNA FISH PIE

4 T. butter
1 slice onion, chopped
4 T. flour
⅛ t. pepper
¾ t. salt
2 chicken bouillon cubes
1¾ c. boiling water

½ c. milk
1 c. celery, chopped
3 hard-boiled eggs, sliced
12 oz. can tuna fish
1 recipe baking powder
  biscuits

Cook onion and butter 2 minutes. Add flour, salt and pepper. Add bouillon cubes dissolved in water and milk. Stir until sauce boils. Add tuna, celery, eggs and top with very small biscuits. Bake until biscuits brown. Serves 6.

Mrs. Robert G. Snowden

TOASTED TUNA LOAVES

6 frankfurter buns
¼ lb. American cheese, cubed
3 hard-boiled eggs, chopped
1 7-oz. can tuna, flaked
2 T. onion, chopped

2 T. stuffed olives, chopped
2 T. sweet pickle, chopped
2 T. green peppers, chopped
½ c. mayonnaise

Slice off top of buns and scoop out soft center. Combine other ingredients and fill bun centers. Replace top slice. Place in shallow baking pan, cover with aluminum foil. Cook at 250° about 30 minutes. Serve hot. Serves 6.

Mrs. John McDonough

SHRIMP PUFFETTES

1 doz. shrimp (cooked) $\frac{1}{4}$ c. grated cheese
$\frac{1}{2}$ c. mayonnaise   1 egg white, well beaten

Fold stiffly beaten egg white into mayonnaise and cheese. Spread on crackers lightly. Place shrimp on top, brush with mayonnaise. Broil until brown. Serves 4-6.

LOBSTER ROUNDS

1 can lobster meat   Salt and pepper
Thick white sauce (p. 129)   Dry sherry
1 beaten egg yolk   Grated cheese

Cut sandwich bread in small circles about $1\frac{1}{2}$ inches in diameter. Shred can of boiled lobster meat and mix with enough thick white sauce to hold meat together. Add a beaten egg yolk, salt, pepper and dry sherry to taste. Pile lobster on the rounds of bread, dust with grated cheese. Toast in 350° oven under broiler until cheese is browned. If desired, this may be frozen.

RULES FOR FREEZING FISH

Cooked fish may be frozen by wrapping the cooked fish in heavy aluminum foil, pressing close to fish to avoid air pockets. Fold under and press tightly as foil need not be sealed with heat or tape. Freeze.

Creamed fish may be prepared by your favorite recipe and frozen after allowing to cool.

Fish pies made from separately cooked fish and vegetables, then frozen in unbaked pie crusts, make excellent left-over dishes.

Casserole combinations of fish with vegetables, noodles or rice, should be slightly undercooked before freezing as the process of reheating to serve will otherwise result in a too-done product. Some people recommend adding noodles or rice after thawing. Be sure to omit potatoes from any of these dishes as potatoes do not freeze well.

Spices and other seasonings often lose their strength during freezing so it is best to season during the reheating process.

All of these dishes can be placed in the oven in the frozen state. If a pyrex dish is used be sure to place them in a cold oven to avoid cracking the dish.

There is a trick to keep uncooked fish from drying out while freezing. Wrap fish for freezing but do not seal. Now freeze. When the fish is hard take it out of the freezer, unwrap it and dip it in ice water for a few minutes. Drain. A thin coating of ice will have formed. A second coating may be desired to act as more insulation. When rewrapping the fish, take care not to break this protective layer of ice. Seal and freeze. Fish frozen in this way should keep a year.

Game and Poultry

Just between us girls — would game be included among our "fair weather friends"? It would seem more femininely accurate to call them "foul — foul weather rivals that is!"

In the cold winter months, just as we wives are needing our husbands to keep the home fires burning, off they creep in the wee, small hours eager to wade deep in muddy waters, sit huddled in charcoal heated blinds or roam through frost-crusted fields — the mighty hunters answering the call of the wild!

Upon their return from such Sportsman's Paradise, laden with good humor, stories and their kill, we would do well, not only to listen breathlessly and admire, but to heed closely the following savory recipes. After all, 'tis only "sportswomanly" to prepare and serve our vanquished rivals in a style fit for our lords!

— 1952

See Table of Equivalents (p. 240) for sugar and cream references.

DOVES

Olive oil	Curry powder
Dry mustard	Pepper
Celery Salt	2 t. Worcestershire sauce
Garlic Salt	Juice of 1 orange
Salt	Juice of 1 lemon

Roll doves in enough olive oil to get them well greased. Sprinkle curry powder, dry mustard, celery salt, garlic salt, salt and pepper over doves. Put in covered dutch oven with a little water and cook for 1½ hours in 250° oven. Add Worcestershire sauce and juice of orange and lemon. Cook for 10 to 15 minutes longer or until tender.

MRS. E. HARRISON HUMPHREYS

ROAST DUCK

Flour	Consommé and water (1 can
Apple	of each for every 4 ducks)
Onion	1 c. sherry wine
Celery	

Clean and pick ducks, rub with bacon drippings, pat with flour (this is done so they will not brown too early). Take a nice sized piece of apple, onion and celery and put them inside each duck, also put in the roaster. Add to this the consommé and water. If you have a self-basting roaster, don't fail to use it as it will improve the ducks 100%. Place ducks in covered roaster in 275° oven for 4 hours, basting frequently. Add sherry wine and cook ½ hour longer. Scrape off flour, brown and serve.

This is the perfect way to cook ducks that have been frozen for any length of time. They are so juicy and good that even rare duck fans rave.

MRS. LAWRENCE K. THOMPSON, JR.

ROAST WILD DUCK

Salt	2 t. butter
Pepper	Garlic clove
1 potato	Bacon strips
1 onion	½ c. sherry

When duck is picked and cleaned, soak in strong salt water for 3 hours. Dry thoroughly inside and out. Rub with salt and pepper. Place a peeled potato and an onion inside the duck. Be sure to remove them before serving as they absorb the strong flavor. Have electric roaster pre-heated, add butter. When butter is hot, place duck in roaster and put strips of bacon across the breast. A small pod of garlic may be added if desired. Cover roaster and cook for 25 minutes at 500°. Reduce temperature to 250° and cook 2½ hours. When almost done, add sherry. Lift out duck and strain gravy, which may be thickened with a light cream sauce (p. 129). Allow half a duck to person.

Since the secret of cooking wild ducks is to get them tender and juicy, an electric roaster is ideal. It steams them and basting is unnecessary. Turn them occasionally. Add a little hot water if pan gets dry. This recipe may also be used with a covered roaster in the oven.

MRS. HENRY LOEB, JR.

WILD DUCK AND DRESSING

2 ducks	2 bay leaves
2 pinches rosemary	1½ T. cornstarch
2 t. thyme	Salt and pepper

Stuff ducks with dressing and sew up tightly so it will not come out during cooking. Sprinkle outside liberally with salt and pepper. Put breasts down in ½ inch water in roasting pan. Add rosemary, thyme and bay leaves to the water, also the giblets if you have them. Preheat the oven to 275°, have the ducks at room temperature. Cover roasting pan and cook for 2 hours. Basting unnecessary. Make gravy from liquid in pan by thickening with corn starch and seasoning with salt and pepper.

DRESSING:

2 c. crumbled corn bread, made with yellow meal	4 T. bacon grease
2 c. dried bread crumbs	1½ t. salt
⅓ c. green pepper, cut fine	½ t. pepper
½ c. onions, cut fine	1 t. rubbed sage
¾ c. celery, cut fine	½ t. poultry seasoning
	½ c. warm water

Cook green peppers, onions and celery in skillet in bacon grease until tender. Add to corn bread and bread crumbs. Add seasonings and warm water. This makes 4 cups of dressing.

MRS. HERBERT HOOD, JR.

DUCK A L'ORANGE

Salt and pepper	1 T. orange marmalade
Butter	2 livers, duck or chicken
Soy sauce	1 T. flour
2 oranges	1 T. Curacao

Rub duck inside and out with salt and pepper, then brush with melted butter and soy sauce. Grate peel from oranges, reserving peel. Slice oranges, discarding seeds, and stuff duck with orange slices and orange marmalade. Place them in roaster, sear at 450° for 10 minutes, cover and cook for 1½ hours, basting occasionally. In the meantime, simmer finely chopped livers in enough salted water to cover until very tender. Pour off pan juices from duck, discarding excess fat. Simmer juices gently and add grated orange peel and chopped livers with their broth. Thicken with flour. Put Curacao in gravy boat, add gravy and serve immediately.

MRS. BETTY BARBER

BLOODY DUCK (wild game only)

Clean thoroughly, remove all pin feathers and rub well with salt. Place in preheated 500° oven in open baking pan and sear 18 minutes by the clock. Remove and serve immediately.

If you have never tried rare duck you have a treat in store. This recipe, allowing ½ to 1 whole duck per person, served with wild rice, red currant jelly, red wine, and a tossed green salad cannot be surpassed. This recipe is only for wild game and cannot be recommended for domesticated fowl.

MRS. SYDNEY R. MILLER, JR.

PRESSED DUCK

The following recipe for Pressed Duck is a combination of two of the world's most famous recipes—The Mud Lake Club and Tour D'Argent Restaurant.

1. Obtain by one means or another some ducks.
2. Carefully cut in one piece from the body of the duck the 2 breasts.
3. Marinate breast in olive oil and chopped onions for at least 2 hours.
4. Cut carcass of duck into medium size portions and warm in skillet or in oven until all portions of carcass are thoroughly heated.
5. Place heated portions of carcass into a duck press and squeeze out, as much as possible, all blood from meat and marrow from bones.
6. To each cup of duck juice add the following approximate amounts:
   A. 1 jigger red wine, preferably French bordeaux or burgundy.
   B. 1 jigger cognac.
   C. ⅛ lb. sweet butter.
   D. Dash of cayenne pepper.
   E. 1½ t. horseradish.
   F. 1 jigger cointreau.
   The above ingredients should be added to the duck juice that has been obtained from pressing the carcass. This should be done after the juice has been cooked for about 5 to 7 minutes and added according to taste.
7. The breast of the duck should be wrapped around the middle with a piece of bacon held in place by a toothpick.
8. An extremely hot charcoal fire should be prepared. This is very important. The duck breasts should be cooked over the charcoal, which should not be over 6 inches away from the duck breast, the coals being absolutely red.
9. For rare duck they should be cooked 4 minutes per side, for medium, 7 minutes per side, for well done, 10 minutes per side. The duck should be served immediately after being taken off charcoal.
10. Duck should be served with wild rice. The gravy made from the duck carcass should be put on the wild rice and on the duck breast itself.
11. An additional item which should be served with the duck is a slice of orange with grape jelly.

MR. J. TUNKIE SAUNDERS

WILD DUCK IN SOUR CREAM

2 ducks	1 t. thyme
2 onions	Salt and pepper
2 c. chicken broth or water	Nutmeg
3 garlic cloves	2 c. sour cream
4 bay leaves	2 T. sugar
Parsley and fennel	2 T. lemon juice

Dress ducks, place onion in each and truss for roasting. Place them in roaster with hot chicken broth or water. Tie in a cloth, garlic cloves, bay leaves, thyme, a little parsley and fennel and place in broth. Salt and pepper birds and sprinkle with nutmeg. Cover and roast for 1 hour at 350°, adding more liquid if necessary. Remove bag of spices and onions. Take birds from roaster, skim off fat and add sour cream, sugar and lemon juice, all blended together, to the broth in the pan. Boil rapidly until thickened, stirring vigorously. Add more liquid if necessary. Return birds to roaster and place in 250° oven for 15 to 20 minutes.

MRS. RICHARD LEATHERMAN, ROBINSONVILLE, MISS.

DUCK BREASTS ROYALE

Breasts of 4 ducks
½ lb. butter
⅔ c. sherry

⅓ c. bourbon or brandy
1 T. currant jelly
1 T. Worcestershire sauce

Make sauce by combining sauce ingredients in a skillet and bring to a boil. Add duck breasts, cover and reduce heat. Cook for 12 minutes, turning once. Place breasts on platter, pour sauce over them and serve immediately. Serves 4.

MRS. CHARLES P. OATES

DUCK BREASTS CHARCOAL BROILED

Cut breasts from duck. Place them on wax paper, cover with chopped onion and garlic, wrap them in the wax paper and let stand for 1 hour. Wipe off onion and garlic, wrap breasts in bacon and secure with toothpicks. Cook over a low charcoal fire on a grill covered with top of roasting pan, 3 minutes per side for rare, 7 minutes per side for medium and 10 minutes per side for well done. Pour melted butter over breasts and serve at once. Serves 2.

MRS. RICHARD LEATHERMAN, ROBINSONVILLE, MISS.

DUCK SAUCE

This sauce may be used with charcoal broiled duck if desired. Mash blood and marrow from remaining duck carcass until you have 2 cups. Cook down to 1 cup. Add ¼ stick butter, 1 teaspoon Worcestershire sauce, 2 tablespoons sherry, salt and pepper. Cook until thick. Serve with wild rice.

MRS. WILLIAM A. LEATHERMAN, ROBINSONVILLE, MISS.

WILD DUCK, WITHOUT WILD FLAVOR

1 t. soda
1 potato, quartered
½ onion
Salt and pepper
Crushed red pepper

¼ onion
¼ cooking apple
Celery leaves
Juice of ½ orange
Bacon strips

Soak duck 30 minutes to 1 hour in salted water to cover, to which soda has been added. Rinse duck. Put it in pan of fresh water with potato and ½ onion. Boil for 30 to 45 minutes. Pour out water, wash duck thoroughly and start all over again. Season cavity of duck heavily with salt, black pepper and red pepper. Insert ¼ onion, cooking apple and sprig of celery leaves. Place duck in roaster in 1 inch of water. Squeeze orange juice over duck, lay a strip of bacon over the breast, and salt and pepper. Cover and cook in 275° oven for 3½ to 4 hours. Baste often. Remove cover the last ½ hour to brown duck. Allow ½ duck per person.

MRS. GEORGE A. COORS

For best results in freezing ducks—place clean duck in empty ½ gallon milk carton, add pinch of salt, ½ t. vinegar and add enough water to cover bird.

BARBECUED DUCK

2 ducks
2 garlic cloves
1½ c. lemon juice
4 t. Worcestershire sauce
4 t. tomato catsup

Tabasco to taste
4 T. butter
Salt
Pepper
Paprika

Combine and stir over heat the sauce ingredients. Cut the breasts from the ducks. Rub them with garlic cloves. Broil them under a flame or cook them over a charcoal fire until done, basting frequently with the sauce.

DUCKS AU MADEIRA

4 small ducks
1 t. Worcestershire sauce
5 drops Tabasco

2 c. sweet wine or sherry
½ lb. butter
Salt

Brown ducks in butter. Add Worcestershire sauce, Tabasco, wine and salt to taste. Cover and put in 400° oven for 30 to 40 minutes. Lower heat to 250° and cook until tender, approximately 1 hour and 45 minutes in all.

Jerusalem root artichokes may be added as they are very nice with duck. Birds or venison may be prepared in the same way.

MRS. EMMETT R. HALL

WILD GOOSE

1st, shoot him.
2nd, pick and clean him.
3rd, wash him in olive oil, rub salt inside.
4th, stuff him with 1 apple and 1 potato.
Steam him in roaster with 1 cup water for 1 hour. Then remove apple and potato and stuff him with dressing (your favorite turkey dressing). Add 1½ cups water to roaster, cover breast of goose with a grease soaked tea towel and cook covered for 2 hours in 275° oven. Uncover and cook 1 more hour in 250° oven. Goose can be cooked by recipe for wild duck on page 53. Simply increase cooking time about 1 hour.

MRS. RICHARD LEATHERMAN, ROBINSONVILLE, MISS.

PHEASANT MARYLAND

2 heaping T. shortening
2 heaping T. bacon fat
½ c. sherry wine
¾ c. hot water

½ t. basil
1 T. lemon juice
1 small can mushrooms

Split bird in half. Flour heavily, using paper bag method. In a dutch oven or heavy skillet melt fat. When hot, brown the pheasant on both sides until outer skin is crisp. Drain about half of excess fat, replace the browned bird and pour over it the sherry mixed with water, basil and lemon juice. Cover tightly and bake at 375° for 1½ hours. Remove and arrange bird for serving. Thicken the pan drippings, if necessary, with flour and water, **not** milk. Add mushrooms and a dash more sherry. Bring to a boil and pour over bird, with chopped parsley sprinkled on top at last moment.

MRS. EDWARD W. COOK

PHEASANTS OR QUAIL IN CREAM

2 pheasants or 4 quail
Bacon strips
4 T. butter
8 shallots (onions)
Cognac

Salt
Pepper
2 c. veal or chicken broth
1 c. XX cream
¼ c. pickled grated horseradish

Clean pheasant or quail well, cover their breasts with strips of bacon and tie them securely. Brown them carefully in an iron skillet with butter and shallots. Pour over them a little cognac and light it. Salt and pepper them, add veal or chicken broth and cook uncovered in 350° oven for ½ hour, basting frequently with the juice. Add cream and horseradish. Let all this cook another 20 minutes, continuing to baste with the sauce. Season to taste. Place birds on a platter, pour sauce over them and serve. Serves 4.

MRS. ROBERTSON G. MORROW

SMOTHERED PHEASANT

1 pheasant
4 small onions
5 stalks celery
Butter
Flour
Thyme

Marjoram
½ c. consommé
½ c. dry red wine
Chopped parsley
Salt
Pepper

Disjoint the cleaned and plucked pheasant, shake the pieces in a bag containing seasoned flour until they are thoroughly coated, then lay them in a roaster or a dutch oven. Around them place peeled onions (as many as can be used, depending on size). Sprinkle the pieces of pheasant with a generous pinch each of thyme, marjoram and chopped parsley. Liberally dot with pieces of butter the size of grapes. Lay stalks of celery, leaves and all, across the pheasant pieces and the onions. Pour into the roaster consommé and red wine. Cover and place in 450° or 500° oven for about 1½ hours, adding more wine as necessary and basting at least every ½ hour. Next, uncover, turn up the oven for a quick browning and remove pheasant, onions and celery to a hot platter. Put roaster on top of stove over a medium flame, add a little more red wine, scraping the pan well to loosen any particles that adhere, and when the gravy is heated, pour over the pheasant, onions and celery.

MR. A. ARTHUR HALLE, CORDOVA, TENN.

LUCILLE'S WILD RICE AND MUSHROOM DRESSING

1 lb. wild rice
1 stalk celery
1 green pepper
1 onion

½ stick butter
Salt and pepper
2 8-oz. cans chopped mushrooms and broth

Cook wild rice according to directions on box. Chop celery, green pepper and onion and sauté them in butter. Add salt and pepper, mushrooms and broth. Mix with rice and stuff bird heavily. Bake as usual. This makes enough for a turkey.

MRS. WILLIAM A. LEATHERMAN, ROBINSONVILLE, MISS.

SMOTHERED QUAIL

2 quail   2 or 3 T. butter
Salt and pepper   1 to 2 T. water

Clean quail. Sprinkle with salt and pepper. Brown slightly in butter in skillet, add water, cover and cook slowly 35 to 45 minutes. Serves 2.

MRS. W. LYTLE McKEE

QUAIL AND BACON

Quail   Salt and pepper
1 T. vinegar   Bacon strips
Butter

Pick, split and clean quail. Wash and soak in water mixed with vinegar. Rinse. Put walnut size piece of butter in quail, sprinkle with salt and pepper, wrap with bacon and secure with toothpicks. Broil under low flame, turning occasionally until done, about 30 to 40 minutes.

MRS. RICHARD LEATHERMAN, ROBINSONVILLE, MISS.

BROILED QUAIL

Split quail, wash and dry. Sprinkle liberally with salt and pepper, sparingly with sugar, paprika and lemon juice. Place in pan close under a hot broiler. Brown slightly on both sides, dot with butter, lower heat and turn frequently, adding butter to each side. Cook about 20 minutes until nicely brown and done.

MRS. HERBERT HOOD, JR.

RABBIT IN WINE AND OLIVE OIL

1 rabbit, cut in pieces   1 c. dry red wine
Garlic clove   Salt
¼ c. olive oil   Pepper
Flour

Put pieces of rabbit in flour seasoned with salt and pepper and coat well. Rub skillet with garlic, add olive oil and brown rabbit. Place rabbit with olive oil, garlic clove and red wine in casserole and cook covered in 375° oven, basting occasionally, until rabbit is very tender. Add more wine if needed. Serves 3 or 4.

MRS. LEO J. BUCHIGNANI

VENISON IN CASSEROLE

2 lbs. venison loin   1 pinch cayenne
Red wine or watered vinegar   ¼ t. pepper
2 T. olive oil   1 T. chopped parsley
2 T. sherry   4 T. flour or sufficient to
2 T. butter   thicken gravy
1 t. salt   1½ pt. stock (bouillon cubes)
1 t. chopped onion   1 small can mushrooms or 1
                                               pt. fresh, chopped

Soak venison in red wine or weak vinegar overnight. Brown cubed venison in skillet in olive oil and butter. Mix flour into ½ cup stock and add to remaining stock, mushrooms, onion and seasoning in skillet. Cover and let simmer 1 hour or until tender. Add sherry before serving.

MRS. E. HARRISON HUMPHREYS

POULTRY

Chickens are such talented creatures—the only ones who can get fried, stewed or boiled and still be socially acceptable; the only ones who can lay an egg with such success that they are the envy of every comedian! 'Tis the only group of which the male sex is the one to tell the world to rise and shine. (Crowing, however, is not uncommon with the human male.)

Chickens could well be included on the best dressed list. They might even belong to the international set—Tetrazzini of Italy, Paprika of France, or Chop Suey of China. Why, they are so ingenious no one has ever figured which came first, the chicken or the egg.

Yes, it can honestly be said, "Versatility, thy name is chicken!"

BRUNSWICK STEW

4 large chicken breasts	Salt
5 large chicken legs	Pepper

Cook chicken slowly until meat falls off bones. Remove all bones and skin. To the broth add:

2 No. 2½ size cans tomatoes	Salt to taste
1 qt. diced Irish potatoes	Red pepper to taste

Cook all this very slowly until stew has thickened, add:

2 large cans cream style corn	1 stick butter

After corn is added carefully watch to avoid burning. After adding corn and butter cook for one hour. Stew should be thick—it is not a soup. Serves 6.

Mrs. John M. Maury, Jr.

CHICKEN CROQUELLE

1 large chicken	Nutmeg
1 lb. fresh mushrooms, cooked	1 wine glass sherry
or 8 oz. can mushrooms	2 T. chicken fat
Parsley, chopped	2 T. flour
Salt	1 c. milk
Cayenne	1 c. chicken stock
Onion juice	3 egg yolks

Cook chicken and cut in pieces. Make cream sauce by putting fat in skillet, blend in flour and add milk and stock gradually, stirring until thickened. Remove from fire and add, separately, yolks of eggs, beating constantly. Add chicken, mushrooms, seasonings to taste and sherry. Mix well and put in long shallow baking dish. Dot with butter and bread crumbs and bake in 350° oven until well heated and brown on top. Serves 6 to 8.

Mrs. William E. Buxton

ARROZ CON POLLO

½ c. olive oil
2 large chopped onions
2 pods garlic, mashed
4 medium roasting chickens
3 T. salt
2 t. paprika
1 t. pepper
4 bay leaves
2 T. minced parsley
8 c. water, boiling

½ t. saffron
4 c. uncooked rice
2 cans pimentoes
1 can asparagus
1 can tiny peas
1 can tomatoes
¼ lb. ham, cut up
¼ lb. butter
Grated Parmesan cheese

Cut chicken in serving portions. Heat olive oil in large kettle. Add onion and garlic and cook to a golden brown. Add chicken, ham, salt, pepper, paprika, bay leaves, parsley and saffron. Cook about 30 minutes, turning occasionally. Add boiling water and tomatoes, cover and simmer for 1¼ hours. Remove chicken from pot and strain broth. Add rice to pot, and continue simmering for about 30 minutes. Add chicken which has been kept warm, serve on platter and arrange pimentoes, buttered asparagus and peas on top and around it. Just before serving, add some sherry or sauterne if desired. Sprinkle cheese over top. Serves 24.

This is directly from Puerto Rico. A variation is to omit pimentoes, asparagus and peas, then serve with 1 pound cooked sausage and 1 pound cooked shrimp, floated on top.

Mrs. Tannen Hollenberg

CHICKEN ROSEMARY

1 2¼ lb. chicken, disjointed
½ stick butter
1 medium onion, chopped
1 garlic clove, optional
6 oz. sauterne or chablis

½ pt. cream
1 t. rosemary
Flour
Salt
Pepper

Wash and dry chicken, sprinkle with salt and pepper. Lightly brown onion and crushed garlic in butter, using heavy skillet or dutch oven. Add chicken, brown and dust both sides with flour and crushed rosemary. Add wine and cook covered in 300° oven for 45 minutes or until tender. Remove chicken to hot platter, add cream to sauce in skillet, heat and pour over chicken.

Mr. Hal W. Hirsheimer

CHICKEN TETRAZZINI

1 large hen
2 green peppers, chopped
2 onions, chopped
1 small bunch celery, chopped
1 can mushrooms
3 slices bacon

2 pts. medium cream sauce
2 c. grated cheese
American or Wisconsin
¾ small pkg. vermicelli

Cook hen until tender and cut up as for chicken a la king. Fry bacon, using grease to cook onions, green peppers, celery and mushrooms until tender. Add bacon to these ingredients. Make cream sauce of chicken fat and broth and after it is of medium consistency, add grated cheese. Cook vermicelli. Mix all ingredients, put in casserole and bake in 400° oven until hot. Before serving, sprinkle over the top a can of Chinese noodles (the kind used in Chop Suey) or toasted almonds. Serves 10 easily.

Mrs. Paul T. Gillespie

BARBECUED CHICKEN IN PAPER BAG

Mix and heat thoroughly the following sauce

3 lbs. chicken	3 T. brown sugar
3 T. catsup	1 t. salt
2 T. vinegar	1 t. mustard
1 T. lemon juice	1 t. chili powder
2 T. Worcestershire sauce	1 t. paprika
4 T. water	½ t. cayenne
2 T. butter	

Cut up 3 pound chicken as for frying. Grease the inside of a medium size heavy paper sack and place in roaster. Set oven at 500°. Salt and pepper the chicken, dip in sauce and place in sack along with remaining sauce. Carefully fold sack so as not to leak. Cover roaster, cook 15 minutes at 500°, lower to 350° and cook 1¼ hours. Do not open sack until finished cooking. Serves 4.

MRS. JOHN H. TERRY, SANTA ROSA, FLA.

CHICKEN SOUFFLE

1 c. cooked, ground chicken	½ t. salt
4 T. butter	¼ t. celery salt
4 T. flour	1 t. chopped parsley
1½ c. milk	2 t. chopped green pepper
3 egg yolks	3 egg whites
¼ t. paprika	

Melt butter, add flour, and when blended add milk and cook until thick. Stir constantly, and add yolks and seasonings. Beat for 2 minutes. Fold in chicken, parsley, green pepper and stiffly beaten egg whites. Pour into oiled mold, set in pan of hot water and bake 35 minutes in 325° oven. Remove and let stand 5 minutes. Carefully unmold and serve with mushroom sauce. Garnish with parsley. Serve at once. Serves 4.

This dish can successfully be made with tuna fish if you put it in colander and pour boiling water over it before using.

MRS. MILLARD M. BOSWORTH

CHICKEN QUEEN

⅛ lb. butter	1 c. almonds
1 lb. fresh mushrooms	1 small onion
½ c. sherry	Salt
1 large hen	Pepper
1 bunch celery, chopped	Flour

Cook hen in water to cover till meat falls from bones. Cut into 1 inch pieces. Broil sliced mushrooms, celery and onion in butter. Add salt and pepper. Blanch and slice almonds. Thicken chicken stock with flour. Combine all ingredients and add sherry when ready to serve. Pour into casserole over tiny, freshly made biscuits, cover with biscuits. Serves 6 to 8.

MRS. J. W. MACQUEEN, BIRMINGHAM, ALA.

HINT FOR LEFT-OVER TURKEY: place a slice of turkey and cooked country ham·on toast, cover with cream sauce (p. 129), grated New York State cheese and sprinkle with paprika. Heat in 400° oven 15 minutes.

CHICKEN CROQUETTES

1 boiled fat hen	Cracker crumbs
½ set boiled calf brains	1 egg
1¼ c. cream sauce (p. 129)	1 T. water

After chicken and brains are cooked, put through meat grinder. Make thick cream sauce. Mix chicken and brains with cream sauce and work into soft mixture. Pat into desired shape and roll in cracker crumbs. Dip into beaten egg, to which 1 tablespoon water has been added for each egg used, and roll again in cracker crumbs. Fry in deep fat until lightly browned. Makes 16 to 20 large croquettes.

MRS. JOHN F. KIMBROUGH

CHICKEN DIVAN

Alternate twice in small individual pyrex pie plates:

1 layer of broccoli, cooked
1 layer of breast of chicken or turkey, cooked

Pour over all of this:

2 cups of Hollandaise sauce to which has been added:
½ pt. XX cream, whipped
5 T. sherry

Cover sauce with grated Parmesan cheese and brown under flame. The breasts of 2 hens will serve 5.

MRS. WALTER LANE SMITH

COUNTRY CAPTAIN CHICKEN

2½ or 3 lb. chicken	1½ t. salt
2 T. fat	1 t. white pepper
2 T. butter	1¼ t. curry powder
1 onion, sliced thin	1¼ t. powdered thyme
1 green pepper, sliced	¼ c. almonds
1 or 2 garlic cloves, chopped	1 T. currants
2 No. 2 cans tomatoes	1¼ t. chopped parsley

Cut up and brown chicken in fat, and put aside. Using clean pan, brown onions, pepper and garlic in butter. Add tomatoes and seasonings and cook for 10 minutes. Place chicken in casserole and pour in sauce, adding fat in which chicken was browned. Cover with brown paper and lid and bake in 350° oven 45 minutes. When ready to serve, add blanched and browned almonds and well-washed currants. Serve with rice. Serves 4 or 5.

MRS. M. M. JAMIESON

CHICKEN WITH NOODLES

1 large hen	6 green peppers, chopped
1 large and 1 small pkg.	1 c. dry mushrooms
noodles	1 large can tomatoes
2 stalks celery, chopped	1 lb. ground beef
6 onions, chopped	1 T. salt
1 soup bunch, optional	1 t. pepper

Cover hen with 2 quarts cold water, add soup bunch and simmer until tender. Mix well, celery, onion, green peppers, mushrooms, tomatoes, beef, salt and pepper. Cook in skillet until well done. Cook noodles, then mix with sauce. Place on platter with slices of chicken on top. Serves 8.

MRS. SADIE BECK TAYLOR

CHICKEN LOAF WITH MUSHROOM SAUCE

1 4-lb. chicken
1 c. cooked rice (p. 105)
4 well-beaten eggs
2 c. bread crumbs
1½ t. salt
3 c. chicken stock

Stew chicken. Remove meat from the bones and dice. Combine all ingredients and pour into an oiled 10-inch pan. Set in pan of hot water and bake uncovered in a 300° oven for 1 hour or until done. Remove from pan and serve with mushroom sauce. Serves 8 to 10.

MUSHROOM SAUCE:

¼ c. butter
1 c. mushrooms, sliced
¼ c. flour
2 c. stock
¼ c. top milk
⅛ t. paprika
½ t. chopped parsley
½ t. lemon juice
Salt
Pepper

Melt butter and add mushrooms. Simmer for 5 minutes. Add flour and blend. Gradually add stock and blend. Cook until smooth, stirring constantly. Add milk, paprika, parsley, lemon juice, salt and pepper.

MRS. WILLIAM A. LEATHERMAN, ROBINSONVILLE, MISS.

CHICKEN WITH MUSHROOMS AND WILD RICE

1 3-lb. fryer, cut in pieces
2 T. butter
2 T. olive oil
2 green peppers, chopped
½ lb. fresh mushrooms,
canned may be used
1½ c. wild rice
¼ c. sherry
½ c. stock or water, if needed
Salt
Pepper
Rosemary

Thoroughly brown chicken on all sides in butter and olive oil in frying pan. Remove chicken and brown mushrooms and green peppers in same skillet. Return chicken to pan, add sherry and seasonings and cook covered over low heat for 20 minutes. If not enough sauce left, remove chicken, add water or stock (canned chicken consommé may be used) and simmer a few minutes. Meanwhile, wash well and cook rice. Mound rice on a platter, surrounding it with chicken, and pour sauce over all. Serves 4.

MRS. WILLIAM A. LEATHERMAN, ROBINSONVILLE, MISS.

CHOP SUEY OR CHOW MEIN

⅔ c. butter
2½ lb. chicken or lean pork,
cooked, cut in thin strips
3 onions, chopped
6 c. chopped celery
1 T. salt
1 T. pepper
3½ c. stock
3 cans mixed Chinese
vegetables
⅓ c. water
6 T. cornstarch
2 T. soy sauce
1 T. sugar

Melt butter in hot skillet. Brown meat lightly, add celery and onions and simmer for 5 minutes. Add to the stock salt, pepper, water, cornstarch, soy sauce and sugar and simmer for 5 minutes. Combine with meat, celery, onions, and well-drained Chinese vegetables and mix thoroughly. Heat to boiling point and serve piping hot with noodles for Chow Mein, or rice for Chop Suey. Serves 10 to 12.

MRS. MILLARD M. BOSWORTH

CHICKEN SPAGHETTI

1 5 to 6 lb. hen
1½ pkg. spaghetti
2 onions, chopped
1 can tomato paste
Worcestershire sauce
Cayenne pepper
8 oz. can mushrooms
½ lb. American cheese, grated

1 pinch sage
Garlic clove
3 or 4 cloves
1 pinch celery seed
12 to 15 stuffed olives
1 T. chili powder
Pepper
1 small can English peas

Stew hen until tender. Dice when cold. Cook and blanch spaghetti. Skim fat from stock, add spaghetti to stock, place in large skillet and simmer. In another pan brown onions in chicken fat, add tomato paste, season highly with Worcestershire sauce and cayenne pepper and add to spaghetti. Add diced chicken and mushrooms, cooking until well blended. Add grated cheese, sage, garlic, cloves, celery seed, stuffed olives, chili powder, pepper and last the English peas. Remove garlic and cloves before serving. Serves 12.

This dish, always delicious, is even better if cooked the day before using.

MRS. JOHN HUCKABEE

CHICKEN WITH ARTICHOKES

1 2-lb. chicken, cut as
for fricassee
½ c. olive oil
4 cooked artichoke hearts,
sliced, fresh or canned
1 green pepper, sliced
1 onion sliced thin
1 c. rice

2¼ c. hot chicken broth,
canned may be used
Juice of 1 lemon
½ box fresh mushrooms,
sliced and sautéed in butter
24 toasted almonds
Salt and pepper to taste

Sauté chicken, onion, and green pepper in olive oil. Remove chicken, pour lemon juice over it. Add washed rice and broth to pan. Cook about 20 minutes. Remove from fire and add mushrooms, artichoke hearts, salt and pepper. Place chicken and rice mixture in large casserole and bake, covered, 1 hour in 350° oven. Sprinkle toasted almonds over top before serving. Serves 4.

MRS. JACK S. GOLTMAN

FONDUE DE POULET A LA CREME

2 roasting chickens
1 stick butter
3 or 4 small white onions,
sliced thin
Salt to taste

Pepper to taste
1 wineglass Cognac
½ t. curry powder
3 c. cream (XX best)
½ stick butter

Clean chickens, cut as for fricassee. Melt 1 stick butter in shallow iron skillet and add chicken, onions, salt and pepper. Cover pan tightly and simmer about 20 minutes or until chicken is tender. Add Cognac, curry powder and cream and simmer 5 minutes longer. Remove chicken to a hot platter. Pass sauce through a fine sieve, pressing hard on onions. Heat it without boiling, stir in ½ stick butter and pour over chicken. Serve at once. Serves 8.

MRS. HUBERT K. REESE

COLD CHICKEN IN A BLANKET

2 5-lb. roasting chickens	Peel of 1 lemon
6 whole carrots	4 T. butter
4 stalks celery	4 T. flour
4 white onions	Salt
Chicken broth or canned	Pepper
chicken consommé	Juice of 1 small lemon
1 pt. cream	½ t. powdered mace

Place chickens in pan and cover with broth. Add whole carrots, celery and onions. Cover and simmer gently until quite tender. Remove from fire and let cool in their own juice. Take chickens from pan and skin them. Remove all meat in as large pieces as possible, arrange it on a platter with the white in the center and dark around the edges. Make cream sauce by heating cream in double boiler with lemon peel. Melt butter and blend in flour, then add hot cream gradually. Continue to cook in double boiler for 15 to 20 minutes, adding a little broth if too thick. Add salt and pepper to taste, mace and lemon juice. Pour sauce over chicken carefully so as to coat it evenly and place in refrigerator. When ready to serve, decorate with whole carrots from the stock, crisp cut bacon curls and parsley. Serves 10 to 12.

Your reputation as a hostess will be made when you serve this.

Mrs. Hubert K. Reese

DRESSING FOR FOWL

5 stalks celery, chopped	1 large onion, chopped
1 recipe cornbread (p. 150)	½ c. drippings from fowl
6 slices toast or dry bread	Salt and pepper to taste

Cook celery and onions in very little water until thoroughly wilted. Crumble breads together with fingers. Stir in celery and onions, plus the water in which they were cooked. Season and add drippings. The mixture should be barely moist, not wet. Cook fowl ½ the required time, then stuff lightly with dressing and continue cooking until done. Cook any left-over dressing in a separate pan. This recipe will stuff a large hen or 2 ducks.

This is a good basic dressing. For variation add ½ pint oysters and liquor, 1 cup chopped pecans or 1 teaspoon sage.

Mrs. William D. Galbreath

FRIED CHICKEN

1 chicken	Flour
1 egg	Salt
Juice of 1 lemon	Pepper
Milk to cover	

Beat egg, add lemon juice and milk enough to cover chicken. Soak at least ½ hour, longer soaking recommended. Remove chicken from batter and place in paper sack into which has been put flour, salt and pepper to taste. Shake thoroughly. Fry uncovered in hot grease about 1 inch deep until tender. If more than 1 chicken is used increase eggs and lemon proportionally and use enough milk always to cover chickens.

Mrs. Frank M. Norfleet

CREAMED CHICKEN, MUSHROOMS AND SWEETBREADS

1 hen	1 large can B in B mushrooms
1 T. salt	2 T. butter
2 bay leaves	2 T. flour
1 clove	1 c. cream
1 sprig parsley	Few drops onion juice
1 stalk celery	½ t. salt
1 onion	⅛ t. pepper
2 lb. sweetbreads	1 pinch paprika
1 T. butter	½ c. cream, whipped

Cover hen with boiling water. Boil 5 minutes, then simmer. When chicken is half done, add salt, bay leaves, clove, parsley, celery and onion. Continue cooking until done. When cool, remove skin and cut meat in bite-sized pieces. Drop sweetbreads in boiling water in skillet and simmer until tender. Place them in cold water 15 minutes to harden, drain and remove skin membranes. Cut sweetbreads in pieces, drain mushrooms and cook together in 1 tablespoon butter for 10 minutes in skillet. Do not brown. Make cream sauce in double boiler by blending flour in 2 tablespoons melted butter and onion juice. Gradually add cream, stirring constantly, and cook until sauce thickens. Add salt, pepper and paprika. To every cup of cream sauce add 2 cups of mixed chicken, sweetbreads and mushrooms. Return all to double boiler and fold in whipped cream very gently. Heat and serve in timbal shells, on buttered toast or in bread baskets. Garnish with parsley. Serves 10.

MRS. WILLIAM L. NICHOL

TAMALE PIE

1 4-lb. baked hen	1½ t. Mexene powder
1 large can tomatoes	3 cans High Power tamales
1 can tomato sauce	1 10-oz. can niblets (corn)
1 can tomato purée	24 to 30 ripe olives, sliced

Save stock from baking hen. Put stock in heavy skillet, add tomatoes, tomato sauce, purée, Mexene powder, and salt and pepper to taste. Let this simmer for 1½ hours. Slice chicken and cut tamales lengthwise. Put into a large casserole a layer of chicken with niblets and sliced ripe olives, then a layer of tamales. Repeat until casserole is filled. Pour sauce over all and bake in 300° oven until very hot, about 40 minutes. Serves 10.

MRS. W. LYTLE McKEE

TURKEY DRESSING

4 small onions	12 oz. box Grapenuts
2 T. butter	1 wine glass French vermouth
¼ lb. pork sausage	1 wine glass cognac
1 lb. fresh mushrooms	Juice of 1 lemon
3 doz. chestnuts	Salt and pepper

Brown slightly in butter chopped onions and sausage. Add chestnuts that have been boiled 15 minutes, skinned and peeled. Add peeled, washed and sautéed mushrooms to onion mixture, then add Grapenuts, lemon juice, French vermouth, cognac, salt and pepper. Stuff turkey, cook with breast down and baste often.

HOT TAMALE LOAF

1 large hen, cooked	1 t. red pepper
8 onions	Salt to taste
6 garlic cloves	3 c. corn meal, sifted
1 No. 2 can tomatoes	3 T. shortening
2 T. chili powder	1 c. chicken stock
1 t. cumin seed	Corn shucks, if available

Grind meat of chicken. Cook onions and garlic (ground together), tomatoes, chili powder, cumin seed, salt and red pepper for 20 minutes. Mix with chicken. Scald corn meal, shortening and salt with chicken stock. Line 2 quart casserole with sterilized corn shucks, if available. Spread thin layer, about ⅛ inch thick, of corn meal at bottom, then layer of chicken mixture, alternating layers until dish is almost full. Leave space at top for swelling. Cover with shucks, cooking paper or casserole lid and steam in moderate oven about 3 hours in covered roaster with water in bottom. Serves 6 to 8.

Ground beef may be substituted for chicken with excellent results. As corn meal swells and is apt to dry out in cooking, dish should be watched and more stock added as needed. Individual tamales may also be made from this recipe.

MRS. SAM COOK, PINE BLUFF, ARK.

POULET A LA GENOISE (Cold Chicken)

1 large fowl or capon	Salt
1 c. salad oil	Pepper
1 c. vinegar	Pickled gherkins
1 small glass white wine	Capers

Boil fowl or capon in salted water, keeping cover of pan tightly closed. When cooked, strain it in a colander. Cut it in pieces, place in a deep dish and pour over it while still hot the following sauce: combine and mix well, salad oil, vinegar, salt, pepper, a few pickled gherkins (finely chopped), some capers and white wine. Let the fowl be completely covered by the sauce and remain in this marinade for at least 24 hours in the refrigerator. Turn occasionally. Serves 4 to 6.

MRS. A. H. ESKELUND, OSAKA, JAPAN

YOUNG GUINEAS

3 guineas, 1 to 2 lb.	1 8-oz. can mushrooms,
¼ lb. butter	chopped
2 c. water	4 T. flour
2 t. Worcestershire sauce	1 c. water
Salt and pepper	4 T. sherry
3 T. chopped parsley	

Cut the guineas in half. Brown both sides in butter in a skillet, add 2 cups water, cover and simmer 20 minutes. Add Worcestershire sauce, salt and pepper, simmering 10 minutes. Add mushrooms, parsley and sherry, cooking for 20 minutes or until guineas are tender. Remove the birds, add flour mixed in 1 cup water to thicken the gravy and a little more sherry if desired. Serves 6.

MRS. W. GORTON BERRY

POULET CHAUD-FROID (Cold Chicken)

1 3½ or 4 lb. hen
2½ c. stock
1 can consommé
1 onion, sliced
6 celery stalks
1 large can B in B
  mushrooms, sliced
½ t. rosemary
½ t. savory
Cayenne

6 carrots
12 stuffed olives
Lettuce
Watercress
Parsley
Anchovies
Cucumber strips
Mayonnaise
3 T. anchovy paste

Cook chicken in water with onion and celery until tender. Remove chicken and when cool, pull off generous sized pieces of meat, discarding skin and bones. Skim fat off stock. Cook stock down to 2½ cups, add consommé, bring to a boil, simmer 10 minutes and strain into a bowl. Immediately add mushrooms, rosemary, savory and cayenne. Allow this to cool while you scrub carrots, slice in half lengthwise and simmer in salted water until barely tender. Pour the cooled broth into a glass casserole and arrange in it pieces of chicken, mushroom slices, carrots and olives so that they show to best advantage. Bake, covered, in a preheated 375° oven 25 to 30 minutes. Remove, cool, then chill in refrigerator. After an hour or so carefully remove light layer of fat that may have risen to the top. Chill at least 6 hours, preferably overnight. The broth will congeal into a beautiful golden brown aspic. Place casserole on a platter or tray, surround it with crisp lettuce cups and garnish with watercress, parsley, anchovies and cucumber strips. Accompany this with a bowl of rich mayonnaise into which anchovy paste has been blended. Serves 6.

A canned whole chicken and its broth may be used for this recipe. For best results make dish day before using.

MRS. JAMES W. MOORE

TOMATO SUPREME

1 cooked hen
3 sets calf brains
1 lb. fresh mushrooms or
  2 8-oz. cans, chopped
4 T. butter
1 onion, chopped
1 T. olive oil
1 T. curry powder
2 T. cream

Salt
Red pepper
½ lb. N.Y. State cheese,
  grated
3 eggs, separated
12 to 14 tomatoes, using 6 to
  8 for juice and pulp
Buttered bread crumbs

Parboil brains in same water used to cook chicken. Broil onions in olive oil. Broil mushrooms in butter. Chop chicken meat and mushrooms very fine (a meat grinder may be used). Mash cooked brains with a potato masher and blend with chicken and mushroom mixture. Add onion, curry powder, dissolved in cream, 8 tablespoons grated cheese, tomato juice and pulp, salt and pepper to taste. Blend thoroughly. Beat in egg yolks, then fold in stiffly beaten egg whites. Cook about 5 minutes over very low flame, stirring constantly. Hollow out rest of tomatoes (the juice of 6 to 8 having been used for filling). Drain and rub lightly with salt. Fill tomatoes with filling, cover tops with buttered bread crumbs and rest of grated cheese. Heat thoroughly and brown in 400° oven about 10 to 15 minutes. Serves 12 to 14.

Filling may be made day before using and stored in refrigerator.

MRS. WILLIAM D. CONNOR, WASHINGTON, D. C.

CHICKEN JAMBOLAYA

1 young chicken
½ lb. raw ham
¼ c. hot lard
⅓ c. minced onion
½ c. skinned, minced tomato
1 c. uncooked rice

1 bay leaf
¼ t. thyme
¼ c. chopped parsley
1 t. salt
¼ t. pepper

Cut chicken into pieces, place in skillet with ham. Sauté for 5 minutes in lard. Remove the meat from the pan. Sauté in the same skillet for 3 minutes the onion and tomato. Stir in the rice. When the rice is well coated with lard, stir in the sautéed chicken and ham. Cover these ingredients well with boiling water. Add bay leaf, thyme, parsley, salt and pepper. Simmer these ingredients until the chicken is tender and the rice is done. Season if necessary with additional salt and pepper. Dry out the jambolaya by placing it for 5 minutes or more in a 350° oven. Serves 10.

This delicious old creole recipe calls for lard but butter or margarine may be substituted.

CHICKEN POT PIE

1 stewing chicken
2 c. flour
2 t. baking powder
⅞ c. milk

2 T. melted butter
2 well beaten eggs
1½ t. salt

Stew chicken making about 3 cups of gravy as the crust is apt to soak up quite a bit of it. Place the chicken pieces in a baking dish, add the gravy and pour the following batter over it.

BATTER:
Sift flour, salt and baking powder. Combine milk, butter and eggs. Add these ingredients quickly to the sifted flour mixture. Stir the batter as little as possible. Bake the pie in 375° oven until it is light brown. Serves 6.

HERB-BAR FARM CHICKEN

1 frying chicken, cut up in pieces
Salt and pepper
Paprika

Sugar
Lemon juice
3 T. butter or oleo

Squeeze lemon juice on chicken on all sides, then sprinkle liberally all over with salt, pepper and paprika and sparingly with sugar. Heat butter in frying pan and brown chicken, then lower heat, cover and cook until chicken is very tender. Add more butter if necessary to keep from burning. Do not use water. Turn chicken occasionally. Serve with gravy on bed of cooked rice.

MRS. HERBERT HOOD, JR.

Meats

Meat is truly the Master of Ceremonies at every meal, introducing the keenest of appetites to the greatest of satisfactions. It is the royal road to any man's heart and the king who crowns every woman queen of her kitchen. Be it beef, pork or lamb, we watch and wait for it at every dinner, and then look back on it with the fondest of memories.

Ever variable and always noble, meat stoops to conquer with the simple hamburger, strives to please with satisfying stews, stays to rule with roasts and chops, and makes a feast with succulent steaks. Young brides cannot wither nor old wives make stale, Meat's infinite pleasures.

— 1952

See Table of Equivalents (p. 240) for sugar and cream references.

RARE ROAST BEEF

For a rare roast, cook, according to the following directions, 17-18 minutes per pound. For a medium roast, allow 20-22 minutes per pound, and well-done requires 25-28 minutes per pound. Select a 3-4 rib roast. Rub it with salt and pepper and place, fat side up, in an uncovered roasting pan. Sear roast in a pre-heated 500° oven for 20-30 minutes. Reduce heat to 325° and cook 10 minutes. Remove from oven for 10 minutes, then return to oven for 30 minutes, out for 10 minutes, back in for 30 minutes, continuing this process until the required amount of cooking time is consumed.

MRS. ROBERTSON G. MORROW

BARBECUED BEEF

2 lb. ground beef
1 large onion, chopped
1 c. celery, chopped (optional)
1 bottle chili sauce or 2 c. catsup
1 green pepper, chopped

2 T. vinegar
2 T. Worcestershire sauce
5-7 drops Tabasco sauce
2 T. horseradish (optional)
2 T. dry mustard (optional)
Salt and pepper to taste

Brown meat in fat. Add rest of ingredients. Cook in 250° oven for 2 hours. Serve on toasted hamburger buns. Serves 6.

MRS. ARCHIBALD McCLURE

BARBECUED SPARERIBS

4 - 5 lb. spareribs
1 t. salt
⅛ t. pepper
1 thin-sliced lemon
1 large onion, chopped fine
1 c. tomato catsup
1 t. chili powder

1 t. celery seed
¼ c. each brown sugar, vinegar, Worcestershire sauce
½ t. mixed herb seasoning
2 c. water

Cut spareribs into serving size pieces. Spread, meaty side up, in large shallow pan. Sprinkle with salt and pepper. Put a slice of lemon on each piece. Sprinkle onion over all. Brown 30-45 minutes at 450°. Mix remaining ingredients and bring to boil for barbecue sauce. After 45 minutes pour off grease, add sauce to ribs and roast uncovered for 1-1½ hours more. Baste, turn occasionally. Add water if sauce gets too thick. Serves 4.

MRS. FRANK M. NORFLEET

CHILI CON CARNE

⅓ lb. beef suet diced
2 lbs. lean ground beef
4 cups water
2 small onions, chopped fine
2 garlic cloves, chopped fine
⅛ t. cumin powder

6 T. chili powder
1 large can tomatoes
1 T. paprika
½ t. salt
2 cans kidney beans

Cook suet until melted, add meat, onions and garlic. Add water, cumin and simmer for one hour. Add chili powder, tomatoes, beans, and simmer 1½ hours longer. Season with paprika and salt.

POUPIETTES OF BEEF

½ lb. bacon
2 T. finely chopped shallots
　or onions
4 T. chopped mushrooms
1 t. butter
2 T. chopped parsley
Dash of Worcestershire sauce

8 thin slices top round of beef
1 t. French's mustard
1 T. tomato sauce or catsup
1 t. beef extract
Juice of ½ lemon
Butter
Salt and pepper to taste

Put bacon through meat grinder. Add to this the onions, mushrooms and 1 teaspoon butter. Cook together for a few minutes then add parsley, salt and pepper, mustard and dash of Worcestershire, and continue cooking 2 minutes longer. Spread this paste on 8 individual very thin slices of beef which have been trimmed and pounded with wooden mallet. Roll, as a blanket, and tie with string. Salt and pepper and place in skillet with large piece of butter, browning evenly on all sides. Then add 12 mushrooms, sliced. Sauté in the butter. Add tomato sauce or catsup, and 1 teaspoon beef extract dissolved in a little boiling water. Simmer for a few minutes, add juice of ½ a lemon and lump of butter. Don't boil. Place poupiettes on hot platter and serve at once. Serves 6-8.

MRS. HUBERT K. REESE

ESCOFFIER BEEF

Rump roast of beef,
　or similar cut
2 carrots, sliced
2 onions, sliced
1 lb. mushrooms, or more,
　depending on size of roast

Several stalks of celery,
　chopped fine
1 garlic clove, chopped fine
Salt, pepper, nutmeg to taste
Red wine

Marinate roast in wine for 5 hours with salt, pepper and nutmeg. Brown carrots, onions, garlic, celery and mushrooms in butter. Sear roast. Put vegetables in bottom of dutch oven. Put roast on top. Pour wine in which roast was marinated over it and bake slowly 2 or 3 hours in 325° oven.

MRS. HUBERT K. REESE

POT ROAST A LA NEW ORLEANS

4 lb. pot roast
½ t. each pepper, ground
　cloves, mace and allspice
1 T. salt
1 large onion
1 or more garlic cloves
½ c. salad oil

2 T. lemon juice
1 T. vinegar
2 c. tomato juice or canned
　tomatoes
2 or 3 bay leaves
1½ c. beef stock

Wipe meat with damp cloth. Mix dry ingredients and rub into scored surfaces. Chop onions and garlic, add lemon juice, vinegar and only ¼ cup of salad oil. Let meat soak in this mixture for 5 hours in ice box. Turn occasionally. Then sprinkle with flour, sear in ¼ cup salad oil, and add liquid in which meat was marinated, tomatoes, beef stock and bay leaves. Cover and simmer for 3 hours. Add carrots, onions, and peeled potatoes 45 minutes before roast is done. Thicken stock with flour and serve as gravy. Serves 8 generously.

MRS. EDWARD W. COOK

BRAISED SHORT RIBS OF BEEF

4 lb. cut of short ribs
2 T. bacon fat
16 small white onions
½ lb. sliced mushrooms
1 scant t. tomato paste
3 T. flour
2 T. sherry with equal water

2½ c. boiling water
1 unbroken clove of garlic
Bouquet garni (carrot, leek,
 celery and parsley)
⅛ t. thyme
Salt and pepper to taste

Salt and pepper ribs and brown in bacon fat. Remove meat and brown onions, garlic and mushrooms. Cook until mushrooms are tender. Mix in tomato paste, flour, sherry and water, then pour in boiling water. Season with thyme, bouquet garni and salt and pepper to taste. Return ribs to pot, cover and simmer 2½ hours or until tender. Remove garlic and bouquet. Place meat on a hot platter, skim off all grease from sauce and pour over the beef. Serves 4.

MRS. HUBERT K. REESE

JELLIED BEEF LOAF

2 lbs. round steak cut in
 1-in. cubes
1 onion, sliced
2 stalks celery, chopped
1 carrot, chopped
3 c. boiling water
Few sprigs parsley
1 c. tomato juice
1 T. vinegar
2 t. salt

⅛ t. pepper
¼ t. dry mustard
½ t. Worcestershire sauce
1 t. horseradish, cream style
1½ T. plain gelatin
½ t. vinegar
¾ t. salt

Place first 9 ingredients in kettle and simmer covered for 1½ hours. Drain, reserving liquid. Chop meat slightly. Cool ½ cup liquid, soak gelatin in it for 5 minutes. Dissolve this in remaining 3½ cups liquid, boiling hot. Add remaining ingredients. Chill until it begins to thicken, add meat, pour into mold and chill until firm. Serve with Horseradish Cream Sauce (p. 135). Serves 8.

MRS. HENRY H. HAIZLIP

BEEF STROGANOFF

1½ lb. beef, filet or sirloin
3 T. prepared mustard
1 c. thin sliced onions
1 can tomato paste, equal
 amount water

1 T. Worcestershire sauce
1 T. paprika
1 can mushrooms
1 c. sour cream

Cut meat in finger strips. Spread mustard over meat and let stand in ice box for 1 hour. Fry onions in butter. Sear meat in hot skillet, add tomato paste and water, Worcestershire sauce and paprika. Simmer beef for 1 hour if top of round, ½ hour for filet. Add mushrooms and sour cream. Stir until well heated. Serve with Boiled Rice (p. 105) or Red Rice (p. 106) or French fried potatoes. Serves 4-6.

MRS. A. H. ESKELUND, OSAKA, JAPAN

BOEUF MORENO

6 ripe olives
¼ c. minced mushrooms
½ green pepper
1 medium onion, chopped
½ T. pan drippings

2 T. flour
1 c. stock
1 c. cooked beef, diced
2 T. sour cream
Dash of whiskey (optional)

Sauté olives and vegetables in drippings. Add flour and stir in stock gradually to make thick sauce. Add beef and bring to a boil. Stir in sour cream and a good dash of whiskey before serving. Serves 4.

Mrs. Hubert K. Reese

MEAT LOAF

2 medium onions
1 or 2 garlic cloves, minced
2 stalks celery with leaves
1 egg
1 lb. ground beef
¼ lb. sausage meat
¼ c. milk

½ c. chili sauce or catsup
2 t. salt
1 t. Accent
½ t. pepper
1½ c. bread, cracker or cheese
    cracker crumbs
1½ can tomato sauce (8 oz.)

Mix thoroughly beef, sausage, crumbs, onions, garlic, celery, slightly beaten egg, milk, chili sauce and seasonings. Stir well and press into well greased loaf pan. Bake 1 full hour in 350° oven. Pour tomato sauce over top and continue baking for another 15 minutes. To serve, take out of pan and place on hot platter, with rich sauce poured over. Serves 6 .

Mrs. R. Carl Dickerson, Jr.

SPICED ROUND

10-12 lb. round of beef
½ t. saltpeter

2 c. brown sugar
2 c. salt

Rub each side with this mixture and let stand overnight in a cool place. Then mix:

3 T. chopped onions
  or chopped celery
3 lb. beef suet
½ T. cayenne
1 T. ginger

1 T. ground cinnamon
1 T. nutmeg
1 T. allspice
2 T. black pepper

Heap spices on top of round and let stand 2 weeks, turning daily. Grind suet and onions or celery. Add spices in which meat has stood with the juice. If necessary add more spices and salt in above proportions. Make holes in round with large skewer and pack them with suet mixture. Tie firmly in heavy pudding rag and boil 15 minutes to the pound. Serve cold.

Recipe dated 1881.

Mrs. Robert H. Jordan

CURRIED ROUND STEAK

2 lb. round steak
3 small onions, minced
¼ lb. salt pork
1 T. curry powder

2 heaping T. flour
Milk, about ½ c.
Salt and pepper

Fry diced salt pork in skillet. Add diced steak and brown. Add onions, curry powder, salt and pepper. Cover with hot water and cook in covered vessel until meat is tender, about 1½ hours. Then thicken with flour and milk. Cook gravy to desired consistency. Serve with rice (p. 105). Serves 6.

MRS. E. HARRISON HUMPHREYS

OLD VIRGINIA CORN SCRAPPLE

2 large onions
½ T. butter
½ T. lard
2 lb. ground round steak

1 c. corn meal
1 large can tomatoes
1 small can mushrooms
Salt and pepper

Brown onion in fat. Add meat then corn meal, tomatoes, mushrooms, 1 teaspoon salt and pepper to taste. Cook for 2 hours in skillet over slow fire. Serves 6-8.

This recipe is over 100 years old.

MRS. A. ARTHUR HALLE, CORDOVA, TENN.

STEAK AND KIDNEY PIE

2½ lb. beef or lamb kidneys
1 lb. beef (less tender cut)
½ onion

1 stalk celery
Stock
1 t. Kitchen Bouquet

Skin and cut in 1 inch pieces the kidneys and beef. Dredge in flour, salt and pepper and brown. Add celery and onion. When brown, add stock to cover. Cook over a very low fire for 2 hours, or until tender. Add Kitchen Bouquet and thicken gravy if necessary. Put filling in a casserole, cover with pie crust (p. 188), brown and serve. Serves 6 amply.

MRS. WILLIAM A. LEATHERMAN, ROBINSONVILLE, MISS.

BARBECUED WIENERS

6 wieners
3 T. butter
½ c. chopped onion
1 can tomato sauce, 8 oz.
4 t. sugar

3 T. vinegar
4 t. Worcestershire sauce
1 t. mustard
½ t. black pepper
1 t. paprika

Boil wieners 10 minutes. Split wieners lengthwise and place in greased baking dish. Brown onion in butter in skillet. Add rest of ingredients and bring to a boil. Pour this sauce over wieners and bake in 350° oven for 30 minutes. Can be served on buns or as a meat dish. Allow 2 wieners per person.

MRS. ROBERT L. TAYLOR

LAMB HASH WITH RICE

HASH:
4 c. left-over roast
1 T. butter
1. T. flour
1 c. lamb broth
   or 1 c. consommé
Left over gravy
Salt, pepper and cayenne

RICE:
1 c. rice
2 T. butter
1 t. chopped onion
1 - 2 T. curry powder
¼ c. chutney
Salt and pepper to taste
2½ c. boiling water

Put chopped left-over lamb in double boiler. Melt butter, add flour and cook together until light golden brown. Add lamb broth (made from lamb bone) or consommé. Add all left-over lamb gravy, season to taste with salt, pepper and pinch cayenne. Pour over lamb and heat gently over boiling water. Pour in platter with rice around it.

RICE: Wash rice well and drain. Melt 2 tablespoons butter in frying pan and brown onions slowly. Add rice and stir over hot fire for 5 minutes. Remove pan from fire and sprinkle curry powder, salt and pepper over rice. Stir well and add water. Cover and cook rapidly for 10 minutes; reduce heat and cook very slowly for 40 minutes, and then stir in chutney. Serves 6.

MRS. HUBERT K. REESE

LAMB SOUFFLE

1 c. finely chopped or coarsely
   ground cooked lamb
1 can condensed mushroom
   soup
½ c. fine dry bread crumbs
3 well-beaten egg yolks
2 T. minced parsley

2 T. minced onions
⅓ c. milk
1 t. Worcestershire sauce
3 stiffly beaten egg whites
1 t. salt
Dash pepper

Combine bread crumbs, egg yolks, parsley, onions, seasonings, and 1 cup of the mushroom soup. Mix lightly but well. Fold in stiffly beaten egg whites. Pour into greased 8-inch casserole. Place casserole in pan with 1 inch hot water in it. Bake in 350° oven for 45 minutes. Serve with mushroom sauce made by combining rest of mushroom soup, milk, Worcestershire sauce and salt and pepper to taste. Heat thoroughly. Serves 4 generously.

MRS. JOHN McDONOUGH

ROAST LAMB PROVENCAL

6 - 7 lb. leg of lamb
1 c. dry white wine
1 c. water
1 lemon
Flour

Garlic
Rosemary
Salt
Pepper

Insert slivers of garlic throughout roast. Sprinkle top with flour, salt, pepper and rosemary. Put in roaster and pour water and wine over it. Cover and cook for ½ hour in 500° oven, until crust begins to form on top. Baste, turn oven to 350° and cook for 2 hours, basting every 30 minutes. Squeeze lemon over roast after each basting. Skim off grease and cook for another ½ hour. If necessary during cooking add more wine and water in equal portions. Serve with mint sauce (p. 134). Serves 8-10.

MRS. A. ARTHUR HALLE, CORDOVA, TENN.

INDIAN CURRY

1 large leg of lamb
3 c. broth
15 t. curry powder (less if
real imported Indian)
3 t. salt
3 T. butter or margarine
8 medium onions, minced
3 cloves garlic, minced
Juice of lemon

7 T. grated coconut
¼ c. salad oil, or fat
Milk of 3 coconuts
1 c. cream or evaporated milk
3 T. sugar
8 apples, chopped
2 c. Hubbard squash, or eggplant or Acorn squash
1 handful seeded raisins

Remove all meat from leg of lamb and boil the bone to make 3 cups of stock. Cut meat into half-inch cubes and sprinkle well with salt and curry. Mix meat and seasonings thoroughly with your hands. Saute onions and garlic 10 minutes. Do not let brown. Brown well in salad oil in another very hot skillet, stirring frequently to keep from burning. Put meat and onions, coconut milk, 2 cups of the stock, cream and sugar, in large pot, cover and simmer ½ hour. Now add apples, squash, raisins, grated coconut and lemon juice. The squash and apples will thicken the sauce naturally. Continue cooking gently for 2 more hours. Add more curry if you like. Curry improves with standing so make ahead of time—the morning of day to be served or the day before. Serve with rice.

RICE:

Wash in a large pot 3 cups rice and rinse in 6 waters, stirring each time before water is poured off. Bring 6 quarts of water and 3 teaspoons salt to rolling boil. Add rice a little at a time so boiling continues. Boil briskly without stirring until rice is tender (about 30 minutes). Strain into colander and rinse with plenty of boiling water. Don't cook rice too far ahead of time and keep it hot by standing the colander over, not in, boiling water, or empty rice into a pan, cover with cloth, and stand in 150° oven. Each grain will be separate and fluffy.

CONDIMENTS:

As this is a ten-boy curry, there should be 10 condiments, each served in a small bowl. They should stand in warm place the last hour before serving.
1. Freshly grated coconut (unsweetened canned or frozen will do).
2. Chopped peanuts or almonds.
3. Avocado, sliced thin with baçon crumbles.
4. Chutney. This is a must.
5. Finely chopped whites of 5 cooked eggs.
6. Yolks of 5 hard-cooked eggs, pressed through ricer.
7. Green pepper, chopped.
8. 5 firm tomatoes, cut into small pieces (leave skins on, but remove seeds and most of watery pulp).
9. Scallions or chives, chopped crosswise.
10. 1 can mushrooms sliced and sautéed in butter. These should be served hot.
11. Bombay dux.
12. Grated orange peel.

MRS. DUNBAR ABSTON, GERMANTOWN, TENN.

LAMB CHOP FINANCIER

4 large lamb chops	¼ stick butter or more
8 chicken livers	2 T. madeira or sherry
1 T. flour	½ bay leaf
1 c. chicken broth	Pinch thyme
8 seeded sliced green olives	Salt and pepper to taste
8 sliced mushrooms	

Broil lamb chops. Sauté chicken livers in butter until brown. Remove and brown flour in the skillet. Add broth, a little at a time. When well blended return chicken livers, add olives, mushrooms, and seasonings. Let simmer 5 minutes; add wine. Pour mixture over lamb chops. The trick to this lamb chop dish is to get the flour really brown. On your first attempts you will stop before it is brown enough. Let it brown until almost burned before adding chicken broth. Do no tampering with the recipe. If you change it one bit, you may as well make lamb stew. This is a one dish meal! Serves 4.

MRS. ROBERTSON G. MORROW

SHISH KEBAB

1 leg lamb (5 - 6 lb.)	1 t. oregano
2 large onions, sliced	½ t. pepper
½ c. sherry or wine vinegar	1 T. salt
¼ c. olive or peanut oil	

This wonderful Caucasian dish may be barbecued or cooked under the broiler. Remove all fat and gristle from lamb. Cut into 1-inch cubes. Marinate in wine, seasonings and onions at least 1 hour, preferably over night. Put 6 pieces on a skewer and broil over charcoal fire or under broiler until crisply brown on all sides. Or you may alternate meat on skewers with squares of tomatoes, onions and bacon. Serve with bulghour pilaf (p. 103) and your favorite green salad. Serves 8.

MRS. WALTER P. ARMSTRONG, JR.

CURRIED RICE WITH CHICKEN LIVERS

CURRIED RICE:

2 T. butter or oleo	1½ c. boiling water
1 T. onion flakes	½ t. salt
1⅓ c. pre-cooked rice	1 t. curry powder

Combine butter, onion flakes, rice, water, salt and curry powder in heavy saucepan with tight fitting cover. Bring to a boil. Cover, turn off heat. Let stand 13 minutes.

LIVERS:

2 8 oz. pkg. frozen chicken livers
2 T. butter
1 t. salt
¼ t. pepper

Brown chicken livers in butter in a skillet. Add salt and pepper. When rice is done, toss chicken livers with rice and serve at once. Serves 4.

MRS. F. PEARSON ALLEN, JR.

COUNTRY HAM

Allow 25 minutes per pound for ham weighing 10-12 pounds; or 20 minutes per pound for a larger one. Cover ham with cold water and soak 12 hours in 2 different waters, to which has been added 1 cup vinegar for each gallon of water. Remove and rinse in cold water. Place in large roaster on top of stove. Pour over ham 1 gallon water, 1 cup black molasses and 1 cup vinegar. Cover and allow to come to a rolling boil, then lower flame and let simmer slowly until skin can be easily removed (about 2 hours). Remove ham from solution, remove skin, puncture at intervals with ice pick and insert very small slivers of garlic. Score, dot with whole cloves and place in pre-heated oven 300° for remaining cooking time, basting every 20 minutes with port wine. Add water in bottom of pan as needed. Frequent basting is most important. A good companion for country ham is sweet mustard sauce.

SWEET MUSTARD SAUCE:

2 t. dry mustard	2 t. flour
½ c. milk	1 t. vinegar
2 t. sugar	¼ stick butter

Melt butter in double boiler, blend in flour, add milk as if making cream sauce. Dissolve mustard and sugar in vinegar. Add to sauce, stirring constantly until right consistency.

Mrs. Millard Hall

HAM SLICE

Spread prepared mustard on one thick slice of ham. Cover with brown sugar. Pour over it 1 cup milk and bake slowly covered for 1 hour.

An added attraction is to bake whole bananas in the dish along with it.

Mrs. Walter Lane Smith

HAM CROQUETTES

2 c. ground ham	4 T. milk
1 c. seasoned left-over potatoes	1 beaten egg
	16 single crackers, crushed

Mix ham, potatoes, and milk, season with salt and pepper if needed. With wet hands form 8 equal balls. Then shape each one into a cone, dip in beaten egg, roll in cracker crumbs, and set in refrigerator for one hour. Fry in hot, deep fat until golden brown. Serve with thin cream sauce (p. 129).

Mrs. W. D. Galbreath

LAMB SHANKS

Allow 1 shank per person. Flour well and brown in bacon grease in roasting pan. When brown add 1 cup water, 1 bay leaf and 1 clove of garlic. Cover and place in 350° oven for two hours.

MRS. ALBERT M. AUSTIN, III

FANCY HAMBURGERS

2 lbs. ground round steak	¼ t. thyme
½ stick butter	¼ t. coarse pepper
2 medium onions, chopped	⅛ t. rosemary
¼ lb. mushrooms, chopped	¾ c. sherry or burgundy
½ t. salt	¼ c. water

Shape hamburger into 6 patties. Broil in skillet until brown and cook to taste. Melt butter in small frying pan. Add other ingredients and simmer until onions and mushrooms are golden brown. Add sherry and water, bring to a boil. Let simmer for 3-5 minutes. Serve sauce over hamburgers. Serves 6.

MRS. WALTER P. ARMSTRONG, JR.

BRAIN FRITTERS

2 sets of calf brains
Batter for French fried vegetables (p. 95).

Soak brains for one hour in salt water. Skin, cover with cold, salted water and cook 30 minutes, or until soft. Cool. Break into bite size pieces, dip in batter and drop in deep hot fat. Fry until golden brown, drain and serve immediately.

MRS. WILLIAM L. NICHOL

SHEPHERD'S PIE

Cut left-over meat in cubes or run through meat grinder. Salt and pepper to taste. Add finely chopped onions, bell peppers and roast gravy. Line inside of casserole with fluffy whipped potatoes. Put meat in center. Dot all with butter. Bake in 350° oven until hot and potatoes are golden brown on top.

MRS. EDWARD W. COOK

BRAISED CALF'S LIVER BOURBONNAISE

1 whole calf's liver or
    sliced liver
Salt and pepper to taste
Small strips of larding pork
2 T. butter
1 c. sliced onions
½ c. sliced carrots
1 small bay leaf

1 stalk celery
4 sprigs parsley
Pinch of thyme
2 T. fat
1 T. flour
2 c. red wine
1 clove garlic chopped fine

Lard liver with small strips of larding pork (p. 242) and season with salt
and pepper. Melt 2 tablespoons butter in casserole and spread carrots
and onions over it. Add clove garlic and celery, parsley, bay leaf, pinch of
thyme. Brown liver on all sides in skillet in 2 tablespoons fat, transfer to
casserole and cook over low heat until onions and carrots begin to brown.
Sprinkle 1 tablespoon flour over vegetables and mix together by shaking
casserole. Add red wine and enough water to come to top of liver. Cover
and cook in 350° oven for 2½ to 3 hours, turning liver several times to cook
evenly. Allow 30 to 40 minutes for sliced liver. When done, strain sauce,
skim off fat and pour over liver in serving dish. This dish may also be
served cold.

LIVER AND ONIONS ITALIAN STYLE

1 lb. thin slices liver
½ c. dry red wine
4 medium onions
6 T. olive oil

Salt and pepper
Flour
Pinch of oregano

Let liver stand in wine for hour or more in ice box, turning occasionally.
Sauté onions ½ hour before serving in 4 tablespoons oil until brown. Remove and keep hot. Add 2 more tablespoons of oil to skillet. Drain liver,
saving wine. Roll in seasoned flour and brown, adding more oil if necessary.
Cook 3 to 4 minutes on each side. Take out liver and keep hot. Add to
skillet 1 tablespoon flour, oregano and wine marinade. Stir until slightly
thickened, season to taste. Pour gravy over liver. Serves 4-6.

MRS. A. ARTHUR HALLE, CORDOVA, TENN.

SCRAPPLE

1 lb. unboned pork shoulder
¼ lb. liver
4 c. boiling water
1 c. meal
2 t. salt

1 c. cold water
½ t. black pepper
1 t. dried sage
Fat or salad oil
Flour

Remove bones from pork. Place bones and pork in kettle with liver. Add
boiling water. Cover and simmer over low heat for 1 hour. Remove bones,
drain off broth, reserving 2 cups. Grind meat fine. Combine meal, salt
and cold water in double boiler over boiling water. Stir in 2 cups broth
slowly, cook until thickened, stirring frequently. Add meats and rest of
ingredients except flour and fat. Cover. Cook for 1 hour. Pour scrapple
into wet loaf pan 9x5x3. Chill until very firm. Cut into quarter-inch slices.
Roll lightly in flour; sauté in fat until golden brown. Makes 35 thin slices.

MRS. ST. JOHN WADDELL

SUKI-AKI

¾ lb. pork or beef tenderloin
3 T. fat or oil
2 t. sugar
½ c. soy sauce
2 bunches green onions and
tops

1 c. celery, cup in strips
1 pkg. frozen French cut
green beans
1 pkg. frozen broccoli
1 pt. mushrooms, cut

Cut meat in cubes. Brown in fat. Add soy sauce. In layers, add vegetables, and simmer until done (time given on frozen food boxes). Serve immediately. A meal complete for 4.

MRS. EDWIN JOHNSON, DETROIT, MICH.

PORK CHOP CREOLE

6 pork chops
1 onion
1 No. 2 can toamtoes
Salt and pepper to taste

1 T. Worcestershire sauce
2 t. chopped green peppers
1 c. rice (p. 105), cooked

Sprinkle chops lightly with flour. Cook in skillet with small amount of fat until brown. Set aside to keep warm. Brown onions in skillet used for chops. Add tomatoes, green peppers and seasonings. Return chops to sauce and cook slowly until thick. Place chops on platter. Cover with 1 cup of cooked rice and pour sauce over all. Serves 6.

MRS. RICHARD LEATHERMAN, ROBINSONVILLE, MISS.

STUFFED PORK CHOPS

1 c. bread crumbs
¼ c. chopped celery
¼ c. chopped onions
2 T. chopped parsley

½ t. sage or poultry seasoning
¼ t. salt
⅛ t. paprika
Milk to moisten dressing

Get butcher to cut pocket in 6 thick rib pork chops. Wipe them with damp cloth. Fill pockets with above ingredients, well mixed. Do not bother to sew up. Sear chops in hot skillet then put them in pan with a little milk or cream. Cover and bake in 350° oven until done (¾ to 1 hour). Gravy may be made by thickening the drippings with flour, but less rich just to use drippings. Serves 6.

MRS. R. CARL DICKERSON, JR.

SAUSAGE

8 lb. lean pork
4 lb. fat
3 T. salt
4 T. freshly-ground sage
1 T. cayenne (scant)

1 T. red pepper pod (ground
fine)
1 T. sugar
1 T. freshly-ground black
pepper

Put all this through meat grinder at least twice to mix well.

MRS. ARCH HENDERSON, HERMITAGE, TENN.

SPAGHETTI I

1 stalk celery, including
  leaves, chopped
2 large onions, chopped
3 green peppers, chopped

2 T. parsley
2 cloves garlic, minced
Olive oil or chicken fat

Brown above in oil, then add:

4 No. 2 cans tomatoes
2 cans tomato paste
½ t. cloves, ground
½ t. nutmeg
¼ t. sage

2 bay leaves, broken
4 T. grated Parmesan cheese
Salt to taste
4 T. chopped olives
¼ t. red pepper

Simmer all for 3 hours. Then make meat balls of:

½ lb. ground veal
1 lb. ground beef

½ lb. ground pork

Brown, add to sauce and cook 1 hour more. Sprinkle with sautéed mushrooms just before serving. Serves 8-10.

Mrs. George S. Bush

SPAGHETTI II

2 lbs. shoulder clod of beef
  (ground)
2 large cans tomatoes
1 can tomato paste
1 can water
3 large onions (red or white)
2 cloves garlic, minced
Enough olive oil to brown the
  meat

2 pkg. dried mushrooms
  (imported)
½ lb. Roman cheese
1 t. salt and pepper (each)
1 t. sugar
1 pkg. Parmesan cheese
  (large)

Brown meat in olive oil, in iron skillet. Add chopped onion and one garlic clove. Put tomatoes through colander and add to meat mixture, then add seasonings. Simmer for 2 hours, then add the mushrooms that have been chopped and simmered in small amount of water, and the other garlic clove. Simmer 2 more hours. Cook 2 packages vermicelli. Just before serving add Roman cheese to sauce. Pour over vermicelli and top with Parmesan cheese. The sauce is better if made the day before. Serves 10-12.

Mrs. D. A. Canale

MACARONI ITALIENNE

½ lb. pkg. macaroni
1 lb. ground lean beef
8 strips bacon
1 large Spanish onion
1 large can tomatoes

1 lb. grated yellow cheese
1 large can mushrooms
Salt to taste
Garlic and red pepper
  (optional)

Pour 1 quart cold water over ground beef and let soak in a bowl over night in refrigerator. Next morning simmer beef and water in which it has soaked for 1 hour. Then boil hard for 1 hour, adding juice from mushrooms and enough water to make 1 quart of beef juice when done. Fry bacon and save grease. Fry onion in this grease and add tomatoes. Cook until the consistency of mush. Add beef and juice, bacon, cheese, and mushrooms to tomato mixture. Cook macaroni in salted water until tender. Drain and add to sauce mixture. Pour in casserole and heat at 350° until hot. This is excellent to make the day before serving.

This is an old family recipe and delicious!   Mrs. James H. Fisher

TORTILLA CASSEROLE

½ lb. can tortillas	1 t. chili powder
2 - 3 onions	1½ c. grated cheese
½ can tomato soup	1½ c. X cream or chicken or
½ brick chili	beef stock

Crisp and brown tortillas in skillet. Mix cream, chili powder, soup, cheese, onions, chili brick, salt and pepper. Put in casserole in alternate layers with tortillas. Bake 1 hour. Serves 6-8.

Miss Marjorie Cooke, Clarksdale, Miss.

HAM LOAF

1 lb. of lean ham, ground	2 eggs, beaten
1 lb. of lean pork, ground	1 cup milk
1 c. rice crispies, crushed	½ t. each salt and pepper

Mix all ingredients together and pack into loaf pan, 8½x4½x2½. Bake in moderate oven (350°) for 30 minutes, reduce heat to very slow (250°) and bake 1½ hours, basting frequently with the following sauce:

½ c. warm water	¼ c. vinegar
½ c. brown sugar	¼ c. Lea & Perrins
1 t. dry mustard	Worcestershire sauce

For the last hour, I like to take the ham loaf out of the loaf pan and into a regular baking pan so that it will brown.

Mrs. Albert M. Austin, III

SPICED TONGUE

1 fresh tongue	1 T. allspice
1 qt. water	1 T. ground cloves
1 teacup brown sugar	½ t. black pepper
½ c. salt	½ t. red pepper
1 oz. saltpeter	

Let spice mixture come to a boil then cool. Pour over tongue in jar or crock. Keep in refrigerator 1 week. Wash off and simmer until tender (about 3 hours). Let cool and skin.

This recipe has been in the Donelson family for over 200 years.

Mrs. M. Ames Saunders, Jr.

NOT QUITE A RECIPE, yet so good—veal or pork chops lightly browned, a slice of Bermuda onion placed on each, a can of tomato sauce or soup poured over all. Simmer until done. Serve with grated cheese sprinkled on top, and a sprig of parsley.

VEAL SHOULDER WITH SOUR CREAM

2 celery stalks   Garlic
Parsley   Salt and pepper
1 green pepper   1 pt. sour cream
1 onion   2 cans mushrooms

Have your butcher bone a veal shoulder. Stuff it with mixture of above seasonings and vegetables, roll and tie. Salt and pepper roast and put in roaster with 1 inch of water or stock in bottom. Cook 2 hours in 300° oven. Then add sour cream and mushrooms. Cook ½ hour more, basting frequently. Serve with sauce in pan poured over it.

Mrs. William A. Leatherman, Robinsonville, Miss.

VEAL CUTLETS PARMESAN

4 individual veal cutlets   ½ t. onion salt
1 egg   ½ t. garlic salt
Cracker crumbs   ½ t. chili powder
2-3 T. butter   1 t. sugar
1 can tomato sauce (8 oz.)   Pinch of basil, marjoram,
1 can water   rosemary, thyme, savory
1 T. chopped onion   Parmesan cheese, grated
1 T. chopped bell pepper   Sharp cheddar cheese, grated
1 T. chopped celery   Pepper to taste

Roll cutlets in egg and crumbs, brown in butter. Make sauce of remaining ingredients, except cheese. Simmer sauce slowly for 1 hour. Put cutlets in baking dish. Pour sauce over them. Top with generous amount of Parmesan cheese, then pile high with Cheddar cheese. Run in 350° oven until cheese is melted and cutlets are thoroughly reheated (15-20 minutes). This dish may be made ahead of time and reheated just before serving. Serves 4.

Mrs. Eugart Yerian

PARTY VEAL ROAST

Leg of veal—10 to 12 lbs.   Parsley
12 garlic pods   Salt and black pepper
4 or 5 hot peppers

Have your butcher bone and roll a veal leg. Make at least a dozen gashes in it with a knife. Into each gash pour salt and pepper, then poke in a garlic pod, a half inch piece of hot pepper, and a wad of parsley. Rub outside of roast generously with salt and pepper. Cook until well done. This is excellent served cold for buffet supper, etc., as it can be made a day or two ahead. Slices beautifully and will serve 25 people.

Mrs. Joseph Hyde

VEAL SCALLOPINI

2½ lb. veal
1 can beef consommé
1 c. mushrooms, sliced
½ t. meat extract

Dash of nutmeg
½ c. sherry
Red wine to taste

Get butcher to cut top round of veal very thin. Place between wax paper and pound well on both sides, then cut in strips. Sauté pieces in butter until golden brown. Add consommé thickened with a little flour. Add seasonings, sherry and wine. Put in a large deep skillet and slowly simmer covered for 1½ hours. Brown mushrooms in butter and add to veal dish about 20 minutes before serving. Serve with rice (p. 105). Serves 6.

VEAL VIENNA

2 large veal cutlets, ½ in.
thick or 4 large chops
1 large onion, chopped fine
½ c. water
¼ c. sherry

½ pt. sour cream
2 T. bacon fat
Pinch of rosemary, salt and
pepper

Sprinkle cutlets with salt, pepper and rosemary. Brown with onions in frying pan, using about 2 tablespoons bacon fat. Add water and sherry and simmer for ½ hour. Add sour cream and serve. Serves 4.

The resulting gravy is perfect on mashed or baked potatoes.

MRS. WALTER P. ARMSTRONG, JR.

WESTERN SANDWICH

5 eggs, slightly beaten
3 T. water
1¼ c. chopped ham
¾ t. salt

1 T. onion, chopped fine
2 T. bell pepper, chopped
¼ t. pepper

Combine water with eggs and beat. Add ham and seasonings, mixing well. Drop from tablespoon on greased frying pan, spreading to form flat cakes. Brown on both sides. Serve over slices of buttered toast.

MRS. JOHN F. BARBEE

SWEETBREADS

Remove sweetbreads from paper as soon as received from market and plunge at once into ice water to which you add 2 tablespoons vinegar or lemon juice. Let stand for 1 hour. Drain and place in boiling salted water. Cook slowly for 20 minutes. Drain, put into cold water and when cool enough to handle, remove thin outer skin with aid of sharp paring knife. Be careful to avoid unnecessary breakage. Place sweetbreads in wax paper and keep cold until time to serve.

Sweetbreads then may be sautéed in butter having been coated first lightly in seasoned flour. When slightly brown, remove at once to preheated platter. A spot of lemon juice, pan butter and a dusting of finely minced parsley complete the dish.

Sweetbreads may also be done in shirred egg dishes with tablespoon of cream poured over each, covered with glass mushroom bell and finished in hot oven. Season with melted butter.

STUFFINGS FOR MEAT

Many kinds of meat may be roasted and served with stuffing. The stuffing may be baked in a separate pan, arranged in alternate layers with the meat, or filled into a pocket or opening in the meat. The shoulder of lamb, pork or veal may be boned, spread with stuffing and rolled, or stuffing put into opening. Stuffing may also be baked in a ring mold and center filled with creamed meats.

CORN BREAD STUFFING

4 c. boiling water
4 c. broken corn bread
1 onion, grated
1 c. diced celery

2 eggs, beaten
½ c. melted butter
Salt and pepper

Pour boiling water over bread and squeeze out fairly dry. Add remaining ingredients and mix well. Use for stuffing pork or lamb. Serves 6-8.

Try adding raw onion to corn bread batter before baking. Onions will never be under-done in dressing this way. Also marvelous just to eat with butter!

BREAD STUFFING

4 c. soft bread crumbs or
cubes
1 t. salt

¼ - ½ c. melted butter or
margarine
1 t. pepper

Combine ingredients and stuff lightly into meat, allowing room for expansion; or use as desired.

APPLE STUFFING:

Use the larger amount of fat in bread stuffing. Add 1 cup chopped tart apple.

CELERY STUFFING:

Add 1 cup minced celery to Onion Stuffing. (See below.)

CHILI STUFFING:

Add ½ cup chili sauce or tomato catsup and 1 tablespoon minced onion to bread stuffing. Use ¼ cup fat.

MUSHROOM STUFFING:

Add ¾ cup chopped mushrooms to Onion or Celery Stuffing.

ONION STUFFING:

Add 2 tablespoons minced onion.

SAGE STUFFING:

Add 2 teaspoons sage, 2 tablespoons chopped onion and 1 tablespoon chopped parsley.

SAUSAGE STUFFING:

Omit fat. Brown 1½ cups sausage slightly and add to bread stuffing.

Vegetables

The vegetable is the Cinderella in the Adventure of Pleasing Palates, and the vegetable garden is a treasurehouse of textures and flavors.

If treated as a step-child, the vegetable is overcooked in too much water and loses its vitamins as well as its eye and taste appeal. However, if the cookpot is employed in the fairy godmother manner, the vegetable becomes tender, yet firm and colorful and wins the princely nod.

The golden coach transporting the vegetable to the feast is the casserole dish, where brews in mysterious alchemy a variety of tempting tastes. Many a yesterday's weed is bubbling in today's casserole as our knowledge of greengroceries has increased.

The cook who brews a toothsome ending to the vegetable vignette can wear the glass slipper of gastronomic approval and her guests will reminisce happily ever after.

— 1952

See Table of Equivalents (p. 240) for sugar and cream references.

ARTICHOKE AND MUSHROOM CASSEROLE

1 can artichoke hearts	½ lb. fresh whole mushrooms
1 c. cream sauce (p. 129)	6-8 "Muffets" or shredded
2 T. butter	wheat biscuits
½ c. N. Y. cheese, grated	

Make cream sauce, adding cheese and artichokes. Sauté mushrooms in butter and add to first mixture, mixing well. Serve on "Muffets" that have been buttered and heated in the oven. Serves 6-8.

Mrs. J. Pervis Milnor, Jr.

ASPARAGUS CASSEROLE WITH NIPPY CHEESE

2 large cans all green asparagus	2 T. butter
	2 T. flour
¾ lb. nippy Wisconsin cheese	2 T. asparagus juice
1 small can mushrooms	Scant cup of cream
Grated blanched almonds	Paprika and red pepper to
Salt and pepper to taste	taste
2 hard-boiled eggs	

Melt butter, add flour, mix well. Add asparagus juice, making a paste. Return to heat, add cream for right consistency, stirring constantly. Season with salt, pepper, paprika and red pepper. Add cheese which has been cut into small pieces; stir until dissolved. Add mushrooms. Drain asparagus and line bottom of casserole with 1 can asparagus, cover with cheese sauce and sliced hard-boiled eggs. Repeat and top with grated blanched almonds. Run in 350° oven 20 minutes before serving. Serves 10-12.

Mrs. St. Elmo Newton, Jr.

ARTICHOKE HEARTS WITH ROQUEFORT DRESSING

1 can artichoke hearts	¼ lb. butter
1 wedge Roquefort cheese	Lemon juice to taste

In double boiler melt butter, add Roquefort and lemon juice. Drain hearts, add to butter sauce and serve hot. Serves 2 to 4.

Good served with steak.

Mrs. Everett R. Cook

ASPARAGUS LUNCHEON SUGGESTION

Roll cooked asparagus stalks in thin ham slices; broil and serve on toast with a medium white sauce (p. 129) to which grated cheese has been added. Allow about 3 stalks per person.

COOKING HINT:

Adding sugar to water in which some vegetables are cooked improves flavor; for sweet potatoes add 1 heaping teaspoon; for peas, cabbage, turnips, beets and corn add 1 level teaspoon.

ASPARAGUS SOUFFLE DELIGHT

2 No. 2 cans of asparagus
6 egg yolks
6 egg whites
1 c. grated cheese

2 c. medium cream sauce
(p. 129)
Salt and pepper to taste

Drain green asparagus very dry; cut in half, removing all tough parts. Use juice from cans and add necessary milk to make 2 cups cream sauce. Then add a scant cup of grated cheese, salt and pepper to taste. Chill, add slightly beaten egg yolks; then asparagus. Fold in stiffly beaten egg whites. Bake in 350° oven for 45 minutes in a pan of hot water on the bottom shelf. Serves 8.

Mrs. Henry H. Haizlip

BLACK BEANS, CUBAN STYLE

2 c. black beans
2 qt. water
½ lb. salt pork
1 c. chopped onion
2 buds garlic, minced

½ T. dried oregano
1 bay leaf
½ c. red wine
2 T. olive oil

Wash black beans in several waters, then cover with 2 quarts water and soak 3 hours. Bring to boil without salting. Turn down heat and allow to simmer until tender. Fry salt pork cut in small pieces until brown and crisp. Remove pork to absorbent paper. In the fat, sauté onion and garlic until tender. Add oregano and bay leaf. Mix well and add cooked beans. To this add salt pork pieces, red wine and olive oil. Simmer ½ hour and serve. Serves 6.

Mrs. Henry H. Haizlip

DANISH BEAN DISH

2 cans baked beans
10 strips of bacon, fried and
   drained
⅔ c. tomato catsup
1 T. Worcestershire sauce

2 medium onions
2 T. butter
1 lb. round steak, ground
1 can chopped mushrooms
1 c. consommé or beef stock

Cut up fried bacon strips. Sauté onions in butter. Fry ground round steak until lightly browned. Mix with beans, bacon, catsup, Worcestershire sauce, onions and mushrooms. Add beef stock or consommé and bake in 300° oven about 1 hour. Optional: grated cheese baked on top. Serves 6 amply.

Quite good as a dressed-up dish for baked beans. The number of bacon strips can be cut in half successfully for economy.

Mrs. Richard Alcott

SUCCOTASH

1 pkg. frozen corn
1 pkg. frozen baby lima beans

⅔ c. XX cream
Salt and pepper to taste

Put corn through meat grinder while still frozen. (Break into pieces with ice pick.) Add cream and lima beans. Add salt and pepper to taste and cook in top of double boiler 20 minutes, stirring 3 times. Serves 6 to 8.

Mrs. Charles B. Dudley, Jr.

CURRIED GREEN BEANS

2 pkg. French style green
   beans
6 stuffed eggs
2 c. cream sauce (p. 129)

1 t. curry
½ c. sharp cheese grated
Salt and red pepper to taste
Mayonnaise to moisten

Cook 2 packages frozen green beans as directed. Put in well buttered 7 inch round casserole dish. Arrange 6 stuffed egg halves on top of beans. Egg yolks should be highly seasoned and have enough mayonnaise to make them moist. Pour cream sauce seasoned with salt, red pepper, and curry over beans and eggs. Top with sharp grated cheese. Run in 350° oven until very hot. Serves 6-8.

Mrs. Keith M. Spurrier, Jr.

GREEN BEAN CASSEROLE

3 cans whole green beans
1 c. consommé
1 pt. fresh mushrooms

1 stick butter
Maggi to taste, if desired
Salt to taste

Drain all liquid from beans. Put in bowl with undiluted consommé and let soak at least 1 hour. Broil mushrooms in butter, add to beans. (1 large can mushrooms can be substituted for fresh ones.) Pour into buttered casserole. Bake 45 minutes at 325°. Serves 6-8.

This dish is best if prepared day before serving.

Mrs. H. Duncan Taylor

GREEN BEAN CASSEROLE WITH SOUR CREAM

½ c. sliced onions
1 T. minced parsley
2 T. butter or oleo
2 T. flour
1 t. salt
¼ t. pepper
½ t. grated lemon peel

1 c. sour cream
5 c. green beans (canned or
   frozen)
½ c. grated yellow cheese
2 T. melted butter
½ c. cracker crumbs or bread
   crumbs

Cook onion (sliced thin) and parsley in 2 T. oleo until tender, not brown. Add flour, salt, pepper, and lemon peel. Add sour cream and mix well. Stir in beans. Put in casserole dish, top with grated cheese. Combine butter and bread crumbs (or cracker crumbs) and put on top of casserole. Bake at 350 degrees for 30 minutes. If using canned beans, drain. Cook frozen beans first. Serves 4-6.

This recipe can be made a day ahead if necessary.

Mrs. Bill R. Bobbitt

FANCY GREEN BEANS

2 pkgs. frozen French style
   green beans
1 can water chestnuts,
   thinly sliced
2 T. butter

1 can cream of chicken soup,
   undiluted
1 pkg. frozen French fried
   onion rings
Parmesan cheese (optional)

Cook beans until tender, mix soup, chestnuts and butter with the cooked beans and put in casserole. Place the onion rings on top with the Parmesan cheese sprinkled over all. Bake at 300° for 30-40 minutes. Serves 8.

BRANDY NAVY BEANS

1 No. 2½ can tomatoes	Salt to taste
1 small can tomato paste	A-1 sauce to taste
Chopped onions to taste	Worcestershire sauce to taste
Chili powder to taste	A soupcon of your favorite
Red pepper to taste	herbs
1 lb. navy beans	Ham hock
Small amount of brown sugar	Brandy to taste

Soak beans overnight. Make a rich tomato sauce using canned tomatoes and tomato paste as a base and add seasonings to taste. Add this sauce to navy beans which have been cooking for 1 hour (or when put in a spoon and blown on, the skin blows off) with the ham hock. Put in casserole, add brandy and bake in 250° oven for about 8 hours. If more liquid is needed during baking time, add more brandy. Serves 10.

Mrs. John M. Maury

RED BEANS AND RICE

1 whole ham hock	¼ c. bacon drippings
1 pkg. large red kidney beans	1 bay leaf
2 large onions, chopped	Salt and pepper
1 T. flour	4 c. cooked rice

Put ham hock and beans in large pot. Cover with water, season with salt and pepper and bay leaf. Cook over low fire 4 or 5 hours, or until meat falls off bone and beans are done. Sauté onions in bacon drippings. Add flour. Add this mixture to bean pot and cook until mixture thickens. Takes about 1 hour. Salt and pepper to taste. Serve over rice (p. 105). Serves 8-10.

Mrs. Thomas R. Price

CASSEROLE SUPREME OF BROCCOLI AND CARROTS

8 thin slices bread	½ stick butter
½ lb. pkg. sliced processed	2 T. flour
American cheese	2 c. sweet milk
2¼ to 3 c. half cooked cut	Dash pepper
broccoli and diced carrots	Paprika

Trim crusts from bread, make 4 sandwiches using slice of cheese (trimmed to fit bread) in each. Cut each sandwich in half diagonally. Make a cream sauce with the flour, butter, milk and seasonings. Add other slices of cheese and pieces cut from sandwich slices to cream sauce, stirring until melted. Add well drained vegetables; pour mixture into rather large shallow casserole. Stand sandwiches in it with their points up. Sprinkle freely with paprika. Cook in 350° oven about 30 minutes or until sandwiches are lightly brown. Serves 8.

Other combinations of vegetables may be substituted.

Mrs. M. Ames Saunders

WHIPPED CREAM IN BEETS

1 can whole beets	Horseradish to taste
½ c. cream, whipped, or	Salt to taste
sour cream	Garlic to taste
Whole cloves to garnish	

Marinate beets in vinegar with cloves, then remove cloves. With a teaspoon hollow out a deep well in top of each beet. Fill with whipped cream which has been beaten with horseradish. Strengthen to your liking with salt, a faint bit of garlic. Stick cloves in each beet. Figure 2-3 beets per person. Serve ice cold.

Substitute this when you don't want to serve a salad.

MISS FRANCES E. SHIELDS

BROCCOLI CASSEROLE WITH ALMONDS

2 pkg. frozen broccoli	1 t. salt
2 T. butter	¼ t. pepper
2 T. flour	¼ c. chopped almonds
2 c. milk	4 slices crisp bacon
¾ c. grated cheese	½ c. buttered bread crumbs

Cook broccoli until just tender. Drain and place in greased casserole. Make a sauce of the butter, flour, milk, cheese, salt and pepper. Sprinkle broccoli with almonds, then pour on the cheese sauce. Sprinkle top with crumbs and bacon. Place in 350° oven for about 20 minutes or until bubbling hot and browned on top. Serves 6.

MRS. JOHN McDONOUGH

BROCCOLI SOUFFLE

1 c. cooked broccoli	1 t. salt
3 T. butter	Few grains nutmeg
3 T. flour	1 t. lemon juice
1 c. milk	4 eggs, separated

Melt butter in saucepan, blend in flour. Gradually add milk, stirring constantly, and cook until smooth and thick. Add salt, nutmeg and lemon juice. Chop cooked broccoli and measure 1 cup. Beat egg yolks, add first mixture to them and let cool. If you are assembling the soufflé hours before serving time, keep it in a cool place; then before cooking, beat egg whites until stiff but not dry, and fold into broccoli mixture. Bake in 300° oven for 1½ hours. If you use the quick method, bake soufflé in 425° oven for 25 minutes. Serve with Hollandaise (p. 129) or Cheese Sauce (p. 45).

MRS. GEORGE S. MILES

OLIVE-RICE CASSEROLE

1 c. long grain rice, uncooked	1 c. tomatoes
1 c. New York State cheese, diced	½ c. onion, chopped
	½ c. salad oil
1 2-oz. jar stuffed olives, sliced	1 c. water
	Salt and pepper to taste

Combine all ingredients and bake in covered casserole for 1 hour at 350°. Do not become alarmed by the soupy appearance of this dish when it goes into the oven as the rice will absorb the moisture. If the recipe is doubled add 15 minutes to the cooking time. This makes a delicious buffet dish. Serves 6.

MRS. GUS MORGAN

AN EASY WAY TO COOK CABBAGE

Shred a nice, green head of cabbage, being careful not to cut too much of the hard white stems with the green part. Drop in boiling, salted water with a dash of cayenne pepper. Cover. You do not have to have too much water as you want to cook the cabbage only about 10-15 minutes and then drain. Pour melted butter over the cabbage when you put it in the serving dish. The vegetable should be eaten immediately and not left to stand. It makes a most delicate dish, not at all like cabbage cooked quartered or whole.

MRS. ERIC BABENDREER

CARROTS AND ONIONS

1 bunch green spring onions, sliced
1 bunch carrots, sliced

2 to 4 T. butter
Salt and pepper to taste
Lemon juice to taste

Cook carrots with onions. Season with butter, salt and pepper. Lemon juice may be added. Serves 4-6.

MRS. EDWARD W. COOK

CARROT RING

2 c. shredded cooked carrots
1½ c. grated American cheese
2 eggs

1 c. sweet milk
1 c. coarse cracker crumbs
Salt and pepper to taste

Thoroughly drain carrots. Beat eggs separately. To yellows, add milk, carrots, cheese and cracker crumbs. Fold in whites. Pour into greased ring mold. Bake in pan of hot water in 350° oven for about 1 hour or until firm. Unmold on chop dish, fill center with peas, bacon curls, mushrooms or other vegetables.

Do not use prepared cracker crumbs as ring will be too dry.

MRS. GUS MORGAN

FRENCH FRIED CARROTS

Scrape or peel carrots, and wash. Cut in strips lengthwise, as for French fried potatoes, but slightly smaller. Drop in boiling salted water and boil until tender. Drain and cool. Dip in batter for French-fried vegetables. (See next page.) Drop in deep hot fat, and fry until a golden brown. Remove from the fat and drain. Serve hot.

MRS. LILBURNE M. VOLLMER

HOT WEATHER CARROTS

3 medium-sized carrots
½ c. butter
½ c. sugar

1 T. chopped, fresh mint leaves
Butter, salt and pepper

Wash, scrape, and cut carrots in ¼-inch slices, then in strips or fancy shapes. Cook 15 minutes in boiling salted water. Drain. Cook slowly with butter, sugar, and mint until soft and glazed. Season with butter, salt and pepper.

BATTER FOR FRENCH FRIED VEGETABLES

1 egg yolk, well beaten
⅜ c. milk
½ c. sifted flour

1 T. melted butter
Salt and pepper
1¼ t. baking powder

To well-beaten egg yolk add milk and melted butter. Mix and sift in flour and baking powder. Beat until thoroughly mixed, and if not smooth, beat with Dover egg beater until it is. Stir in salt and pepper.

MRS. LILBURNE M. VOLLMER

CAULIFLOWER A LA BELGIQUE

1 head cauliflower
Mayonnaise to mask

1 lb. cooked ham
Tarragon vinegar to marinate

Cook cauliflower in slightly salted water until firm but not overcooked. Drain and cool. Marinate whole cauliflower in tarragon vinegar for 30 minutes. Cut ham in small wedges 2 inches long, about 1 inch wide at top. Insert ham wedges between each fleurette of cauliflower. Mask with mayonnaise (much better if mayonnaise is homemade).

Excellent way of using up leftover ham. Garnish with watercress, sliced cucumbers and tomatoes. This can be used as entrée for buffet supper on hot night or as first course for formal dinner. Serves 4-6 depending on size of cauliflower.

MRS. JOHN D. MARTIN, JR.

CAULIFLOWER AND ONION IN CHEESE SAUCE

1 lb. grated American cheese
1 large head cauliflower
2 bunches large spring onions
  or 1 large can young onions
4 T. butter

4 T. flour
1½ c. milk
Salt and pepper to taste
Worcestershire sauce to taste

Break cauliflower into bite size pieces, and cook about 10 minutes in salted water. Remove tops from onions, cook onions about 10 minutes in salted water. Make a cream sauce from the butter, flour, and milk. Add seasonings and grated cheese. Place in layers in casserole dish, first the cauliflower, then onions then cream sauce. Cook about 30 minutes in 350° oven, or until dish is thoroughly heated. Serves 8-10.

Left-over ham may be added to make a main dish. Excellent dish served with spinach.

FRENCH FRIED CAULIFLOWER

Dip cauliflower flowerets in batter (see above) and fry in deep hot fat for an unusual taste treat.

CHESTNUTS SERVED AS A VEGETABLE

5 lb. chestnuts
Sherry to cover

Toast
½ pt. XX cream

Soak chestnuts overnight in sherry after they have been blanched. Cut toast into crisp fingers. Arrange toast and chestnuts in alternate layers in casserole dish. Pour in ½ pint cream. Cook in 300° oven about 30-45 minutes. Serves 12-14.

MRS. CHARLES M. KORTRECHT, COLLIERVILLE, TENN.

FRESH CORN CAKES

1 egg
1 c. thick buttermilk
½ t. soda
½ t. salt

½ t. sugar
3 ears fresh sweet corn
½ c. flour
2 t. grease

To cut corn: hold the ear upright in a shallow bowl and cut downward with a sharp knife, cutting off only the tip of each kernel. Then using the back of the knife, scrape downward until you have removed all the milk from each kernel. To the corn mixture add whole egg, buttermilk and sifted dry ingredients, beating after each addition. Stir in grease. Drop by spoonfuls into very hot, very greasy iron skillet. Turn when brown and eat while piping hot.

These batter cakes make a wonderful summer breakfast with crisp bacon and sliced tomatoes. This will serve 4 hungry people.

MRS. PERCY GALBREATH

CORN AND HAM FRITTERS

2 egg yolks
½ c. milk
1⅓ c. sifted flour
2 t. baking powder
¾ t. salt

¼ t. paprika
2 T. minced parsley or onion
¼ c. drained cream-style corn
¾ c. minced ham
2 stiffly beaten egg whites

Beat egg yolks until light. Add to milk, flour, baking powder, salt, and paprika, using a few swift strokes. Fold in parsley or onion, corn, ham, and egg whites. Fry fritters in deep fat until browned. Serves 6.

MRS. LESLIE MILLER

CORN PUDDING

2 c. fresh young corn cut
    off cob
3 T. butter
2 eggs

¼ c. sugar
½ t. salt
1½ c. milk

Cream butter and sugar, then beat in eggs. Add milk, salt and corn last. Bake in 350° oven for 35 minutes or until pudding is firm. If canned corn is used, add 2 t. flour for each 2 cups corn and cream it well with the butter and sugar. Serves 6.

MRS. EDWIN B. PHILLIPS

CORN FRITTERS PIERRE

1 12-oz. can corn
  or 6 ears corn, scraped
  and sieved
2 eggs, well beaten
1 t. salt
½ t. pepper

2 t. baking powder
Scant T. sugar
2 T. XX cream
1 c. flour
2 T. rolled corn flakes

Beat eggs well, add cream, corn flakes, and dry ingredients sifted together. Add grated and sieved corn. Cook on lightly greased and wiped griddle. Make the fritters small. Serves 4-6.

Serve in mounds of 3 with pitcher of melted butter in center. These are especially good with fish or hash.

MRS. HENRY H. HAIZLIP

EASY CORN PUDDING

1 can cream-style corn
2 eggs
½ c. milk
1 T. sugar
½ t. salt

Paprika
Bread crumbs
½ green pepper, optional
1 t. bacon fat

Grease baking dish with bacon fat. Put corn into dish, break in eggs and stir until mixed. Pour in milk; while stirring add sugar, salt and sprinkle top with dry bread crumbs and paprika. Pepper may be chopped up into corn if desired. Put dish in pan of hot water and bake 1 hour in 350° oven. Serves 4-6.

MRS. GEORGE S. MILES

CORN SOUFFLE

1 can cream-style corn
1 t. minced onion
1 T. chopped green pepper,
  sautéed

Salt and pepper to taste
2 t. pimento
2 eggs
½ c. XX cream

Season canned corn with salt, pepper and onion; then beat in green pepper and pimento. Beat eggs slightly, add cream and stir in corn mixture. Bake it in greased casserole dish at 325° for 10 minutes; then increase heat to 350° and bake 10 minutes longer or until firm. Serves 4.

MRS. HUBERT K. REESE

DOUBLE BOILER CORN SOUFFLE

1 pkg. frozen corn
⅓ jar of XX cream

Salt and pepper to taste

Put corn through meat grinder still frozen (break into pieces with ice pick). Put in top of double boiler, add cream, seasonings. Cook 20 minutes, stirring 2 or 3 times. Serves 4.

This is not firm like an orthodox soufflé but has delicious flavor.

MRS. C. P. STEWART, HARTFORD, CONN.

ZUCCHINI CASSEROLE

2 lbs. slender zucchini   3 large onions
⅓ lb. bacon

Wash but do not peel zucchini. Cut into slices. Cut bacon into pieces, and thinly slice onions and separate into rings. Cook bacon in skillet over medium heat, add onions and cook five minutes. In a large casserole place layer of zucchini slices, sprinkle with salt, pepper, dried basil and dot with catsup. Cover with layer of onions and bacon and repeat until casserole is filled. Cover and cook at 350° for 1½ hours.

MRS. ALBERT M. AUSTIN, III

BROILED EGGPLANT

1 large eggplant   1 c. grated American cheese
¼ c. melted butter   6 slices bacon, broiled and
6 slices of large ripe tomato   chopped
Salt and pepper to taste

Peel eggplant and slice crosswise ½ inch thick. Soak slices in salted water for ½ hour. Brush slices with melted butter on both sides. Broil lightly, turn, broil until almost tender. Top each slice with a thick slice of tomato. Salt and pepper to season, cover with generous amount of grated cheese and bacon pieces. Broil under flame until cheese melts and bacon browns. Serve at once, allowing one slice per serving. Serves 6.

MRS. GEORGE P. PHILLIPS

EGGPLANT CASSEROLE

1 eggplant   1½ c. grated cheddar cheese
1 onion, chopped   Salt and pepper to taste
1 can condensed mushroom   ½ c. cracker crumbs
   soup

Peel and cube eggplant. Cook in very little water with salt and chopped onion. Cook until soft, drain, and save liquid. Put in layers in casserole: eggplant, undiluted soup, cheese, cracker crumbs, salt and pepper. Top with cheese. Use liquid only if dry while cooking—rarely needed. Cook about 1½ hours in 350° oven. Serves 4-6.

I mix the day before serving. Take out of refrigerator long enough before cooking for it to get to room temperature.

MRS. A. BARLOW TREADWELL

FRIED GREEN PEPPERS

Wash and remove seeds from 4 green peppers. Cut in long strips about ½ inch wide. Sauté in butter in skillet until tender and edges are slightly brown. Drain on absorbent paper, salt and pepper to taste, and serve piping hot. Delicious with meat loaf. Serves 4-6.

MRS. CHARLES B. DUDLEY, JR.

CLARA'S EGGPLANT

2 eggplants
2 eggs
½ lb. chicken livers (or to taste)
½ stick of butter

⅓ c. cream
1 small can mushrooms
½ c. bread crumbs
½ c. grated cheese
¼ t. nutmeg
Salt and pepper to taste

Peel and cut the eggplants into cubes. Cook until tender in salted water. Drain well and mash. Broil livers in small amount of butter, reserving enough butter to dot top of casserole. Season with salt and pepper while broiling. Chop fine. Beat eggs, cream and seasonings together. Add drained mushrooms, eggplant and liver with the butter it was cooked in. Mix well, put in quart casserole. Cover with bread crumbs, dot with butter and cook in a 350° oven for 20 or 30 minutes. You will find this casserole slightly liquid before cooking, but don't worry. Serves 6-8.

The nutmeg gives a wonderful elusive flavor but must be used sparingly. This dish is a specialty of the Hunt and Polo Club.

CLARA OF THE HUNT AND POLO CLUB, MEMPHIS, TENN.

EGGPLANT SOUFFLE

1 medium sized eggplant
2 T. butter
2 T. flour
1 c. milk
1 c. grated American cheese
¾ c. soft bread crumbs

2 t. grated onion
1 T. tomato catsup
Salt, pepper, cayenne
2 eggs
Broiled bacon

Peel eggplant, cut in small pieces and cook in boiling, salted water until tender. Drain thoroughly and mash. Make a cream sauce with the butter, flour and milk. When thickened and smooth, add the mashed eggplant, cheese, crumbs, onion, catsup, seasoning to taste; then add egg yolks well beaten. Fold in stiffly beaten egg whites, pour into a buttered casserole and bake in 350° oven about 45 minutes. Garnish with broiled bacon and serve immediately. Serves 8.

MRS. JAMES W. WRAPE, COLLIERVILLE, TENN.

FRITO DISH

1 large onion
1 or 2 pods garlic
Butter for browning
1 green pepper
1 No. 2 can tomatoes

4¼ oz. pkg. Fritos
1 t. Worcestershire sauce
1½ c. sharp cheese
Cayenne and Tabasco to taste

Chop onion; brown onion and garlic in butter in a skillet. Add chopped green pepper and tomatoes. Cook over medium flame. Add fritos and cup of cheese. Let fritos absorb liquid. Pour into casserole. Sprinkle remaining ½ cup cheese on top. Bake in 375° oven until cheese melts. Serves 4-6.

MRS. J. SEDDON ALLEN, JR.

HOMINY GRITS SOUFFLE—KENTUCKY STYLE

¾ c. grits   1 T. sugar
1 t. salt   1 egg
1 c. boiling water   2 c. milk
¼ c. butter

Add salt to water. Pour in grits gradually, constantly stirring. Let cook until water is absorbed. Add 1 cup milk and cook in double boiler 1 hour. Remove from fire, add butter, sugar, slightly beaten egg and remaining milk. Turn into buttered casserole and bake in 275° oven 1 hour. Serves 6.

MRS. BETTY BARBER, GERMANTOWN, TENN.

BAKED MUSHROOMS

1 pt. XX cream   2 T. sherry
3 boxes fresh mushrooms,   Salt and pepper
  peeled   Butter to spread
4 paper thin slices dried toast

Put layer of mushrooms in buttered casserole. On top of this put layer toast, quartered and spread generously with butter. Salt and pepper to taste. Repeat layers. Pour cream over this and bake in 350° oven for 40 minutes. Add sherry immediately before serving. Serves 4-6.

MRS. W. LYTLE MCKEE

MUSHROOMS FLAMBE

3 T. butter   1 t. tarragon (chopped) or
2 T. olive oil   chives
1 lb. large whole mushrooms   1 t. parsley, chopped
Salt and pepper to taste   4 T. sherry
Few grains of sugar   Brandy to ignite
1 t. lemon juice

Put in chafing dish and heat butter and olive oil. Add whole large mushrooms, peeled and caps removed. Sauté, moving about with a fork from time to time. When almost done (about 7 minutes), season with salt and freshly ground pepper, chopped tarragon or chives and chopped parsley, sherry and lemon juice. Cook another 3-4 minutes, covered. Remove cover, pour over it a little heated brandy and a few grains of sugar and ignite. Serve on toast. Serves 3-4.

MRS. EDWARD W. COOK

BROILED GARLIC MUSHROOMS

1 lb. fresh mushrooms   2 cloves garlic, crushed
1 stick butter   4 or 6 slices toast

Wash mushrooms quickly in cold running water. Remove stems and peel the caps. Sauté the garlic in the butter over a very low flame. Fill mushroom caps with garlic butter mixture. Place in shallow baking pan and broil 5 to 7 minutes. The butter will run out of the caps into the pan. Soak this up with the toast, place the mushrooms on toast and serve piping hot. Serves 4 to 6.

This is a wonderful luncheon dish or Sunday night supper dish, but you have to like garlic.

MRS. JOHN MCDONOUGH

MUSHROOM SOUFFLE WITH SHRIMP SAUCE

2 T. fat
3 T. flour
½ c. milk
½ c. mushroom liquid
½ t. salt

3 beaten egg yolks
1 c. canned mushroom
pieces
3 stiffly beaten egg whites
Maggi to taste, optional

Make white sauce of fat, flour, liquids and salt. Blend slowly into egg yolks. Add mushrooms. Fold in egg whites. Pour into ungreased casserole. Bake in pan of hot water in 350° oven until mixture does not adhere to knife. Serve with shrimp sauce. Serves 6-8.

SHRIMP SAUCE:

Slice 1 four ounce package American cheese; add to 2 cups hot medium white sauce (p. 129); stir until cheese melts. Add 2 pounds cooked shrimp and 4 hard-boiled eggs. Heat thoroughly.

MRS. PHILIP P. McCALL

NOODLE RING

2¼ c. very small cut noodles
1 T. butter
¼ lb. pimento cheese

3 eggs
¼ c. tomato catsup
2 T. Worcestershire sauce

Boil noodles in salted water for 10 minutes. Drain. Cream butter and cheese. Beat eggs well. Add butter and cheese to noodles, then catsup and Worcestershire sauce. Add well beaten eggs and mix well. Put in well buttered ring mold; set mold in pan of hot water and bake in 350° oven for 45 minutes. Serve creamed chicken or broiled mushrooms in center of ring. Serves 6-8.

MRS. WALTER P. ARMSTRONG

FRIED OKRA

Cut 2 cups okra into small pieces crosswise. Dredge with flour or corn meal, salt and pepper. Drop in deep hot fat. Drain. Serves 4-6.

This is marvelous okra as it has none of the slipperyness to which some people object.

MRS. WILLIAM A. LEATHERMAN, ROBINSONVILLE, MISS.

FRENCH FRIED ONIONS

4 large white onions
1 c. milk
1 c. flour
½ t. salt

⅔ c. water
2 T. salad oil
1 egg white, beaten stiff

Slice large Bermuda onions ¼ inch thick. Separate and soak in milk for ½ hour. Drain. Dip in batter made out of rest of ingredients, folding in egg white just before ready to fry, then fry in hot fat until lightly browned. Serves 8 generously.

MRS. M. A. ISAACS, BLYTHEVILLE, ARK.

ONIONS GLACE

18-20 young tender white
onions
1½ T. powdered sugar

1 stick butter
1 qt. canned consommé

Clean onions, leaving whole. Fry in butter until brown; add sugar. Continue to fry until quite brown; then put in baking dish with consommé. Put in 325° oven for about 1 hour. Onions must be so well cooked they will glaze in their own juice. Serves 4.

MRS. HUBERT K. REESE

STUFFED ONIONS

8 large mild onions
½ lb. sausage

1 box chopped frozen spinach
2 t. lemon juice (optional)

Wash and peel onions, cover with water, cook 20 to 25 minutes (careful not to overcook, so that onions will not fall apart). Drain, cut root end off, remove centers from root end, and chop fine. Cook spinach, drain. In skillet, break sausage into small pieces, cook and crumble, add spinach, lemon juice, chopped onion, salt and pepper to taste. Fill onions with stuffing. Arrange in greased baking dish, bake in 350° oven 25 minutes. This is better if stuffed hours before serving.

MRS. HAL PATTON

PEAS A LA BONNE FEMME

2 pkg. frozen peas
¼ lb. fresh peas
¼ head lettuce in small
chunks
2 green onions, chopped
1 t. m.s.g. (monosodium
glutamate)

1 t. sugar
2 T. butter
2 T. chopped parsley
2 T. chopped chives
⅛ t. Java cracked pepper
1 bay leaf, optional
4 T. butter, added last

Put lettuce, chopped onion, sugar, 2 tablespoons butter, m.s.g., pepper, bay leaf, fresh peas and pods into frying pan. Break frozen peas in as small bits as possible. (This is easily done if peas are unwrapped 15 minutes before ready to cook.) Add to above mixture in frying pan. Put lid on, bring to a quick boil (about 5 minutes), lower flame and cook 20-25 minutes longer or until peas are tender. Turn off heat and allow to steam 1 minute. Add chives, parsley and rest of butter. Stir well. Remove pods and serve at once. Serves 6-8.

BAKED POTATOES SUPREME

For each baked potato to be served, place in 3 separate condiment bowls and serve each guest along with potato:

1 strip of crisp bacon, broken in bits
1 T. grated Parmesan cheese
1 T. chopped chives

MRS. WALTER P. ARMSTRONG, JR.

STUFFED BELL PEPPER CREOLE

2 buttons garlic
16 medium sized peppers
4 onions, chopped
1 No. 2 can tomatoes
1 c. tomato juice
1 c. water
4 c. cracker crumbs

1 stick butter
1 c. chopped ham
Salt and pepper to taste
2 eggs
1 t. sugar
Dash of Tabasco
Dash of paprika

Wash and chop onions, garlic and 4 peppers, leaving in the seeds. Cook with butter until tender in skillet. Add tomato juice, tomatoes, ham, water and cook until all ingredients go to the bottom. Take off fire, add cracker crumbs, beat eggs well and add to mixture. Scald the remaining 12 peppers with a pinch of salt and a little sugar. Stuff the peppers with the filling and sprinkle cracker crumbs over and add a little melted butter and a dash of paprika. Bake 20 minutes in 350° oven. Serves 12.

MRS. MARY McKAY, OLD SOUTHERN TEA ROOM, VICKSBURG, MISS.

BULGHOUR PILAF

3 c. bulghour (cracked wheat)
¼ lb. butter
1 small onion, chopped fine

6 c. broth (chicken, lamb, beef)
Salt and pepper

Melt butter in heavy skillet, then add dry bulghour. Braise well until butter begins to bubble. Fry onion in separate pan until golden brown. Mix with bulghour; add broth and seasonings. Stir well and bake in 375° oven for 30 minutes. Remove from oven, stir well, bake again for 10 minutes. Serves 8.

The bulghour is a good substitute for wild rice, having a strong and distinct flavor.

RICE PILAF—Same as above, substituting rice for bulghour.

PINK PILAF—Same as above, substituting 3 cups tomato juice for broth.

MRS. WALTER P. ARMSTRONG, JR.

IDEAL POTATOES

4 medium sized potatoes
1½ c. cream sauce (p. 129)
½ c. grated N. Y. State cheese

1 t. paprika
1 T. butter
Salt and pepper to taste

Cut potatoes in shoe strings. Drop in hot grease as for French fried potatoes. Cook until lightly brown, but not crisp. Put into shallow casserole, cover with cream sauce about ½ inch deep. Sprinkle with grated cheese, paprika, and dot with butter. Cook in 375° oven for 15 minutes. Just before serving, place in broiler to brown. Serves 4.

MRS. ROBERTSON G. MORROW

TO FRESHEN WILTED GREENS: douse quickly in hot and then ice water, with a little vinegar added.

POTATO CAKES

3 medium sized raw potatoes	1 t. salt
1 T. flour	Pepper to taste
1 T. cream	Grated onions to taste
1 egg	

Grate potatoes, add other ingredients. Mix well. Cook by spoonfuls in an iron skillet in hot fat turning once. For variety 3-4 pieces crumbled bacon may be mixed in.

Mrs. George S. Miles

POTATO PUFFS

1 c. well seasoned mashed potatoes	½ c. flour
½ stick melted butter	1 t. baking powder
	2 eggs

Mix all ingredients and chill (can be done hours before serving). Drop from teaspoon and fry in deep fat until golden brown. Drain and serve hot.

Mrs. William L. Nichol

YORKSHIRE POTATO PUDDING

6 medium size potatoes	1 t. salt
⅓ to ½ c. hot milk	¼ t. pepper
1 bouillon cube	1 to 2 eggs, slightly beaten
3 T. melted butter	½ t. paprika

Boil and mash potatoes. Dissolve bouillon cube in hot milk, add butter, salt and pepper, and beat into potatoes. Reserve 1½ tablespoons of the beaten egg; add remainder to potatoes and beat again. Pile into well greased 8 or 9-inch cake tin. Brush with egg, combined with the paprika. Brown in hot oven. Cut in wedges. Serves 6-8.

Mrs. John Coulter Wyckoff II

ALMOND-CONSOMME RICE

1 c. unwashed rice	2 cans beef consommé
¾ stick butter	2 scant cans water
1 small pkg. blanched almonds	

Brown rice in butter in skillet. Add almonds and place in ungreased casserole. Cover with consommé and water. Bake covered for ½ hour. Stir, bake uncovered for 45 minutes in 350° oven. Serves 6.

Mrs. Wallace C. Pollard

GREEN RICE

2 c. raw rice	3 or more chopped garlic cloves
1 c. milk	
½ c. salad oil (Wesson Oil)	1 lb. grated snappy cheese
1 c. chopped parsley	Salt
1 c. chopped green peppers	Pepper

Cook rice and when done add remaining ingredients. Mix well and bake in casserole at 350 degrees for 1 hour. Serves 16.

Mrs. Ed McKinley

SWEET POTATO CROQUETTES

4 large sweet potatoes
1 c. broken pecan meats
1 c. crushed corn flakes
1 heaping T. flour
½ c. sugar, or to taste
2 T. milk

1 t. cinnamon
1 t. vanilla
1 egg
Bourbon whiskey to taste
¼ t. baking powder

Boil potatoes until thoroughly done. Drain and peel; mash until they are smooth. Add remaining ingredients and mix well. Shape into croquettes and roll in additional coarse corn flake crumbs. Place in refrigerator to set. Fry in hot fat. Drain. Serves 8.

These proportions are approximate. This is one of those recipes that has been used for years and made only by taste, not by written proportions, but always makes a hit. Sweet potato mixture may be molded around a marshmallow and proceed as above.

MRS. JULIAN C. WILSON

SWEET POTATO CASSEROLE

6 medium sweet potatoes,
   grated
½ stick butter, melted
3 eggs, separated
½ c. sugar

1 t. ginger
1 t. nutmeg
Grated rind of 1 orange
½ c. molasses
¼ t. salt

Mix all ingredients except egg whites, stirring until well blended. Fold in stiffly beaten egg whites and bake in greased casserole in moderate oven for 20-30 minutes.

MRS. JOHN M. MAURY, JR.

RICE—CHINESE METHOD

½ c. rice, white, brown or wild
1 c. water

½ t. salt
1 T. salad oil

Boil salted water in top of double boiler. Pour in rice; add oil, stir with fork, place over boiling water; cover. Cook for 35 minutes with top on. Take off and stir again with fork. Continue to steam for 10 minutes uncovered. This is all you have to do. Rice is dry and fluffy, ready to serve. If you add 15 minutes or so to cooking or steaming, rice is still all right. Serves 2.

MRS. WALTER P. ARMSTRONG, JR

NEW TASTE FOR VEGETABLES: add a pinch of dried thyme to fresh carrots; cook a sprig of fresh mint with green peas; add ¼ teaspoon minced fresh marjoram to butter when melting and pour over cooked spinach.

RED RICE

1 #5 can tomato juice	1 c. rice
Salt to taste	Sugar to taste

Cover rice with tomato juice in heavy iron skillet. Salt to taste. Cook with cover until done, stirring every 5 minutes or so, adding tomato juice as needed. Rice should be done in about 25 minutes. The tomato juice should be judged as to being absorbed by the rice by the time the rice is done. This requires watching. Toward the end I find it improves the flavor considerably to sprinkle a little sugar over the rice; stir it in carefully. Serves 6-8.

Red rice was always served with Beef à la Stroganoff (p. 73) in China. These two and a green salad with hot French bread make a most satisfying meal.

MRS. SYDNEY R. MILLER, JR.

RICE RING

1 c. rice	1 c. grated cheese
1 c. grated carrots	2 eggs, well beaten

Cook rice in salted water and drain. Cook carrots 5 minutes in boiling water and drain. Mix carrots, rice and cheese. Add 2 beaten eggs, season to taste. Place in greased mold lined with wax paper. Cook in pan of hot water in 350° oven until well heated. Serves 6.

MRS. LEWIS K. MCKEE

ORANGE RICE

1 can frozen orange juice	1 stick butter or oleo
1 pkg. "Minute Rice"	

Make orange juice following directions on can. Follow directions on package of "Minute Rice" substituting orange juice for water and increasing salt $\frac{3}{4}$ t. to 1 t. (according to taste). Add butter in proportion to amount made. (Must use butter and salt generously to bring out orange flavor.)

Excellent served with game.

MRS. C. B. DUDLEY, JR.

WILD RICE CASSEROLE

2 c. uncooked, wild rice	12 stuffed olives
1 No. 2 can tomatoes	2 large cans B in B
A little butter	mushrooms
$\frac{1}{2}$ lb. N.Y. cheese cut fine	

Rub baking dish with butter. Add all ingredients, mixing well. Cook in 350° oven for 1 to 1½ hours. Put extra grated cheese on top, if desired, and let brown. Serves 12.

MRS. LOUIS E. WITTENBERG

SPANISH RICE—DRY TYPE

2 to 3 T. olive oil
1 c. raw rice
1 small onion
2 stalks celery, chopped
2 T. bell pepper, chopped
1 t. salt

1 t. chili powder
1 pinch red pepper
1 small can tomato paste
2 c. boiling water
1 small pod garlic, chopped

Use heavy skillet. Heat oil, add rice, cook and stir with fork until rice is light golden brown. Add chopped onion, celery, pepper, and garlic. Stir and heat well. Add tomato sauce and seasonings. Stir well. When hot and bubbling, quickly add boiling water. Mix well. Transfer to preheated, greased casserole and cover. Cook in preheated 350° oven for 1 hour or longer. Do not stir again or rice will be sticky. When mixture is dry and fluffy it is done. Serves 4-6.

Any one of the following may be added to Spanish rice just before boiling water to make a one dish meal:

1-2 c. cooked ground beef
1-2 c. minced clams
or oysters
1-2 c. left-over-roast, ground
1-2 c. cooked, chopped
shrimp

1-2 c. cooked bacon
or sausage
1-2 c. cooked chicken
or turkey

MRS. WILLIAM L. QUINLEN, JR.

SPINACH WITH CHEESE

1 box frozen chopped spinach,
cooked, drained
2 T. butter
1 T. flour

1 T. or more of grated onion
3 beaten eggs
½ c. grated sharp cheese
Salt and pepper to taste

Melt butter in skillet; add flour and stir until smooth. Add onions and brown lightly. Add spinach, eggs, cheese, salt and pepper. Cook and stir together for at least 5 minutes. The spinach may also be placed in a round mold, served on a platter with creamed beets or mushrooms in the center. Serves 4.

Be sure to stir spinach or will stick to bottom. A very attractive and tasty party dish.

MRS. LEO J. BUCHIGNANI

SPINACH SOUFFLE

2 lb. spinach
1 T. chopped onion
1 c. cream sauce (p. 129)
½ bud garlic, chopped
3 eggs separated

Salt to taste
Pinch nutmeg
1 c. grated sharp cheese
(optional)

Cook spinach and chop very fine. Make cream sauce, adding onion and garlic if desired. Add to spinach in skillet and mix well. Reduce heat and stir in beaten egg yolks; cook for a few minutes until yolks thicken. Add seasonings and cheese if desired. Fold in stiffly beaten egg whites. Put in ring mold or casserole, set in pan of hot water and bake in 325° oven until set, about 30 minutes. Use Hollandaise sauce (p. 129). Serves 6.

CASSEROLE OF SQUASH

3 lb. fresh or 1 qt. frozen
squash
½ stick butter
Salt and pepper to taste

1 can condensed cream of
chicken soup
Cracker or bread crumbs

Boil squash until tender. Mash and drain well, and add other ingredients.
Put in casserole, cover with crumbs and bake ½ hour at 400°. Serves 8.

Mrs. William L. Nichol

CURRY SQUASH

3 good sized summer squash
1 t. curry powder, or more

½ c. milk
1 beaten egg

Cut squash into small pieces. Boil in little salted water until soft. Drain
well and mash. Add curry, milk and egg. Mix thoroughly and pour into
greased casserole. Bake it in 350° oven for ½ hour. This dish is easy to
prepare, good with cold meats. Serves 4.

Mrs. A. Arthur Halle, Cordova, Tenn.

SQUASH SOUFFLE

2 lb. squash
2 egg yolks
1 T. flour
1½ T. butter

½ t. onion juice, optional
½ t. Worcestershire sauce
Salt and pepper to taste
2 egg whites, beaten stiff

Cook squash and run through ricer. Melt butter in skillet, add onion juice
(or chopped onion), Worcestershire sauce, blending in flour and seasonings. Beat egg yolks, add to squash, mixing well. Fold in stiffly beaten
egg whites and put in casserole dish. Cook in 375° oven for 30-40 minutes.
Serves 4 generously.

*Mushroom sauce may be made quickly and easily by using a small can of B in B
sliced mushrooms. Make medium cream sauce (p. 129), add contents of can with
about ½ of liquid therein. Season to taste. This makes ample amount to serve
over the above souffle.*

Mrs. A. Arthur Halle, Cordova, Tenn.

STUFFED SQUASH

4 yellow squash
1 pkg. frozen spinach
2 hard-boiled eggs
¼ c. cracker crumbs

1 t. chopped shallots
½ stick butter
Salt and Tabasco to taste
½ c. Parmesan cheese

Boil whole yellow squash until tender. Cool, then halve. Remove center.
Mash cooked spinach. Add chopped eggs, shallots and butter; add seasonings. Stuff squash with this mixture. Sprinkle Parmesan cheese mixed
with crumbs on top. Bake in 300° oven for 25 minutes. Allow one squash
per serving, depending on its size.

Mrs. Edward A. Hall

SUMMER SQUASH WITH SOUR CREAM

4 lb. summer squash
2 T. salt
¼ c. butter
1 t. paprika

2 T. flour
2 c. sour cream
2 medium onions, chopped

Peel squash, cut in matchlike strips. Sprinkle with salt and let stand 1 hour. Drain and sauté in butter 15 minutes or until almost soft. Stir flour to a paste with a little of the sour cream and add with remaining sour cream to the squash. Add onions and let simmer 5 minutes, stirring carefully. Serve at once. Serves 6.

MRS. CHARLES M. KORTRECHT, COLLIERVILLE, TENN.

JOSEPHINE'S STUFFED TOMATOES

6 medium tomatoes
1 beaten egg
2 T. parsley
1 medium onion

¼ c. bread crumbs
Salt, pepper, paprika
2 T. butter
½ c. grated American cheese

Cut the top from tomatoes. Scoop out, chop and add egg to pulp. Then add parsley, onion, bread crumbs, salt, pepper, about a tablespoonful paprika, and butter. Mix well; fill each tomato with mixture. Bake in 350° oven in greased baking dish (filled with ⅜ c. water) until tender. Cook ½ hour. During last 5 minutes, put grated cheese on top.

MRS. EDWARD W. COOK

STUFFED TOMATOES

1 avocado, diced
4 slices bacon, diced
2 t. lemon juice
Salt and pepper

1 c. cooked chopped ham
4 tomatoes
4 T. chopped tomato pulp
¼ c. hot butter

Combine avocado with broiled bacon, lemon juice, salt, pepper and ham. Cut tops off tomatoes, scoop centers and add pulp to avocado mixture. Mix well. Fill tomatoes, replace tops and pour hot butter over them. Bake in 350° oven 25 minutes. Serve with hot Garlic Tomato Sauce (p. 130). Serves 4.

MRS. HUBERT K. REESE

ZUCCHINI WITH SHRIMP

Take the number of squash you need and boil until done. Scoop out center, add butter, salt, pepper, curry powder to taste. Chop up 2 or 3 cooked shrimp to each squash and return to squash shell. Top with buttered bread crumbs and run in oven to brown. Serve at once.

MRS. A. ARTHUR HALLE, CORDOVA, TENN.

TO PEEL TOMATOES:

Drop in boiling water for a few seconds (do not let cook), remove, peel and chill. Another method is to hold tomato over gas flame until skin wrinkles and splits. Put into cold water. Peeling will come off easily.

Salads and Dressings

If you scratch a cook, a recipe you'll get.
We scratched dozens, our salads to net,
And acquired a collection equalled by none!
Just try them, Gourmets — one by one.
Most popular of all is the tossed variety —
The pride of both high and low society.
Then, the ''girls to lunch'' type, made of fruit
Or spicy vegetables — each one we salute!
Or tangy seafoods adding their zest
To creations that rival Escoffier's best,
From the tiny and appetizing teaser
To the big and hearty, masterful ''Caesar.''
All with their dressings so perfect in flavor
With herbs divine for your tongue to savor.

— 1952

SALAD SECRETS

These are the secrets of the salad maker.

Mix the dressing thoroughly in the bottom of the salad bowl before putting in the salad plants. Chop a small onion very fine, add $\frac{1}{4}$ teaspoon salt, rather less pepper (freshly ground is best), $\frac{1}{2}$ teaspoon sugar, and all the finely chopped herbs you can get—chervil, chives, tarragon, parsley and spring onions. Over all this pour 2 tablespoons vinegar and $\frac{1}{2}$ teaspoon mustard.

We can seldom buy fresh herbs in our markets, but we can have their flavor by using herb vinegars. Garlic may be used in seasonings, but it must be used sparingly. The wise salad maker only rubs a cut clove of garlic over the inside of the bowl, or rubs it over a crust of bread, called a chapon, and leaves it in the dressing for the first few minutes. Garlic must be elusive, and that is not its distinguishing quality. Chopped pimento, green pepper, capers, olives or pickles may be used sparingly to take the place of the herbs which we do not have.

Mix the seasoned vinegar thoroughly and let it stand for about 5 minutes. Then put in the well-washed greens, thoroughly dried and broken into pieces with the fingers. A fresh salad must never be cut with a knife. Allow this to stand in a cool place so that the salad will absorb the flavors of the onions and herbs. Pour in the oil quite at the last—just before tossing the salad—and count 3 tablespoons of oil to 1 of vinegar. To stir the contents of a salad bowl with the dressing is an offense that ought to be punished by law. A light tossing with forks is the only right way.

In the south of France, lemon juice is often used in placed of vinegar. In the north, in the pasture lands of Normandy especially, thick fresh cream is used instead of oil for lettuce salad.

When making a salad, remember the old French saying: "Be a spendthrift with the oil, a miser with the vinegar, a wise man with the salt and a madman when you toss the salad together." If the salad is to be garnished, as with quartered tomatoes, hard-boiled eggs, pickled beets, or filets of anchovies, lay these on top of the tossed salad and serve it as quickly as you can.

Many good vegetable salads are spoiled because we do not use a "Marinade" or, as we have changed it, "marinate" our meat or vegetables in the seasoned vinegar and oil before the final dressing—oil, mayonnaise or cooked dressing is added.

Remember in making a dressing for marinating that the oil should be used sparingly, because vegetables or meat coated with oil will not absorb the vinegar and flavors of the herbs. Make a French dressing but use only $\frac{1}{2}$ tablespoon oil to $\frac{1}{4}$ cup of vinegar. The rest of the oil may be added later if mayonnaise is not to be used. With mayonnaise, the oil in that dressing is sufficient.

The salad is better if several cooked vegetables are used instead of only one. Combine potatoes with watercress, or add a bit of tomato to string beans and carrots. Lettuce and chickory combine well with cauliflower and peas, and a very decorative salad they make, too. There should never be a question as to whether the lettuce leaf served with the salad is eaten. That is its raison d'etre.

Bon appetit!

See Table of Equivalents (p. 240) for sugar and cream references.

EGGS EN GELEE

2 T. unflavored gelatin
½ c. cold water
1 c. hot chicken broth
10 hard-cooked eggs, coarsely
grated

½ c. chili sauce
½ c. mayonnaise
1 t. salt
1 T. grated onion
¼ t. pepper

Soften gelatin in cold water, then dissolve in hot broth. Allow to cool. Combine remaining ingredients and add to gelatin mixture. Pour into oiled mold. Chill until firm. Serve on lettuce with mayonnaise. Serves 8.

COOL AS A CUCUMBER SALAD

1 3-oz. pkg. lime flavored
gelatin
¾ c. hot water
¼ c. lemon juice
½ pt. (1 cup) sour cream
1 t. onion juice

1 c. chopped unpeeled
cucumber
6 slices canned pineapple,
drained
Lettuce

Dissolve gelatin in hot water. Add lemon and onion juices. Chill until partially set. Stir in sour cream and cucumber. Pour into 6 individual servings and chill until firm. Unmold each on pineapple ring atop a ruffle of lettuce. Garnish with ripe olives.

Mrs. William Leigh Smith

MILLIONAIRE SALAD

1 large can pineapple, cut
1 large can Queen Anne
Cherries
(may be bought seeded)

1 lb. marshmallows, cut
1 lb. almonds, blanched and
slivered
1 pt. XX cream, whipped

Drain fruits well, add marshmallows, almonds, dressing (see below), and lastly, fold in whipped cream.

FRUIT DRESSING:

5 T. lemon juice
2 T. sugar
3 egg yolks

1 heaping T. cornstarch
1½ t. salt
Juice from pineapple

Cook in double boiler until very thick. Make this salad the day before it is to be used and place in refrigerator or freezer. Stir once or twice. Serves 12.

Mrs. George A. Coors

GREEN GAGE PLUM SALAD

1 pkg. lime jello
1½ c. very hot water
½ c. plum juice
⅛ t. salt
1 t. vinegar

1 No. 2½ can green gage
  plums, drained
Blanched, toasted almonds
1 3-oz. pkg. cream cheese
½ t. ground ginger

Dissolve jello in water, add juice, salt and vinegar. Cool. Pit plums and insert almonds in each. Arrange in bottom of mold. Pour ½ of the jello over them and chill until firm. When rest of jello begins to thicken, whip in ginger and creamed cream cheese and pour over plums. Chill until firm. Serves 8.

This is a tart salad and good with game or turkey.

MRS. WILLIAM W. AYCOCK

APRICOT SALAD

1 pkg. lemon jello
1 can (1 lb. 1 oz.) apricot
  halves
1 pkg. cream cheese

Juice of 1 lemon
Juice of 1 orange
¾ c. nut meats

Use 1 cup of hot apricot juice instead of water in dissolving jello. Use cold orange, lemon and apricot juices instead of 1 cup cold water called for in jello directions. (If juices are insufficient, add water to make correct amount.) Mash apricots with fork to paste consistency and add to jello. When mixture begins to thicken, add nuts. Drop ball of cream cheese in individual molds and fill with fruit and jello mixture. Serves 6 to 8, depending upon size of molds.

MRS. EDMUND ORGILL

CREAM CHEESE RING FOR FRUIT

2 3-oz. pkg. cream cheese
3 T. powdered sugar
1½ c. milk
1 T. gelatin
¼ t. salt

½ t. vanilla
½ c. XX cream, whipped
Fresh or frozen peaches and
  raspberries

Mash cream cheese with fork and work in sugar. Soften gelatin in ½ cup of the milk (cold) and dissolve over hot water. Beat remaining cup of milk into cream cheese; add dissolved gelatin. Beat until very smooth. Add salt and vanilla, then fold in whipped cream. Turn into a 1-pint ring mold and chill until firm. Unmold on a serving plate and fill the center with juicy sliced peaches and raspberries (both lightly sugared if fresh ones are used). Serves 6.

MRS. EDWARD W. COOK

ORANGE-CRANBERRY MOLD

3 c. raw cranberries
3 large seedless oranges,
   peeling and all
1 c. sugar

2 pkg. lemon jello
2 c. hot water
2 c. ice water

Grind cranberries and oranges coarsely in meat grinder. Add sugar. Add to jello which has been dissolved in hot water and added to ice water. Pour into oiled ring mold or individual molds. Chill until firm. Serve on lettuce with mayonnaise. Serves 6 to 8.

MRS. SADIE BECK TAYLOR

CITRUS-AVOCADO MOLD

1 T. unflavored gelatin
¼ c. cold water
1 pkg. lime jello
1 c. hot water
1 large, soft avocado

3 T. lemon juice
1 t. salt
1 c. cream, whipped
½ c. mayonnaise
Grapefruit and orange sections

Soften gelatin in cold water. Dissolve jello in hot water and add gelatin. Stir until completely dissolved and allow to cool. Mash avocado through sieve, add jello mixture, lemon juice and salt. Chill until partially congealed. Fold in whipped cream and mayonnaise. Pour into slightly oiled ring mold and chill until firm. Unmold on lettuce. Surround ring and fill center with grapefruit and orange sections, using French Dressing on fruit and mayonnaise on molded salad. Serves 8.

MRS. E. CARL KRAUSNICK

HAWAIIAN DELIGHT

2 pkg. lemon jello
2 c. hot water
2 c. ice water

1 large can crushed pineapple
   drained
½ pt. sour cream

Dissolve jello in hot water. Add ice water. When jello begins to thicken, whip with egg beater until fluffy. Mix pineapple with sour cream and fold into whipped jello. Pour into mold. Chill until firm. Before serving, garnish with fresh fruits. Serves 8.

MRS. ADELE ORGILL

LIME AND CUCUMBER RING

1 pkg. lime jello
1 c. very hot water
1 medium sized cucumber,
   grated

2 T. lemon juice
½ c. cold water
1 small can drained, crushed
   pineapple, if desired

Dissolve jello in hot water. Put grated cucumber in cup, add lemon juice and ½ cup cold water (or sufficient amount to make 1 cup). Add to jello. Add pineapple, if desired. Pour into small oiled ring mold or individual cups and chill until firm. Good served with cottage cheese. Serves 4 to 6.

MRS. CAREY G. BRINGLE

HOT WEATHER SALAD

1 large can salmon   ¼ c. chopped scallions
(or 2 tuna fish)   1 c. chopped cucumbers
½ c. chopped peppers   1 pkg. gelatin
½ c. chopped celery   1 T. lemon juice

Dissolve gelatin in cold water, add hot water. Add fish and other ingredients. Place in refrigerator to jell. Serve with following sauce:

1 pt. sour cream   1 bunch radishes

Mix sour cream with sliced radishes.

MRS. WILLIAM LEIGH SMITH

TONGUE AND CHICKEN MOLD

ASPIC FOR TONGUE:

1 envelope unflavored gelatin   1 T. lemon juice
2 T. cold water   ¼ t. Worcestershire sauce
1 c. chicken stock   ¼ t. scraped onion
½ c. beef bouillon   12 slices cooked tongue

Soften gelatin in cold water. Dissolve in hot chicken stock. Add remaining ingredients, except tongue. Season to taste with salt and pepper. Set aspic in a bowl of ice to speed the thickening. When thick, but not stiff, dip slices of tongue in the aspic to coat. Then place tongue in oiled quart-size ring mold so that the slices cover the bottom and sides of the mold, overlapping slightly. (Tongue slices should be as large as possible. If whole tongue is small, slice diagonally.) Place in refrigerator to set, saving the remaining aspic for the salad.

CHICKEN SALAD:

2 c. cooked, cubed chicken   Salt and pepper to taste
1½ c. chopped celery   ½ c. cooked salad dressing
3 T. minced parsley   (recipe below)
1 t. scraped onion   2 T. mayonnaise

Toss the first four ingredients. Add salt and pepper to taste. Then add cooled, cooked dressing and mayonnaise and blend well. Fold salad into thickening aspic, and pour over tongue in ring mold. Chill until firm. Serves 8.

COOKED SALAD DRESSING FOR TONGUE AND CHICKEN MOLD:

2 eggs, well-beaten   Pinch cayenne pepper
⅓ c. cider vinegar   Dash black pepper
2 t. sugar   1 t. French's mustard
¼ t. dry mustard   1 T. butter

Put all ingredients, except butter, in saucepan and cook over low heat until mixture thickens, stirring constantly to prevent the eggs from scrambling. Lastly, stir in the butter. This makes ½ cup dressing.

This is a perfect dish for a very hot summer day. Serve on a bed of lettuce with dressing in a dish in the center.

MRS. WILLIAM A. LEATHERMAN, ROBINSONVILLE, MISS.

EGYPTIAN SALAD

1 3-lb. chicken	1 qt. chopped celery
1 pair sweetbreads	2 t. salt
2 bay leaves	½ t. paprika or white pepper
1 slice onion	½ t. curry powder (optional)
4 cloves	Juice of 2 lemons
¼ lb. almonds	1 pt. mayonnaise

Boil chicken until tender. Cool and remove meat. Cut in ½-inch cubes. Wash sweetbreads in cold water, then simmer in water seasoned with bay leaves, onion and cloves for ½ hour. Let cool and remove membrane. Chop up sweetbreads and mix with chicken, then add blanched, slightly browned almonds. At serving time add chopped celery, seasonings and mayonnaise and serve on lettuce leaves. Serves 8.

MEATY SALAD RING

1 T. unflavored gelatin	½ t. salt
½ c. cold water	1 12-oz. jar diced,
2 T. lemon juice	cooked tongue
2 t. horseradish	1 c. diced celery
2 t. prepared mustard	2 T. minced onion
1 c. mayonnaise	

Soften gelatin in cold water. Dissolve over hot water. Add lemon juice, horseradish, mustard, mayonnaise and salt. Mix thoroughly. Add remaining ingredients. Pour into oiled 8-inch ring mold and chill until firm. Unmold on crisp lettuce and garnish with tomato wedges and hard-cooked egg slices. Serves 6 to 8.

This can be made with equal success substituting 2 cups ham, chicken, tuna, salmon, or shrimp for the tongue.

Mrs. John McDonough

PRESSED CHICKEN

1 large or 2 small hens	3½ T. unflavored gelatin
1 garlic button	1½ T. lemon juice
1 medium-sized onion	6 hard-cooked eggs, sliced
1 t. salt	1 small bottle stuffed olives,
½ t. paprika	sliced
¼ t. pepper	

Boil hens with garlic, onions, salt, pepper and paprika until tender. Reserve broth, strain through cloth, and when cool, soften the gelatin in a cup of the broth, then dissolve over hot water. Add lemon juice and 3 cups of broth to gelatin mixture and mix well. (There should be at least a quart of the broth, but if amount is insufficient, more may be obtained by boiling the bones with seasonings after the meat has been removed.) Remove chicken from bones in nice large slices. Arrange egg and olive slices in bottom of oiled mold. Then place chicken in mold, using white slices first. Cover with a little gelatin mixture, let congeal, and continue this process until all gelatin is used up. Serve on lettuce with mayonnaise. Serves 8.

Mrs. George A. Coors

VEGETABLE ASPIC

1 T. unflavored gelatin	2 parsley sprigs
¼ c. cold water	1 bay leaf
3½ c. tomatoes, canned or	1 t. salt
fresh	¼ t. pepper
½ c. celery tops	1 c. chopped celery
1 medium-sized onion,	½ c. shredded cabbage
chopped	1 t. minced parsley

Soften gelatin in cold water. Simmer together slowly for 30 minutes: the tomatoes, celery tops, parsley sprigs, onion and bay leaf. Sieve and add hot juice (there should be about 2 cups) to gelatin. Add salt and pepper and set in refrigerator to cool. When mixture begins to thicken, add chopped celery, cabbage and minced parsley. Mix well and pour into slightly oiled mold or pan. Chill until firm. Serves 6.

VARIATION: Chicken: substitute 2 cans chicken broth for tomatoes. Proceed with regular recipe for vegetable aspic. When mixture is cool, substitute 1 cup minced chicken or veal for the vegetables. Add ½ cup chopped celery and 1 tablespoon minced parsley.

Mrs. Charles M. Kortrecht, Collierville, Tenn.

BING CHERRY SALAD

1 No. 2½ can black bing	2 T. Knox gelatin
cherries, pitted	Blanched almonds
2 c. orange juice, fresh	1 small pkg. cream cheese
or frozen	3 T. mayonnaise
1½ c. sherry wine	3 T. XX cream
1 c. sugar	

Oil a ring mold. Blend cream cheese, mayonnaise, and cream. Line bottom of mold with cheese mixture. Dissolve gelatin in ½ cup orange juice. Drain juice from cherries, mix with 1½ cups orange juice, wine, sugar, and bring to boil. Add gelatin mixture and pour into mold and place in refrigerator. Stuff each cherry with a whole blanched almond and add to gelatin mixture when it begins to thicken. Serve with fruit dressing (p. 125). Serves 8.

Mrs. Cooper Y. Robinson

TOMATO SOUP ASPIC

2 T. unflavored gelatin
½ c. cold water
1 can tomato soup
3 3-oz. pkg. cream cheese
1 c. chopped celery
½ c. chopped green pepper
½ c. chopped stuffed olives

1 heaping T. grated onion
2 T. lemon juice
1 c. mayonnaise
1 T. Worcestershire sauce
1 or 2 t. Tabasco
Salt to taste

Soften gelatin in cold water. Heat soup in double boiler, then add cream cheese. Whip with rotary egg beater and add gelatin. Stir until dissolved. Cool, then add other ingredients. Pour into oiled mold or pan. Chill until firm. Serves 6 to 8.

VARIATION: 1½ pounds (or 2 cups) cooked shrimp may be added to the above recipe, or the same amount of lobster.

Mrs. Frank L. Williams

FRESH TOMATO ASPIC

½ T. unflavored gelatin
¼ c. cold water
6 or 8 fresh tomatoes
1 c. chopped celery
1 green pepper, chopped

Few drops garlic juice
(if and as desired)
½ pkg. cream cheese
¼ c. mayonnaise
Salt and pepper to taste

Cut tomatoes in small pieces over a bowl, conserving and using all the liquid. Add celery, green pepper, garlic juice and cream cheese, broken in pieces. Soften gelatin in cold water and add to it sufficient hot water (approximately ¼ cup) to dissolve the gelatin. Add to tomato mixture, add mayonnaise, season to taste with salt and pepper, and pour into an oiled quart size ring mold. Serves 8 to 10.

Marinated cucumbers in the center make a tasty as well as a pretty salad plate.

Mrs. Hubert K. Reese

PARSLEY POTATO SALAD

5 or 6 lbs. potatoes
½ c. cider vinegar
1 onion, chopped
¼ c. water
Salt and pepper

½ c. salad oil
½ c. sour cream
or 3 T. mayonnaise
¼ c. minced parsley
Riced egg

Boil potatoes in jackets, peel and slice very thin while warm. Bring vinegar, onion, and water to a boil. Put layers of potatoes in a bowl; sprinkle with salt, pepper, a little oil, and a few spoons of the vinegar mixture. Continue in layers until all the potatoes are used. Fold in sour cream or mayonnaise at the last and sprinkle generously with parsley and riced egg. Chill well. Serves 8.

Mrs. John McDonough

SUMMERTIME VEGETABLE ASPIC

2 T. unflavored gelatin
½ c. cold water
1 c. boiling water
1 t. salt
¼ c. tarragon vinegar
¼ c. cider vinegar
⅓ c. sugar
2½ c. grated cabbage

1 stalk celery, chopped
2 pimentos, chopped
1 green pepper, chopped
1 c. pecans, chopped
2 3-oz. pkg. cream cheese
1 3-oz. pkg. Roquefort cheese
Cream to soften

Soften gelatin in cold water. Dissolve in boiling water. Add salt, vinegars and sugar. Allow this mixture to cool. Then add cabbage, celery, pimentos, green pepper and pecans. Pour into oiled mold and chill until firm. Serve with cream cheese and Roquefort cheese which have been mixed together and softened with cream. Serves 8.

Mrs. H. Duncan Taylor

ASPARAGUS SALAD MOLD

1 T. unflavored gelatin
¼ c. cold water
2 c. chicken or beef
consommé
2 small cans green asparagus
tips
6 strips crisp bacon, crumbled

¾ small can almonds,
blanched, toasted and
slivered
Mayonnaise seasoned with
juice from Major Grey's
Chutney

Soften gelatin in cold water. Dissolve over hot water. Add to melted consommé and mix well. Drain asparagus well and place in oiled mold or pan, sprinkling each layer with bacon and almonds. Cover with gelatin mixture. Chill until firm. Serve on lettuce with mayonnaise seasoned with juice from Major Grey's Chutney. Serves 8.

Fresh asparagus may be used. Cook in salted water until done, drain well and chill. This is a delightful luncheon dish.

Mrs. Willis H. Willey

STUFFED LETTUCE

1 small head Iceberg lettuce
½ lb. bleu cheese
1 3-oz. pkg. cream cheese
2 T. milk

1 T. chopped chives
(or green onion tops)
1 whole pimento, chopped
French dressing (p. 127)

Hollow out center or heart of lettuce, leaving a 1-inch shell of green. Beat cheese and milk together until smooth. Add chives and pimento and mix thoroughly. Fill lettuce hollow and chill in refrigerator until cheese is solid. When ready to serve, cut in crosswise slices about ¾ inch thick and serve with French Dressing. Serves 4 or more, depending upon size of head of lettuce.

Mrs. James W. Moore

GUACAMOLE

3 ripe avocados
2 tomatoes, peeled, seeded,
and finely chopped
2 green onions and tops,
finely chopped
½ clove garlic, finely minced

3 T. olive oil
Mayonnaise
Salt, red pepper, chili powder,
cumin and lemon juice to
taste

Peel avocados, mash with a silver fork. Add the next 4 ingredients. Mix in enough mayonnaise to make a paste. Add lemon juice, salt, red pepper, chili powder and cumin to taste. Serves 10 to 12 when used as a cocktail dip. Serves 8 when used as a salad.

This recipe was given to me by the chef of the Mexican Room at LaFonda Hotel in Santa Fe, New Mexico, where I think Mexican food at its best is found. It is delicious served in a bowl, surrounded by Fritos, as an accompaniment for a cocktail—or it may be piled on slices of ripe tomato on lettuce leaves for a dinner salad.

Mrs. Jack S. Goltman

MUSTARD RING

¾ c. sugar
1½ T. dry mustard
⅔ c. cider vinegar
⅓ c. water
4 eggs

1 T. unflavored gelatin
1 T. cold water
½ pt. XX cream
Salt to taste

Mix dry ingredients through fine sieve. Add vinegar and water, then add well beaten eggs. Put gelatin in top of double boiler with tablespoon of cold water and stir vigorously over boiling water until gelatin melts. Add vinegar mixture slowly, stirring constantly and being careful to keep gelatin from forming. When thoroughly mixed, remove from heat and set in cold water to cool. When mixture begins to show signs of setting, add whipping cream. Add salt to taste and pour into oiled ring mold. Chill until firm. Serves 6 to 8.

Serve shredded cabbage or cole slaw in center. Delicious with ham or barbecue.

Mrs. A. Arthur Halle, Cordova, Tenn.

ROQUEFORT ICE

½ pt. heavy cream, whipped   ¼ lb. Roquefort cheese

Mash cheese and mix well with whipped cream. Season to taste with salt and pepper. Freeze in refrigerator tray. Serve with artichoke hearts and French Dressing (p. 127) on lettuce with poppy seed sprinkled lightly over the top. Serves 6.

Mrs. Robert G. Snowden

FROZEN TOMATO SALAD

1 T. unflavored gelatin	⅛ t. dry mustard
¼ c. cold water	¼ t. dry ginger
2 c. tomato juice	Good dash red pepper
1 small can crushed pineapple, drained	1 t. onion juice
½ c. mayonnaise	¾ t. salt
½ c. cottage cheese, sieved	Tabasco to taste

Soak gelatin in cold water and dissolve in a little hot tomato juice. Add this to the other ingredients, stirring well. Pour into freezing pan and stir 3 times, 30 minutes apart, to prevent flaking, or, better still, freeze in an ice cream freezer. Serves 8.

MRS. JAMES W. WRAPE, COLLIERVILLE, TENN.

SHRIMP MOLD

1 T. unflavored gelatin	¼ t. salt
¼ c. cold water	1½ c. fresh shrimp, cooked and cleaned
Juice of 1 lemon	
1 pimento, chopped	½ c. chopped celery
1 T. grated onion	1 c. mayonnaise
1 small bottle stuffed olives, chopped	2 hard-cooked eggs, chopped
	Cayenne to taste

Soften gelatin in cold water. Dissolve over hot water. Stir in lemon juice. Combine remaining ingredients and add to gelatin mixture. Pour into oiled mold and chill. Serves 6.

MRS. H. DUNCAN TAYLOR

SHRIMP-AVOCADO MOUSSE

2 T. unflavored gelatin	1 T. lemon juice
½ c. cold water	1½ T. chopped chives
1 c. boiling water	2 c. mashed avocado pulp
1½ t. salt	1½ c. cooked, chopped shrimp
⅛ t. curry powder	¾ c. heavy cream, whipped
2 t. Worcestershire sauce	¾ c. mayonnaise

Soak gelatin in cold water to soften, then stir it into the boiling water to dissolve. Cool slightly and add salt, curry powder, Worcestershire sauce, lemon juice, chives, avocado and shrimp. Chill until it begins to set, then fold in whipped cream and mayonnaise. Adjust seasoning to taste and pour into an oiled mold. Chill until firm. Serves 8 to 10.

MRS. DUNBAR ABSTON, GERMANTOWN, TENN.

CRABMEAT EN AVOCADO

2 avocados
2 c. crabmeat, canned or fresh

½ c. chili sauce
2 T. lemon juice

Peel avocados and cut into halves. Fill with crabmeat which has been mixed with chili sauce and lemon juice. Serve very cold with French Dressing (p. 127) on lettuce. Serves 4.

MRS. HENRY EISENBEIS

CAVIAR-AVOCADO SALAD

2 avocados
2 3-oz. pkg. cream cheese
Cream

Mayonnaise
Lemon juice
1 small can or jar caviar

Break up cream cheese with fork. Add a little cream, some mayonnaise and lots of lemon juice until all is a consistency of heavy mayonnaise. (Use plenty of lemon juice because avocado is bland in taste). Add caviar and mix well. Fill peeled avocado halves with mixture and serve on lettuce with mayonnaise. Serves 4.

MRS. HUBERT K. REESE.

CAESAR SALAD

1 c. French fried croutons
6 c. mixed salad greens,
    broken up
Salt and pepper to taste
1½ cloves garlic, minced
¾ c. olive oil

¼ c. wine vinegar
2 t. lemon juice
1 c. cut, drained anchovies
3 t. grated Parmesan cheese
1 egg, coddled for 1 min.
2 t. Worcestershire sauce

Place croutons and greens in bowl, then salt and pepper to taste. Mix other ingredients, pour over croutons and greens, toss lightly to distribute dressing, and serve immediately. Serves 6.

MRS. MARION N. CRADY, PIEDMONT, CALIF.

SPINACH SALAD

1½ lbs. baby leaf fresh
    spinach
4 to 6 T. Dore's French
    Dressing (p. 124)
3 T. warm bacon grease

¼ t. garlic salt
4 strips bacon, fried crisp
    and crumbled
2 grated hard-cooked eggs, or
4 quartered ones

Wash spinach thoroughly, remove stems, drain well and place in refrigerator to crisp. When ready to serve, add Dore's French Dressing and toss gently. Then add bacon grease, garlic salt and bacon crumbles and toss gently. Garnish with grated eggs or egg quarters. Serves 4.

Very filling one-dish summer lunch.

MRS. DORE FLY

MAYONNAISE

2 egg yolks (or 1 whole egg
   and one yolk)
Juice of 1 to 1½ lemons
1 t. salt

Dash Tabasco
¼ t. paprika
¼ t. dry mustard
1 pt. salad oil

Place egg yolks in bowl and beat with a wire whisk. Beat in salt, Tabasco, paprika, dry mustard and ½ teaspoon of the lemon juice. Beat in, ½ teaspoon at a time, 1 cup oil. Then beat rest of oil into mixture, ½ teaspoon at a time, alternating with the balance of the lemon juice. Yield: 2 cups.

ELECTRIC BEATER METHOD: When making mayonnaise with an electric beater, beat the egg yolks at medium speed for 4 minutes. Add dry ingredients and 1½ tablespoons cold water. Adjust oil dripper. Place half the oil in the container, adding drop by drop. When dressing begins to thicken, add lemon juice. Place remaining oil in container, let it flow more freely, and beat constantly at medium speed. Time required: about 20 minutes.

MRS. ADELE ORGILL

ROQUEFORT DRESSING

2 egg yolks
½ t. salt
1 t. mustard
Pinch sugar

Juice of 2 lemons
1 qt. salad oil, very cold
½ lb. Roquefort cheese

Make first 6 ingredients into thick mayonnaise. Crumble the cheese, add it to the mayonnaise, and mix well. Keep in the refrigerator. Yield: slightly more than 1 quart.

This is nice on most salads, but especially good on combination salad and frozen pear salad. If used to top a combination salad, the combination should be marinated in French Dressing and not so much lemon juice is then required for the mayonnaise.

MRS. GEORGE HOLMES, SHADOWHILL, HERNANDO, MISS.

RUSSIAN DRESSING

1 c. mayonnaise
½ c. catsup
¼ c. chili sauce
½ pimento, minced
2 T. chopped chives
1 T. minced parsley

1 hard-cooked egg, chopped
1 T. lemon juice
2 T. caviar
Salt
Dash of cayenne
Paprika

Mix all ingredients together. Chill before serving. Serve with seafood salads, avocado, or on plain lettuce. Yield: approximately 1 pint.

MRS. JOHN MCDONOUGH

GREEN GODDESS SALAD DRESSING

1 c. mayonnaise
½ c. heavy cream
1 T. lemon juice
2 T. tarragon vinegar
2 T. garlic vinegar

2 T. eschalot vinegar
1 rounded T. anchovy paste
⅓ c. chopped or dried parsley
¼ c. chopped onions

Add lemon juice to cream, then mix with other ingredients. Serve on very crisp lettuce or other salad greens, making sure to coat delicately each leaf, immediately before serving. This is also good on asparagus and broccoli. May be kept in the refrigerator about 2 weeks. Serves 8.

This dressing was invented by the chef of the Palace Hotel in San Francisco especially for the testimonial dinner given in honor of George Arliss on the opening night of his famous play, "The Green Goddess."

MRS. WALTER P. ARMSTRONG, JR.

DORE'S FRENCH DRESSING

6 oz. vegetable or salad oil
2 oz. cider vinegar
Juice of 1 lemon
1 whole clove garlic

½ t. salt
¼ t. black pepper
½ t. Dash or Accent (available seasoned salts)

Mix together well and serve on any tossed green salad, but this is a "must" for Spinach Salad (p. 122). Makes ½ pt.

MRS. DORE FLY

EXCELLENT FRENCH DRESSING

1 t. salt
½ t. sugar
¼ t. black pepper
½ t. paprika

½ t. dry mustard
¾ c. salad oil
¼ c. vinegar
½ t. Worcestershire sauce

Mix dry ingredients with vinegar, add oil and Worcestershire sauce (optional). Shake well before using.

GARLIC FRENCH DRESSING

2 t. red pepper
8 t. salt
1 t. black pepper
¾ c. lemon juice (6 lemons)
1 clove garlic, cut in half

3 c. salad or olive oil
½ t. sugar
¼ c. vinegar (½ tarragon, ½ cider)

Mix well with garlic, then remove pod. Shake well before using.

MRS. SADIE BECK TAYLOR

ROQUEFORT-ANCHOVY DRESSING

Small bottle anchovies,   1 c. mayonnaise
   drained and chopped   1 c. French dressing
¼ lb. Roquefort cheese,   Dash of Worcestershire sauce
   crumbled

Mix thoroughly. Serve on any green salad.

Mrs. Dunbar Abston, Germantown, Tenn.

LORENZO DRESSING

⅔ c. olive oil   ¼ t. paprika
⅓ c. vinegar   1 c. chili sauce
1 t. salt   1 c. chopped watercress

Combine all ingredients and stir until well mixed. Chill and serve on lettuce or on grapefruit and avocado salad.

CHIFFONADE DRESSING

1 c. basic French Dressing   2 T. cooked, minced beet
1 hard-cooked egg, riced   1 t. chives
2 t. minced parsley   1 T. grated onion
1 T. minced pimento

Combine ingredients and serve on chilled asparagus tips on lettuce.

ROSSEAU DRESSING

2 eggs, hard-cooked   ¼ t. salt
2 T. brown sugar   ½ c. vinegar
1 T. butter, melted   ½ c. cream

Mash egg yolks with sugar, butter and salt. Mix until smooth. Then add vinegar and mix well. Add cream and chopped egg whites.

This is nice on lettuce served with cold lamb or roast beef.

Mrs. Joseph C. Lougheed

FRUIT DRESSING

¼ c. mayonnaise   2 T. crushed pineapple
½ c. heavy cream, whipped

Fold mayonnaise into whipped cream, then fold in pineapple. Yield: 1 cup.

Mrs. Cooper Y. Robinson

ORANGE-NUT DRESSING

¾ c. orange juice
6 T. finely chopped pecans
   (or black walnuts)
6 T. olive oil

1½ t. curry powder
1½ t. salt
1 T. basil wine vinegar
¾ t. dry mustard

Combine all ingredients and mix well. Use with a tossed green salad. Yield: approximately 1 cup.

This is a very unusual dressing—as near like the specialty at "Fanny's" in Evanston, Illinois, as I could make it. "Fanny" serves hers with her superb spaghetti dinner.

MRS. JOHN MCDONOUGH

COOKED SLAW DRESSING

1 egg or two egg yolks
2 t. sugar
1 T. melted butter
¼ c. cider vinegar
1 t. salt

Few grains cayenne pepper
2 t. corn starch
1 t. dry mustard
1 c. milk

Beat egg in top of double boiler. Dissolve corn starch in ⅓ cup milk, add to egg, then add other ingredients. Place over boiling water and cook, stirring constantly until thick. Remove from heat at once. When cool you may add chopped parsley, chives, celery, dill, or other seasonings. Yield: 1½ cups.

MRS. WILLIAM D. GALBREATH

FRENCH DRESSING FOR FRUIT

⅓ c. sugar
1 t. celery seed
1 t. salt
1 t. dry mustard

1 t. paprika
1 t. grated onion (optional)
4 T. cider vinegar
1 c. salad oil

Mix ingredients thoroughly. Serve on fruit salads. Yield: 1½ cups.

MRS. H. DUNCAN TAYLOR

PINEAPPLE SALAD DRESSING

2 well-beaten egg yolks
2 T. flour

1 c. pineapple juice
½ pt. cream, whipped

Cook egg yolks, flour and pineapple juice in top of double boiler until thick, stirring constantly. When cold, thin down with whipped cream. Yield: about 2½ cups.

This is a delicious dressing for frozen, or any fruit salad.

BASIC FRENCH DRESSING AND VARIATIONS

½ c. wine, cider   ¼ t. white pepper
  or malt vinegar   1½ c. olive or salad oil
¾ t. salt

Mix vinegar and spices, stir well with a fork and add oil. Beat the mixture with a fork until it thickens.

VARIATIONS for use as suggested or to taste. To 1 cup French dressing, add:

BAR-LE-DUC—¼ cup Bar-le-Duc. Lemon juice may be substituted for the vinegar in French dressing. For fruit salad and cottage or cream cheese salad.

BELLEVUE—6 tablespoons sour cream and 1 tablespoon finely chopped chives. For citrus fruit salad.

CAPER—2 teaspoons chopped capers, anchovy paste the size of a pea, 1 large clove garlic, finely grated, 2 tablespoons chopped hard-cooked egg yolk, and a few drops Tabasco. For green salad or fish salad.

CHUTNEY—Use half lemon juice and half vinegar and add ¼ to 1 cup imported Chutney, according to taste.

COTTAGE CHEESE—3 tablespoons cottage cheese and 1 tablespoon each chopped sweet pickles and parsley or water cress. For tomato salad.

CURRY—1 teaspoon curry and 1 tablespoon finely chopped shallots. For green salads.

GRENADINE—2 tablespoons grenadine, 1 teaspoon each grated orange rind and grated lemon rind, and Tabasco to taste. For fruit salad.

HORSERADISH — 3 tablespoons well-drained horseradish, 2 teaspoons paprika, and a few drops Tabasco. For meat salad.

HOT FRENCH DRESSING—Heat 1 cup French dressing to the boiling point and add 2 hard-cooked eggs, chopped, 1 tablespoon each finely chopped parsley and green celery leaves, ½ teaspoon Worcestershire sauce, and 1 teaspoon dry mustard. Beat well and serve hot, with asparagus, broccoli, or cauliflower or with hot potato salad.

MARTINIQUE—2 teaspoons each parsley, green pepper, shallots and chervil, all finely chopped. For mixed vegetable salads and greens.

MUSHROOM—¼ cup thinly sliced raw mushrooms. For green salad.

SARDINE—2 generous tablespoons mashed sardines and 1½ teaspoons caraway seeds. For fish salad.

SHERRY—¼ cup sherry, 2 teaspoons chopped chervil and a pinch of sugar. For fruit salad.

VINAIGRETTE—1 teaspoon each finely chopped green olives, capers, chives, parsley, gherkins and the yolk of 1 hard-boiled egg, finely chopped. For green salad.

Sauces

*Here are sauces — simple ones, fancy ones — all superb;
the exception to that rule, ''Never gild the lily.'' For a sauce,
properly made, emphasizes flavor, provides contrast, and
makes perfection complete.*

*The French say that the English have a dozen relishes and
just one sauce, and, in rebuttal, the English claim that sauces
serve the French instead of a state religion. Of course, there is
no truth to either, but there is a legitimate connection between
sauces and religion, for the making of a sauce is a matter to
be approached with religious fervor and reverent care.*

*So, heed closely the directions. Never cease watching your
sauce in its making. Stir it and stir it as it simmers to perfection, and even a novice in fine cookery will be rewarded with
the self-satisfaction of one endowed with infinite culinary
wisdom.*

— 1952

See Table of Equivalents (p. 240) for sugar and cream references.

CREAM SAUCE

THIN:

1 T. flour	1 c. hot milk
1 T. butter	

Make a roux by cooking butter with flour in top part of double boiler, over low heat, stirring constantly for a minute or two. Then add the hot milk gradually, stirring constantly. Place over hot water and cook 10 minutes, stirring frequently. Season to taste with salt and pepper. Use this in making base for cream soups, creaming vegetables, fish, etc.

MEDIUM:

2 T. flour	1 c. hot milk
2 T. butter	

Follow directions for thin sauce. Use this in making soufflés.

THICK:

4 T. flour	1 c. hot milk
4 T. butter	

Follow directions for thin sauce. Use this in making croquettes.

HOLLANDAISE SAUCE

2 egg yolks	½ c. melted butter or
½ t. salt	margarine
Dash cayenne pepper	1 T. lemon juice

Beat egg yolks until thick and lemon colored with hand beater or electric beater at high speed. Add salt and pepper. Then add 3 tablespoons of the melted butter a little at a time, beating constantly with the beater. Slowly beat in the remaining melted butter alternately with the lemon juice. If made the day before, chill until serving time, then stir until softened in top of double boiler over luke-warm, never hot, water. Hot water will cause curdling. Any leftover sauce may be stored in the refrigerator and reheated.

This recipe has been fool-proof to all who use it and the sauce keeps a long time in the refrigerator.

MRS. ROBERT Z. T. ANTHONY

FANNY'S HOLLANDAISE SAUCE

2 beaten egg yolks	⅛ t. nutmeg
⅛ t. salt	1 or 2 T. lemon juice to taste
¼ c. cream	2 T. butter

Cook in double boiler over hot, not boiling, water all the ingredients except butter until thick, stirring constantly. Remove from heat and add butter gradually, stirring. Yield: approximately ½ cup.

MRS. WILLIAM C. CHANEY

GARLIC TOMATO SAUCE

1 T. butter or oil
1 t. tomato paste
1 t. meat glaze (a
   concentrated meat stock)
½ t. minced garlic
Salt to taste

Freshly ground black pepper
   to taste
2 t. potato flour
   or instant potato
1 c. light stock or water
1 t. butter

Melt butter or oil in saucepan. Remove from heat and add tomato paste, meat glaze, garlic, salt, pepper and potato flour. Stir to a paste, add water or light stock and butter. Return to heat and stir until smooth and thickened. Pour over Stuffed Tomatoes (p. 109).

MRS. HUBERT K. REESE

RED DEVIL SAUCE

1 can tomato soup
   (undiluted)

2 c. sharp cheese, grated

Place soup and cheese in double boiler and cook until cheese is melted. Pour on toast or crackers as you would Welsh Rarebit.

MRS. JOSEPH C. LOUGHEED

VEGETABLE SAUCE

1 can condensed cream of
   mushroom soup
½ lb. New York State cheese
½ medium onion, juiced

1 to 2 T. Worcestershire
   sauce
Salt and pepper to taste

Heat soup, add cheese and stir until cheese is melted. Add Worcestershire sauce, salt, pepper and onion juice. Heat to boiling before serving. Serve with spinach, broccoli, asparagus, etc.

MRS. J. PERVIS MILNOR, JR.

HERB BUTTER

Sweet butter
Lemon juice

Chopped herbs

Soften butter, cream in lemon juice to taste and add chopped herbs such as savory, thyme, marjoram or dill. This should set before using. Serve hot on vegetables, or cold, speard on bread in place of mayonnaise for cucumber or watercress sandwiches.

MRS. HUBERT K. REESE

BIGARADE SAUCE

3 c. thin brown drippings
from roasting pan
1 c. currant jelly
3 oranges

2 lemons
1 jigger Burgundy
1 jigger Madeira
½ jigger Cointreau

Mix drippings with jelly and simmer slowly for 1¼ hours. If necessary, skim from time to time. Peel rind from oranges and lemons without disturbing white pulp. Cut into fine strips. Squeeze juice from fruit into separate pan; add rind strips. Simmer 15 to 20 minutes. Add fruit juice, strips, wines and Cointreau to beef-jelly mixture and simmer 10 minutes. Strain through fine cheesecloth. Dip slices of bird into sauce prior to serving. Two cans condensed bouillon plus enough water to make 3 cups can be substituted for drippings. Serve with duck or pheasant. Approximate yield: 2 cups sauce.

"Pump Room", Ambassador East Hotel, Chicago, Ill.

BREAD SAUCE

3 well-filled c. soft bread
cubes
1½ c. milk
2 T. cream
2 small peeled onions

2 whole cloves
1 T. butter
Salt and pepper to taste
Nutmeg or powdered mace

Remove crusts from bread before cutting into cubes. Put peeled onions with clove stuck in each one, into top part of double boiler and add milk. Bring to a boil over direct heat, then place over boiling water and add bread. Cover and cook for 20 minutes stirring lightly now and then. Remove onion and season to taste with salt and pepper. Add butter and cream and toss lightly with fork and serve at once. Nutmeg or mace may be added as desired. Delicious with quail or chicken.

Mrs. Hubert K. Reese

CRANBERRY SAUCE

4 c. fresh cranberries
2 c. sugar

1 c. water

Bring cranberries and water to a boil and cook 10 minutes. Strain and add sugar. Cook 5 minutes—no longer. Pour into mold and place in refrigerator until set.

Mrs. Edward W. Cook

DUCK SAUCE

½ lb. butter
2 T. Worcestershire sauce
1 T. currant jelly

2 c. wine (or 1 c. wine and
1 c. brandy)
1 jigger Benedictine

Melt butter, add remaining ingredients and mix well. Cut raw duck breast, cook in sauce 12 minutes if small, 20 minutes if large.

Mrs. Robertson G. Morrow

EAST INDIA SAUCE

2 c. red currant jelly
2 c. red raspberry jelly
Juice of 2 oranges
2½ lb. granulated sugar
½ lb. raisins, seeded

Rind of 1 orange, chopped
fine
Juice and grated rind of
1 lemon

Mix currant and raspberry jellies with orange juice. Bring to a boil and boil steadily for 20 minutes. Add sugar and boil 5 minutes longer. Add raisins, orange rind, lemon rind and juice. Pour into tumblers and seal. Serve with game or turkey.

MRS. SIDNEY W. FARNSWORTH, JR.

GLAZED PEARS FOR MEAT OR POULTRY

1 10-oz. glass currant jelly
1 t. almond extract

1 large can Bartlett pears,
drained

Melt jelly in saucepan. Add almond extract and place drained pears in jelly. Simmer for 20 minutes. Serve hot or cold.

MRS. H. DUNCAN TAYLOR

WINE SAUCE FOR BROILED CHICKEN

3 T. melted butter
1 T. beef extract
½ c. white wine
¼ c. Mushroom Sauce

1 T. sugar
Juice of 1 lemon
Salt to taste
Cayenne pepper to taste

Mix all ingredients thoroughly and baste chicken while it is cooking. Yield: approximately 1 cup.

MRS. EDMUND ORGILL

HERB GRAVY

1 c. turkey gravy
1 c. chicken broth
2 pinches tarragon
1 t. dry mustard
2 t. sugar

Juice of 1 lemon
2 t. grated lemon peel
1 T. horseradish
1 c. thick cream sauce
(p. 129)

Mix all ingredients but cream sauce and heat over slow fire. Add to cream sauce, heat thoroughly and serve over turkey. Yield: 3 cups.

MRS. HUBERT K. REESE

KATY'S BARBECUE SAUCE

2 pts. Worcestershire sauce
1 pt. salad oil
1 pt. A-1 sauce
1 can tomato paste
1 bottle catsup
1 lb. butter
1 pt. vinegar
4 lemons, quartered

4 garlic cloves, minced
1 9-oz. jar French's mustard
1 T. red pepper
1 T. black pepper
1 T. salt
1 T. sugar
1 T. chili powder

Combine all ingredients and add enough water to make a gallon. Simmer slowly 45 minutes. Keep in refrigerator or freeze. Keeps indefinitely and is delicious to baste broiled chicken as well as any pork roast.

MRS. JAMES K. DOBBS, JR.

PIT BARBECUE SAUCE

½ lb. butter
1 pt. catsup
1 pt. vinegar
1 T. Tabasco
1 small bottle Worcestershire sauce

1 T. brown sugar
1 T. onion juice
1½ cloves garlic, chopped fine
Dash red pepper
Dash black pepper
1 to 3 T. salt

Bring all ingredients to a boil. Add more salt if desired. Refrigeration is not necessary for the part that isn't used. Save it for the next time. Yield: slightly less than 2 quarts.

This is the recipe Bob Ellis used at the Pit and was a trade secret for years. Have had more requests for this than any other recipe I have.

MRS. CHARLES B. DUDLEY, JR.

MUSTARD SAUCE

½ c. brown sugar
½ c. mild vinegar
¼ c. dry mustard

½ c. butter
3 egg yolks

Put all ingredients in double boiler and cook until consistency of custard. If it should curdle, beat with rotary egg beater until smooth again. Good with tongue or ham. Yield: approximately 2 cups.

MRS. JOSEPH LOUGHEED

ENGLISH MUSTARD SAUCE

6 T. dry mustard
½ c. cream
1 whole egg, beaten

1 T. butter
3 T. vinegar
1 t. salt

Combine ingredients and cook over boiling water, stirring constantly, until thick. Serve with tongue or ham.

MRS. CHARLES M. KORTRECHT, COLLIERVILLE, TENN.

JEZEBEL'S SAUCE

1 jar pineapple preserves
1 small jar yellow mustard
1 jar apple jelly

½ bottle fresh horseradish
Salt to taste
Freshly ground pepper to taste

Mix all ingredients in electric mixer. This is particularly good with ham, and it keeps indefinitely in the refrigerator. Makes about 3 cups.

Miss Marjorie Cooke, Clarksdale, Miss.

RAISIN SAUCE

¼ c. sugar
1 T. flour
1 c. boiling water

Juice and rind of 1 orange
½ c. seeded raisins
1 T. butter

Mix sugar and flour. Add boiling water and cook in double boiler until thick. Add orange juice, grated rind, raisins and butter. Allow to simmer a few minutes. Serve hot with tongue or ham. Makes about 2 cups.

Mrs. Andrew O. Holmes

RAISIN-PINEAPPLE SAUCE

1 c. orange juice
1 c. water

½ c. crushed pineapple
½ c. raisins

Combine all ingredients and heat until raisins swell. Serve with tongue or ham. Yield: approximately 3 cups.

Mrs. Walter Lane Smith

MINT SAUCE FOR LAMB

½ c. fresh mint leaves, crushed
¼ c. sugar

½ c. water
½ c. vinegar

Let stand overnight. Cook over very low flame about 2 hours. Thin, if necessary, with equal parts of water and vinegar. Cool for 1 hour.

Mrs. H. Duncan Taylor

SHERRY-MINT SAUCE

Currant or crabapple jelly
Sherry wine

Chopped fresh mint leaves

Mix enough sherry with the jelly to make it the consistency of a thick sauce. Then sprinkle mint over it. Serve with lamb.
VARIATION: This may be varied for use with duck by substituting grated orange peel for the mint.

Mrs. Sidney W. Farnsworth, Sr.

HORSERADISH CREAM SAUCE

½ c. heavy cream
3 T. mayonnaise
1 T. tarragon vinegar
1 t. prepared mustard

½ t. salt
Dash cayenne pepper
2 T. bottled horseradish, drained

Whip cream until thick. Fold in mayonnaise, then slowly add remaining ingredients. Serve very cold. This is particularly good with roast beef or cold cauliflower. Yield: approximately 1 cup.

MRS. HENRY H. HAIZLIP

HORSERADISH MOUSSE

2 t. unflavored gelatin
2 T. cold water
½ c. heavy cream, whipped
½ c. grated horseradish

1 t. salt
½ t. lemon juice
1 T. chopped onion

Soften gelatin in cold water; dissolve over hot water. Cool slightly. Whip cream, then fold in remaining ingredients. Stir in gelatin and pour into oiled mold. Place in refrigerator until firm. Delicious as an accompaniment to hot Roast Beef (p. 71); or any cold meat. Yield: 6 to 8 servings.

MRS. JAMES A. HUSTON

SOUR CREAM AND HORSERADISH SAUCE

½ c. heavy sour cream
1 T. tarragon vinegar
¼ t. salt
⅛ t. white pepper

2 T. freshly grated horse-radish, well drained
Chopped chives
Tabasco, if desired

Combine all ingredients and serve cold with roast beef (p. 71).

MRS. EDWARD W. COOK

WATERCRESS SAUCE

1 bunch watercress
12 oz. chili sauce

¼ t. Tabasco
1 t. grated horseradish

Mince the watercress, add remaining ingredients and serve with hot or cold Roast Beef (p. 71).

MRS. H. DUNCAN TAYLOR

MADEIRA SAUCE

2 T. butter
1 c. leftover gravy
½ c. sour cream

1 c. fresh cream
¼ c. Madeira wine
Sliced veal, beef or lamb

Brown butter in skillet. Add remaining ingredients and pour over meat, either hot or cold.

CHILI SAUCE

24 large ripe tomatoes
6 large green peppers, chopped
8 onions, sliced
10 heaping T. sugar
6 c. cider vinegar

¼ c. salt
1 t. ground cloves
1 t. ground cinnamon
1 t. ground nutmeg
1 t. ground allspice

Skin tomatoes and combine with other ingredients and boil for about 3 hours. Stir to keep from sticking. Add red pepper pod if desired. Pour into sterilized jars while hot and seal. Yield: approximately 6 pints.

Mrs. Edward G. Willingham

COCKTAIL SAUCE

½ c. tomato catsup or chili sauce
3 T. lemon juice
Few drops Tabasco

¼ t. salt
½ c. finely chopped celery
2 t. Worcestershire sauce
Horseradish to taste

Combine ingredients and store in jar in refrigerator. Use for oysters, clams, shrimp, crabmeat or lobster. Yield: about 1 cup.

Mrs. J. Richard Walker

CUCUMBER SAUCE

2 medium onions, grated fine
¼ c. chopped parsley
4 T. capers
4 T. prepared mustard
8 T. mayonnaise

Lemon juice and cold soup stock
4 cucumbers, diced fine
Salt and pepper to taste

Combine onions, parsley, capers, mustard and mayonnaise. Thin to desired consistency with lemon juice and cold soup stock. Add cucumbers and salt and pepper to taste. Serve with cold salmon (p. 44).

Mrs. A. Arthur Halle, Cordova, Tenn.

REMOULADE SAUCE

3 or 4 T. parsley, chopped fine
3 or 4 T. kosher dill pickle, chopped fine
1 hard-cooked egg, chopped fine

3 or 4 T. dry mustard
1 medium sized onion, grated
Juice of 1 lemon
Garlic salt to taste
1 pt. mayonnaise

Grate onion on paper towel and let it stand until moisture is absorbed. Add to mayonnaise with remaining ingredients. If too thick, add juice from jar of dill pickles. Serve cold with seafood, or it may be used as a delicious dressing for head lettuce by mixing ⅓ cup Remoulade Sauce, ⅓ cup tomato catsup, or 1 hard-cooked egg cut in coarse pieces.

Mrs. Solon A. Person

SAUCE VERTE

Fresh spinach   Mayonnaise

Toss a handful of fresh spinach into water and boil until barely tender. Hold under cold water tap to set the color, then force through a strainer. Add this to mayonnaise and serve with cold salmon (p. 44).

VARIATION: Use capers and horseradish to taste in place of spinach.

MRS. ROBERTSON G. MORROW

HERB SAUCE FOR BOILED FISH

4 shallots
1 T. butter
1 T. flour
1 c. hot milk
2 egg yolks
½ c. XX cream

4 doz. tarragon leaves,
  chopped fine
1 T. chopped parsley
Grated rind of 1 lemon
Juice of 1 lemon
Salt and pepper to taste

Chop shallots very fine and cook very slowly in butter, but do not brown at all. Add flour and cook together a minute or two as you gradually add hot milk. When smooth, place over boiling water and cook a little longer. Beat egg yolks with cream, add a little of the hot sauce, then gradually pour all of the egg-cream mixture into the cream sauce and continue cooking over boiling water, stirring constantly until it thickens. Season to taste with salt and pepper and add lemon rind. When ready to serve, add parsley, tarragon leaves and lemon juice. Serve with boiled fish.

MRS. HUBERT K. REESE

APRICOT GLACE

1 large can apricots with juice   ½ c. sugar

Mix apricots, juice and sugar. Cook rapidly for 20 minutes, or until quite thick. Remove from heat and run through sieve. This is very easy and quite delicious served over gingerbread, angel food cake, sponge cake or ice cream.

MRS. ELIZABETH DANTZLER GRAYSON, BILOXI, MISS.

VANILLA SAUCE

1 c. sugar
2 T. cornstarch
⅛ t. salt

2 c. boiling water
6 T. butter
2 t. vanilla

Combine sugar, cornstarch and salt in pan. Add boiling water gradually. Simmer over low heat, stirring constantly for 5 minutes or until clear and thickened. Add butter and vanilla. Serve either hot or cold on gingerbread or other cake.

MRS. JAMES K. DOBBS, JR.

BUTTERSCOTCH SAUCE

⅔ c. brown sugar
⅔ c. white sugar
⅔ c. white corn syrup (Karo)

4 T. butter
1 c. cream

Boil brown sugar, white sugar, white syrup and butter until syrup threads, then add cream. Boil 3 minutes or until thick. Serve hot or cold over cup cakes or ice cream.

MRS. A. ARTHUR HALLE, CORDOVA, TENN.

CARAMEL SAUCE

1 c. sugar
¾ c. XX cream

1 heaping T. butter
1 t. vanilla

Caramelize ½ cup of the sugar by placing it in a heavy skillet over very low heat and stirring it constantly as it melts and browns. Place the other ½ cup sugar and all the cream in the top of a double boiler over boiling water, and heat until very hot. Add the caramelized sugar and stir until all the caramel is melted. Remove from heat and add butter and vanilla. Beat well. Keep in jar in refrigerator. Can be heated over hot water. Yield: 1¾ cups.

MRS. JAMES E. STARK

CHOCOLATE SAUCE

2 cakes bitter chocolate
½ c. sugar

½ pt. X cream

Melt chocolate over low fire, and add sugar and cream. Heat and stir until sugar is dissolved and sauce is smooth. Serve hot or cold over cake or ice cream. Yield: approximately 1½ cups.

MRS. DUNBAR ABSTON, GERMANTOWN, TENN.

AUNT MARJ'S CHOCOLATE SAUCE

2 squares chocolate
2 T. butter
⅔ c. sugar

1 c. coffee cream
½ t. vanilla (optional)

Melt butter and chocolate slowly in sauce pan over open flame. Add sugar and stir until dissolved. Add cream and cook slowly, stirring until smooth and thickened. Remove from heat and add vanilla. Yield: approximately 2 cups.

MRS. ARCHIBALD McCLURE

REGAL CHOCOLATE SAUCE

2 squares bitter chocolate	½ t. salt
6 T. water	3 T. butter
½ c. sugar	¼ t. vanilla

Melt chocolate with water in pan; add sugar and salt. Stir constantly and add butter. Don't over-cook. Cook only until creamy. Remove from stove, add vanilla and serve hot. Yield: approximately ¾ cup.

Recommended especially for those who like a creamy, semi-sweet chocolate sauce.

MRS. GEORGE A. COORS

SABAYON SAUCE

1 whole egg	½ c. Curacao or Grand
3 egg yolks	Marnier
½ c. sugar	1 t. grated orange peel

Combine ingredients and place in double boiler over warm water. Heat mixture, beating constantly until sauce is thick and smooth. Serve over fresh fruit compote. Makes approximately 1 cup.

MRS. ELIZABETH DANTZLER GRAYSON, BILOXI, MISS.

SHERRY SAUCE SUPREME

2 egg yolks	½ c. sherry wine
1 c. powdered sugar	½ pt. cream, whipped

Beat egg yolks, sugar and sherry together until smooth. Fold in whipped cream. Serve on sponge cake or angel food cake. Yield: approximately 3 cups.

MRS. EDWARD A. HALL

LEMON SAUCE

¾ c. sugar	2 T. lemon juice
2 T. cornstarch	½ t. grated lemon rind
⅛ t. salt	2 T. butter
2 c. boiling water	½ t. nutmeg

Mix sugar, salt and cornstarch together in a saucepan. Add the water gradually and boil 5 minutes while stirring. Remove from heat. Add remaining ingredients and serve hot on gingerbread, pound cake or pudding. Yield: approximately 3 cups.

MRS. JOHN McDONOUGH

GERMAN STRAWBERRY SAUCE

½ c. butter
2 c. sugar

1 c. strawberries, riced or
crushed (more or less as
desired)

Cream butter and sugar, add strawberries to taste and serve on Cottage Pudding, pound cake, or dessert pancakes. If the sauce appears curdled, that is as it should be. Yield: approximately 3½ cups.

This recipe originated in Germany and has been used in my family over a hundred years.

MRS. CHARLES B. DUDLEY, JR.

HARD SAUCE

1 c. powdered sugar or ¾ c.
granulated sugar
⅓ c. butter
⅛ t. salt

1 t. or more, according to
taste, of vanilla, rum,
whiskey, sherry, brandy,
lemon, or orange juice

Sift sugar. Cream butter until soft, and add sugar gradually, beating until well blended. Add salt and flavoring. If a richer sauce is desired, beat in 1 well-beaten egg or ¼ c. cream at this point. When sauce is very smooth, chill it thoroughly. Yield: about 1 cup.

MRS. GEORGE S. MILES

MY MOTHER'S PLUM PUDDING SAUCE

1 c. butter
2 c. sugar

1 c. rich cream
Sherry or whiskey to taste

Cream butter until light. Add sugar and continue to cream until light and foamy. Add cream and beat well together. Season highly with sherry or whiskey. Cook slowly over hot water, stirring continually until sauce is like thick cream. Yield: approximately 4 cups.

MRS. EDWARD H. CRUMP

EGGNOG SAUCE

1 c. sugar
½ c. butter
4 egg yolks
1 wine glass wine or brandy

Pinch salt
1 c. hot cream
Nutmeg to taste

Cream butter and sugar, and when light and creamy, add egg yolks. Mix well and stir into this the wine or brandy, salt and cream. Beat this mixture well, place in a double boiler, and cook over low heat, stirring constantly until it is thick like cream. Do not let the water boil or the sauce will curdle. Flavor with nutmeg and serve with gingerbread or plum pudding. Yield: approximately 3 cups.

MRS. CHARLES P. J. MOONEY

Breads

To satisfy the men
As Grandma was aware,
Took a certain, special smell
That floated on the air.

It wasn't Toujours Moi
That entranced Grandpapa.
Nor was it Chantilly
That made him act silly.

The scent that made strong men
As meek as any mouse,
Was the smell of baking bread
Wafted through the house.

Whether raisin, wheat or spoon,
Or a chewy cinnamon bun,
Hot biscuits for a party
Or corn muffins just for one.

It drew men like a magnet
(And just between us two)
What it did for Grandma,
It will do for you!

— 1952

See Table of Equivalents (p. 240) for sugar and cream references.

WHITE BREAD

1 cake yeast	1 egg
2½ c. milk	½ c. lard
½ c. plus 1 t. sugar	2½ t. salt
About 7½ c. flour	Melted butter

Dissolve yeast in ½ cup of lukewarm milk. Add 1 teaspoon sugar and ½ cup of flour. Mix well and let rise for 30 minutes in a warm place. The mixture will become light and full of bubbles. Heat ½ cup sugar, ½ cup of lard or other shortening and 2 cups of milk over low heat, stirring well until sugar and shortening are dissolved. Cool this to lukewarm. Meanwhile, add 1 well-beaten egg to yeast mixture and beat well. Pour in the lukewarm milk mixture and add enough flour to make dough. The amount of flour required will vary from 6 to 7 cups. Grease dough lightly, cover, and place in the refrigerator overnight. Next morning knead dough on lightly-floured board. When the dough is smooth and elastic, divide it in halves and shape into 2 loaves. Place loaves in well-greased pans and let rise until doubled in bulk. Loaves may be brushed with melted butter before rising. Bake at 375° for 45 minutes. Melted butter may be brushed on the bread at intervals during its baking. Remove from pans as soon as the bread is cooked. Yield: 2 loaves.

This rich bread is delicious plain or toasted and may be frozen with great success. The dough also makes delicious rolls.

Mrs. John E. Brown

QUICK WHITE BREAD

1½ cakes yeast	3 T. lard and butter mixed
3¼ to 4¼ c. flour	½ c. milk
2 t. sugar	½ c. plus 2 T. water
1½ t. salt	

Measure 3¼ cups sifted flour into a bowl and resift with 2 teaspoons sugar and 1½ teaspoons salt. Dissolve yeast in 2 tablespoons of lukewarm water and combine it with ½ cup of lukewarm water and ½ cup of lukewarm milk. Stir this liquid into the dry ingredients and add melted lard and butter. Blend these ingredients until a smooth dough is formed. You may add as much as a cup of sifted flour in order to obtain a manageable dough. Knead dough for several minutes and shape into a ball. Cover and let stand in a warm place for 15 minutes. Knead dough for 10 minutes. Shape into a loaf and place in a greased, 5 x 10 inch pan. Let rise for 1 hour. Bake for 40 minutes at 375°. Yield: 1 loaf.

RAISIN BREAD:

This easily made bread may be changed to raisin bread by the addition of a cup of raisins. Wash the raisins, drain them well, sprinkle them with flour and mix them into the dough after the addition of the shortening.

Mrs. George S. Miles

WHOLE WHEAT BREAD

4 c. white flour, sifted
4 c. whole wheat flour,
   unsifted
1 yeast cake
½ c. water (lukewarm)

2 t. salt
½ c. mild molasses
4 T. shortening
2 c. hot water

Dissolve yeast in lukewarm water. Pour hot water over salt, molasses and shortening. Cool to lukewarm. Beat in ½ of white flour and all of whole wheat flour. Add yeast mixture and enough of the remaining 2 cups of white flour to make a stiff dough. Knead on a floured board for several minutes. Cover and let rise for 2 hours. Punch dough down and let rise for another hour. Divide into 2 loaves, place in loaf pans and let rise for 1 hour longer. Bake at 375° for 1 hour or until bread is well-browned. Yield: 2 loaves.

Mrs. Maryan E. Hill, Jr.

OATMEAL BREAD

1 c. oats
6 c. unsifted white flour
2 t. salt
1 yeast cake

2 T. shortening
½ c. molasses
½ c. lukewarm water
2 c. boiling water

Pour boiling water over oats, molasses, shortening and salt. Cool to lukewarm. Dissolve yeast in ½ cup of lukewarm water and add to first mixture. Beat in all of the flour and knead until smooth. Place in greased bowl, cover and let rise for 1 hour. Divide dough in half, shape loaves and place in greased loaf pans. Let rise until doubled in bulk. Bake at 350° for 1 hour. Yield: 2 loaves.

Mrs. Maryan E. Hill, Jr.

WILLIE'S SHREDDED WHEAT BREAD

1 yeast cake
1 t. sugar
¼ c. lukewarm water
4 shredded wheat biscuits
2 c. boiling water

3 T. shortening
2 T. sugar
1 T. salt
⅓ c. molasses
5½ c. sifted flour

Crumble yeast into the lukewarm water and add 1 teaspoon of sugar. Let this become spongy. Pour boiling water over shredded wheat and add shortening, salt, the remainder of the sugar and molasses. When this is lukewarm, stir in the yeast mixture. Add flour, a cup at a time, until the dough is stiff enough to work. Knead gently in the bowl for a few minutes, then cover and let it rise until doubled in bulk. This will take from 2 to 3 hours. Knead dough; shape into loaves and place in greased loaf pans. Butter loaves and allow to rise until doubled in bulk. Bake at 425° for 15 minutes; reduce oven temperature to 375° and bake for 30 minutes longer. Remove from pans and cool. Yield: 1 large or 2 small loaves.

This bread keeps well if stored in bread box wrapped in foil and is grand hot from the oven or toasted.

ORACHNICA (SWEET BREAD)

1½ c. milk	4 eggs
½ c. sugar	8 c. flour
1 yeast cake	1 t. salt
½ c. butter	Walnuts, finely ground
1 c. honey	Cinnamon

Scald milk. Cool to lukewarm and add sugar. Dissolve yeast in 1 cup of this mixture and let stand until bubbly. Add melted butter, beaten eggs and yeast mixture to the scalded milk and sugar. Sift flour, measure, and re-sift with salt. Add flour, a cup at a time, to the liquid ingredients and stir until smooth. Place in a greased bowl, cover, and allow to rise until doubled in bulk. Divide dough in half and roll out thin on a well-floured cloth. Brush dough with finely ground walnuts, add honey and cinnamon. Roll like a jelly roll and place both rolls in greased pans or on a greased cookie sheet. Let rise until doubled in bulk. Bake at 350° for 45 minutes. Yield: 2 sweet rolls.

Mrs. Sidney W. Farnsworth, Jr.

ICEBOX ROLLS

1 c. boiling water	1 egg
⅓ c. sugar	1 yeast cake
1½ t. salt	⅛ c. warm water
1/6 c. shortening	½ t. sugar
4 c. sifted flour	

Mix first 4 ingredients and cool to lukewarm. Dissolve yeast in warm water with ½ teaspoon of sugar. Combine this with the first mixture in a large bowl. Add the egg and mix all well. Add the flour, 2 cups at a time, and beat well. Cover closely and place in the refrigerator for 24 hours. Toss dough on a well-floured board and roll out to ½ inch thickness. Cut rolls with a biscuit cutter, dip in melted butter, and fold over. Let rise for 4 hours in a warm place. Bake at 400° for 15-20 minutes. Yield: 40-50 small rolls.

Mrs. Sydney R. Miller, Jr.

BAKING HINTS:

When cutting rolls with a biscuit cutter, dip cutter in melted shortening at frequent intervals. A light cut with a knife and a generous brushing with melted butter before folding over helps make pocketbook rolls look and taste better. Try letting all yeast breads and rolls rise over the pilot light of your gas range. It's the ideal warm spot! Never forget to preheat your oven to the temperature called for in your recipe. 20 minutes is a safe length of time for this preheating and it's a "must" for successful baking of any kind.

SWEDISH ROLLS

1 yeast cake	3 well-beaten eggs
1 c. milk	½ c. sugar
1 c. melted butter	1 t. salt
1 T. sugar	5 c. flour

Scald milk, add butter and cool to lukewarm. Crumble yeast with 1 tablespoon of sugar until it liquifies, then add to first mixture. Gradually add the half cup of sugar to the beaten eggs, beating all the while. Continue to beat while adding the salt. Combine milk and egg mixtures and stir in the flour. If the rolls are to be served at noon, let this mixture stand, covered, overnight in your refrigerator. If the rolls are to be served in the evening, mix the dough before noon and allow to stand a few hours, covered. Divide dough into 3 parts and knead each one. Roll each portion of dough into a circle, approximately a quarter of an inch thick. Cut each circle into pie shaped wedges and roll each wedge, large end toward its point. Let the rolls rise for 4 hours in a warm place. Bake at 350° for 15 minutes. Yield: 50 small rolls.

These rich, pretty little rolls make perfect party fare.

Mrs. A. Barlow Treadwell

HOMEMADE BISCUIT MIX

3 T. baking powder	1 T. salt
6 c. sifted flour	1 c. vegetable shortening

Sift dry ingredients together and cut in shortening until the mixture looks like coarse corn meal. Store in any covered container. The mix does not require refrigeration. Yield: 6½ cups mix or enough to make 60 biscuits. To use this mix, add ¾ cup of milk to 2½ cups of mix. Blend well, knead lightly and roll out ½ an inch thick. Cut and bake at 425° for 15 minutes. 2½ cups of mix and ¾ cup of milk makes 20 biscuits. (Note: Use either sweet milk or buttermilk.)

Mrs. Charles B. Dudley, Jr.

BISCUITS

2 c. sifted flour	2 t. baking powder
¼ t. soda	4 T. and 1 t. lard
¼ t. salt	½ c. buttermilk

Sift dry ingredients together. Work in lard with fingers until mixture resembles corn meal. Stir in buttermilk. Turn dough out on floured board and knead **only until dough can be rolled.** Roll out ½ inch thick and cut with floured cutter. Prick the top of each biscuit with a fork. Bake at 450° for 8 minutes. Yield: 16 biscuits.

Mrs. William D. Galbreath

ORANGE BREAD

3 c. flour
4½ t. baking powder
⅓ c. shortening
¾ t. salt
1 c. sugar

1 egg, slightly beaten
⅓ c. grated orange rind or
⅔ c. shredded orange rind
1 c. orange juice

Sift flour before measuring, then re-sift with baking powder and salt.
Cream shortening and add sugar gradually, beating until mixture is fluffy.
Add slightly beaten egg and continue to beat. Add orange juice and rind.
Combine with flour mixture, stirring only enough to moisten the latter.
Do **not** beat. Pour batter into greased loaf pan. Bake 1 hour at 350°. Yield:
1 loaf.

*This light, cake-like bread is as good toasted as it is plain and makes a fine
accompaniment to a cup of tea.*

MRS. R. P. BUCKLEY, DULUTH, MINN.

DATE NUT BREAD

1 lb. pecans
2 small pkg. dates
3 eggs
1 c. flour

1 c. sugar
1 t. salt
1 t. baking powder
1 T. vanilla

Break pecans. Chop dates. Mix these together. Sift flour and baking powder
and sprinkle over date-nut mixture. Separate eggs and beat yolks, gradually
add sugar, beating well all the while. Add vanilla. Fold dates and nuts
into this mixture, then fold in stiffly beaten egg whites, into which the
salt has been beaten. Pour into greased, paper-lined loaf pans and bake
40-50 minutes at 325°. Yield: 1 large or 2 smaller loaves.

MRS. DONNELL McCORMACK

BANANA NUT BREAD

¼ lb. oleo or butter
1 c. sugar
2 eggs
½ c. pecans, finely chopped

2 c. flour
1 t. soda
3 very ripe bananas, crushed

Whip bananas until light. Cream butter and sugar and add eggs. Sift flour
and soda. Add to butter and eggs. Combine this mixture with the finely
chopped pecans, then add crushed bananas. Pour into greased loaf pan
and bake at 350° for 1 hour. Yield: 1 loaf.

This banana bread is quite moist and not very sweet.

MR. WALTER L. BERRY

NUT BREAD

3 c. flour
1 c. sugar
4 t. baking powder
1 t. salt

3 eggs
¾ c. milk
2 T. melted shortening
1 c. chopped nuts

Beat eggs with sugar. Sift baking powder and salt with flour and add this, alternating with milk, to the egg and sugar mixture. Add melted shortening, then nuts. Pour batter into 2 greased loaf pans and let stand for 15 minutes. Bake at 325° for 40-45 minutes. Yield: 2 loaves.

MRS. GEORGE P. PHILLIPS

BROWN BREAD

1 c. flour
1 c. graham flour or oats
1 t. salt
1 t. soda

1 c. sour milk
¼ c. molasses
1 c. sugar
2 eggs

Mix dry ingredients together. Beat eggs, add molasses and milk, then beat well. Add dry ingredients and beat all together. If the milk used in this recipe is quite sour, use a heaping teaspoonful of soda. Very sour milk makes delicious brown bread. Pour batter into generously greased loaf pans and bake for 45 minutes to 1 hour at 300°. This batter also makes delicious muffins. Bake muffins for 45 minutes at 300°. Yield: 1 large or 2 small loaves of bread.

MRS. GEORGE KENDEL, GRAND RAPIDS, MICH.

CINNAMON BUNS

2¼ c. bread flour
4 t. baking powder
¼ t. salt
2 T. sugar
3 heaping T. shortening
1 egg

½ stick of melted butter
¼ c. milk
¾ lb. dark brown sugar
Cinnamon to taste
½ box seedless raisins

Sift together flour, baking powder, salt and sugar. Work shortening into this mixture, using fingers. Beat egg and add with milk, using a knife to mix dough. Roll out ¼ inch thick on floured board. Spread dough with melted butter and sprinkle generously with brown sugar and raisins. Roll as for jelly roll and cut into 1¼ inch buns. Place buns in a pan which has been heavily greased with lard and spread with brown sugar. Bake at 350° for 50-60 minutes. Turn out of pan as soon as done and serve warm. These buns are moist and more flavorsome if basted with butter several times during baking. Yield: 9 buns.

MRS. CHARLES B. DUDLEY, JR.

PLAIN MUFFINS

2 c. cake flour or 1¾ c. bread flour	2 t. baking powder
¾ t. salt	2 eggs
¼ c. sugar	2 T. melted butter
	¾ c. milk

Measure sifted flour. Re-sift with remaining dry ingredients. Beat eggs until light; blend in melted butter and milk. Stir liquid into dry ingredients with a few swift strokes. Batter will be lumpy but do **not** attempt to beat out lumps. Overhandling makes muffins tough and soggy. Pour batter into greased muffin tins, filling them about half full. Bake 15 to 20 minutes at 425°. Remove from pans as soon as baked. Yield: about 2 dozen muffins.

VARIATIONS FOR PLAIN MUFFINS

APPLE MUFFINS: Add ½ cup chopped apple and ½ t. cinnamon.

BLUEBERRY MUFFINS: Increase sugar to ⅓ cup, butter to 4 tablespoons, and add 1 cup of flour-coated blueberries.

HAM MUFFINS: Add ½ cup of chopped, cooked ham.

PINEAPPLE MUFFINS: Add ½ cup well-drained, crushed pineapple.

ORANGE-PECAN MUFFINS: Make batter using juice of 1 orange and decrease milk to ⅜ of a cup. Add ⅔ of a cup of chopped pecans.

BACON MUFFINS: Add 3-4 tablespoons of diced, cooked bacon.

DATE MUFFINS: Add ½ cup of sliced, pitted dates.

VANILLA MUFFINS

¾ c. sugar	1 c. flour (measured after sifting)
½ c. (1 stick) butter	½ t. lemon juice (fresh)
3 eggs separated	1 t. baking powder
¼ c. milk	¼ t. salt
1 t. vanilla	

Cream butter and sugar **well**. Add beaten egg yolks, milk, vanilla and lemon. Re-sift dry ingredients, add to mixture. Last, fold in well-beaten egg whites. Stir quickly, make no attempt to beat out lumps completely. (Unnecessary handling of batter causes tough muffins.) Bake in well-greased muffin pans, filling about one-third full. 375° oven for 15-20 minutes. Remove immediately from pan. Yield: 24 muffins.

To reheat, place in paper bag, colse bag and place in hot oven for 5 minutes.

Mrs. Charles B. Dudley, Jr.

NUT MUFFINS

3 T. butter
1 c. sugar
1 egg
½ c. pecans
½ t. salt

1 t. soda
2 t. cream of tartar
1 c. milk
2 c. flour
3 t. ground cinnamon

Cream butter until light. Continue to beat while gradually adding sugar, then beaten egg yolk. Sift dry ingredients together and add, alternately, with milk, to butter mixture. Stir in coarsely chopped nuts, then fold in the egg white, beaten until stiff. Bake in greased muffin tins at 400° for 20 minutes. This recipe makes 2 dozen small muffins.

MRS. RICHARD C. BUNTING

POPOVERS

3 eggs
1 c. flour
1 t. shortening

Pinch of salt
1 c. milk

Mix flour and salt. Beat eggs until light and add milk. Add this slowly to flour, stirring until well-blended. Beat mixture vigorously for a minute or two. Pour batter into buttered, **hot** muffin tins or custard cups. Bake for 30 minutes at 450°. Remove from pans immediately.

MRS. DUNBAR ABSTON, GERMANTOWN, TENN.

SALLY LUNN

¼ c. sugar
½ c. butter
4 t. baking powder
1 c. milk

1 egg
¼ t. salt
2 c. flour

Cream butter and sugar. Sift dry ingredients and add to first mixture, alternating with the milk. Add well-beaten egg and stir until mixed. Bake in well-greased bread or biscuit pan for 25 minutes at 375°. Yield: 12 muffins. Serve hot and break with a fork.

CLOVELLY TOAST

A marvelous toast novelty is this! Quarter one-inch thick bread slices and brown in butter in a skillet. Roll them in a cinnamon-powdered sugar mixture and serve piping hot.

MRS. HUBERT K. REESE

HELPFUL HINT!

If you are plagued by butter browning too much when you preheat pans for popovers or corn bread, try greasing your tins or custard cups with olive oil. It heats to extremely high temperatures without burning.

COFFEE CAKE

1 c. sugar	2 beaten eggs
¼ c. butter or shortening	1½ c. cake flour
½ c. milk	1 t. baking powder
Cinnamon	Chopped nuts

Cream butter and sugar. Sift flour with baking powder and add to butter mixture, alternately with milk. Add beaten eggs and beat all together. Pour batter into an 11 by 8 inch pan and sprinkle sugar, cinnamon and chopped nuts over batter. Bake at 350° for 25-35 minutes. Should be moist and soft.

MRS. GEORGE P. PHILLIPS

SPOON BREAD

2 eggs	1 t. baking powder
½ c. corn meal	½ t. salt
½ c. boiling water	¼ t. soda
1 c. buttermilk	

Sift dry ingredients together, gradually add boiling water, stirring constantly. Beat eggs until light and add to mixture. Stir in buttermilk and pour batter into a casserole in which you have melted enough butter to generously grease the pan and also melt into the batter. Set casserole in a pan of water and bake at 400° for 45 minutes. Yield: 4 generous servings.

A family recipe, this is real Southern spoon bread!

MRS. MILLARD HALL

FRENCH TOAST

1 cup flour	¼ t. salt
2 t. baking powder	1 T. maple syrup
1 egg	1 cup sweet milk

Sift dry ingredients together, add all the liquid ingredients and stir until blended. Dip slices of dry bread (crusts trimmed) into batter and fry in deep fat (370 degrees). Batter may be thicker than desired; if so, thin with milk until it is the right consistency.

MRS. JOHN MAURY, JR.

CORN BREAD

1 c. corn meal	1 t. baking powder
1 heaping T. flour	1 c. buttermilk
1 egg	1 T. melted grease
½ t. baking soda	½ t. salt

Sift dry ingredients together. Add buttermilk, then egg, and beat until batter is smooth. Add grease and blend in well. Pour batter into very hot, greased skillet and bake at 475° until brown. Serves 4.

MR. JAMES K. DOBBS, JR.

HUSH PUPPIES

1 c. corn meal	2 t. baking powder
1 onion, chopped	1 egg, beaten
¾ T. salt	¾ c. milk
¼ t. pepper	2 T. melted fat

Mix dry ingredients thoroughly and gradually add milk, blending well. Add beaten egg, then chopped onion. Drop from teaspoon or tablespoon into hot, deep fat and fry until golden brown. Serves 4-6.

AUNTA'S PANCAKES

2 c. sifted flour	¼ c. sugar
1 c. yellow corn meal	2 eggs
2 t. baking powder	¼ to ½ c. melted butter
1 t. soda	3 c. buttermilk or sour milk
2 t. salt	

Sift dry ingredients together. Beat eggs slightly and add the melted butter and the milk. Beat well. Combine the liquid and dry ingredients, stirring only until all ingredients are moistened. Drop on a hot, ungreased griddle, making cakes 3 to 4 inches in diameter. Yield: 24 pancakes.

MRS. ROBERTSON G. MORROW

WILLIE'S BREAD CRUMB GRIDDLE CAKES

2 c. stale bread crumbs	½ c. flour
2 eggs	½ t. salt
1½ c. scalded milk	3 t. baking powder
2 T. butter	1 T. sugar

Soak crumbs in milk and melted butter. Add egg yolks and beat well. Sift flour with baking powder, salt and sugar and blend into liquid mixture. Fold in stiffly-beaten egg whites and drop mixture by spoonfuls on a greased, hot griddle. Yield: 18 pancakes.

COTTAGE CHEESE PANCAKES

4 eggs	¾ c. flour
1 c. cottage cheese	1 T. sugar
1 c. sour cream	¼ t. salt

Beat eggs. Add cottage cheese and sour cream. Blend in the dry ingredients and beat mixture until it resembles thick cream. Drop mixture by spoonfuls on a hot griddle. Yield: 36 medium-sized pancakes.

These make an unusual and tasty addition to your pancake repertoire and are sure to be a hit with both family and guests.

MRS. ADELE ORGILL

BUCKWHEAT CAKES

1 c. buckwheat flour	1 T. molasses
1 c. white flour	1 t. soda
1½ T. lard or other shortening	1 c. warm water
1 yeast cake	1 t. salt
1 c. milk	

Scald milk and lard together. Cool to lukewarm and dissolve yeast in mixture. Add both kinds of flour and let rise overnight. In the morning add molasses, salt and soda, all dissolved in 1 cup of warm water. Bake on a lightly greased griddle. Serves 6.

CHEESE WAFFLES

1¾ c. sifted flour	1 c. American or Cheddar
3 t. baking powder	cheese, grated
Pinch of salt	1½ c. milk
2 eggs	6 T. melted shortening

Sift together first 3 ingredients. Beat eggs until light and stir in grated cheese, milk and shortening. Gradually add this to the dry ingredients, stirring only until the batter is smooth. Yield: 6 waffles.

MRS. McKAY VAN VLEET

HASH HOUSE WAFFLES

4 well-beaten eggs	3 T. sugar
1 qt. milk	1 scant T. salt
5 c. sifted flour	¾ c. salad oil
5 T. baking powder	¾ c. melted butter
3 T. corn meal	

Beat eggs. Add 1 cup flour and 1 cup milk, alternately, until 4 cups of flour and all of the milk are added. Add the corn meal, sugar and salt, blend in well. Add the oil and melted butter. Add the fifth cup of flour, which has been sifted with the baking powder. These waffles may be made ahead of time and stored in the refrigerator if you do not stir in the fifth cup of flour and the baking powder until you are ready to make the waffles. Yield: 8 or 9 waffles.

Hash House Waffles have been served for years at Calvary Church Waffle Shop with great success.

MRS. ADELE ORGILL

Desserts

Now's the time to collaborate
On dishes most elaborate.

We don't pretend they're ''nothing to fix''
None are made with one-quick-mix.

The cost is not ''next to nothing''
If we said that, we'd be bluffing!

But the results are tasty and tantalizing
For once let's forget our economizing.

Let the butter be real and the cream double X
Tie on your apron and follow the text.

Mousses, meringues or feather-like cake
Flaky rich pies — a variety to bake.

An ice or a torte — to read is to try it
Peruse with restraint if you're on a diet!

— 1952

See Table of Equivalents (p. 240) for sugar and cream references.

ICE BOX PUDDING

2 4½ oz. chocolate bars
  (sweet)
1 c. boiling water
½ c. blanched and parched
  almonds

2 eggs
1 doz. lady fingers
1 t. vanilla
½ pt. whipped cream

Melt chocolate in double boiler, add boiling water and cool. Beat yolks and add to chocolate. Cook until thick (about 15 minutes). Add beaten whites, nuts and vanilla. Place whipped cream and lady fingers on top. Almond chocolate bars may be substituted instead of using blanched almonds. Serves 4 to 6.

This is quick and easy and more of a custard consistency than the other ice box puddings.

MRS. ROBERT SMITHWICK

ICE BOX CUSTARD PUDDING

1 T. (1 envelope)
  unflavored gelatin
¼ c. cold water
2 c. scalded milk
⅓ c. sugar
3 egg yolks

⅛ t. salt
1 t. vanilla
1 T. brandy or rum
5 lady fingers
6 almond macaroons

Soften gelatin in cold water. Make custard of milk, sugar, egg yolks, salt and flavorings. Add gelatin to hot custard and stir until gelatin is dissolved. Cool. Place lady fingers and macaroons in layers in mold. Pour custard mixture over lady fingers and macaroons. Chill in refrigerator until set. Unmold and serve with whipped cream. This may be flavored with two squares of melted chocolate if chocolate pudding is desired. Serves 6.

MRS. ARCHIBALD McCLURE

POOR MAN'S PUDDING

1 t. soda
1 c. molasses
1 egg
2 T. butter, melted
1 c. flour

½ c. chopped nuts
  (preferably pecans)
1 finely chopped raw apple
1 T. cinnamon
Dash of nutmeg

Dissolve soda in molasses. Beat egg, then add to mixture above. Add butter, flour, nuts, apple, cinnamon and nutmeg. Bake slowly and break into pieces to cool. It is better broken in large pieces than cut in slivers. It should be soft and moist but done. Serve cold with whipped cream or a sauce seasoned with grated orange or lemon rind. Serves 6.

MISS MARJORIE COOKE, CLARKSDALE, MISS.

AUNT HARRIET'S BREAD PUDDING

2 c. very fine bread crumbs
4 c. milk
Rind of 1 lemon, grated
¼ c. sugar

2 eggs, whole
2 eggs, separated
Strawberry or raspberry jam
2 T. sugar

Bring milk to the boiling point. Pour over the crumbs. Add lemon rind and ¼ cup sugar, then egg yolks and whole eggs beaten together. Bake as a custard in a pyrex dish in a 350° oven for about 45 minutes. Remove from oven and cover with jam. Top with stiffly beaten egg whites to which 2 tablespoons sugar have been added. Return to oven until meringue is browned. Serves 8 to 10.

MRS. ARCHIBALD McCLURE, SOUTH BEND, IND.

CARAMEL BREAD PUDDING

½ c. sugar
4 c. scalded milk
2 c. stale bread crumbs
2 eggs

⅔ c. sugar
½ t. salt
1 t. vanilla

Caramelize ½ cup sugar. Add scalded milk. When caramel sugar has melted, add stale bread crumbs and let soak for 30 minutes. Beat eggs slightly, add sugar, salt and vanilla. Add this to first mixture and bake in a 300° oven for 1½ hours. Serve with whipped cream flavored with sugar and vanilla, or with Cointreau or Curacao, if desired. Serves 8 to 10.

MRS. HUBERT K. REESE

BANANA PUDDING

2 eggs, separated
½ c. sugar
Pinch salt
1 T. flour
2 c. milk

1-2 t. vanilla
3 or 4 bananas, sliced
Vanilla wafers (optional)
3 T. sugar

Cream yolks and sugar; add salt, flour and milk. Cook over slow to medium heat until thickened. Add vanilla. Pour into baking dish alternately with bananas and wafers. Beat egg whites with 3 tablespoons of sugar until stiff, cover pudding and brown in oven. Serves 6 to 8.

MRS. FERD HECKLE, JR.

MOCHA PUDDING

½ c. strong coffee, boiling
2 doz. marshmallows, quartered
½ pt. XX cream, whipped

¾ c. chopped pecans
Macaroons
Pinch of salt

Pour hot coffee over marshmallows and stir until dissolved to small bits. Set in refrigerator until slightly jelled. Beat until smooth, fold in whipped cream, nuts and salt. Line bowl with macaroons, pour in coffee mixture, place in refrigerator to set. Serves 6 generously.

MRS. WILLIAM M. McKINNEY, CLAYTON, MO.

DATE NUT PUDDING

2 boxes pitted dates
1¾ c. sugar
1 c. bourbon whiskey
2 c. broken pecans

6 eggs
6 T. flour
2 t. baking powder

Cut dates and mash into whiskey. (If allowed to set several hours, whiskey is absorbed.) Add sugar, nuts, egg yolks and flour sifted with baking powder. Fold in beaten egg whites and pour into buttered ring mold. Bake at 350° about 1 hour. Serve cold with whipped cream. Serves 8.

MRS. H. DUNCAN TAYLOR

BLACK CHERRY MOLD

2 envelopes unflavored
  gelatin
¾ c. cold water
¼ c. boiling water
Juice of large lime or lemon

1⅔ c. sherry wine
1 large can black bing
  cherries
Sugar to taste

Soften gelatin in cold water and dissolve by adding boiling water. Cool, add lime or lemon juice, sherry, cherries (pitted), cherry juice and sugar to taste. Stir well. Put in ring mold and chill thoroughly. Unmold and serve with whipped cream. Serves 6 to 8.

MRS. HUBERT K. REESE

PEACH CRISP

4 c. fresh peaches
¾ c. sugar
½ t. cinnamon

1 c. flour
1 stick butter

Peel and slice peaches, add ½ the sugar and all the cinnamon. Cut butter into flour and add remaining sugar. Put peaches in well-greased baking dish and cover with flour mixture. Bake in 375° oven for 30 minutes. Serves 6 to 8.

STRAWBERRIES ROMANOFF

1½ qt. of strawberries,
  halved
½ rind of grapefruit
Rind of 1 orange
1 wineglass of rum

1 pt. XX cream
3 eggs
1 doz. macaroons
3 oz. of sugar

Remove all pulp from orange and grapefruit rinds, cut in thin strips and boil until tender in 2 or 3 cups of water, change water after rind has boiled 5 minutes. Cool, add strawberries. Pour rum over the mixture and allow to stand at least 3 hours. Scald ½ pint of cream. Beat eggs and sugar together until light, add to cream and cook in double boiler until thick. Cool. When ready to serve, add remaining ½ pint of cream, well beaten, to custard. Pour over fruit mixture and cover with powdered macaroons. Serves 6 to 8.

A real treat. Frozen strawberries may be used.

MRS. HERBERT P. JORDAN

MACAROON PUDDING

1½ T. unflavored gelatin
¾ c. cold water
3 c. milk, scalded
4 eggs, separated
12 T. sugar

⅓ c. rum or whiskey
1 c. nuts
½ c. maraschino cherries
12 or more macaroons

Soften gelatin in cold water. Beat egg yolks and sugar together and add to hot milk. Let boil 1 minute, then add gelatin and stir until it is dissolved. Cool slightly and add rum and stiffly beaten egg whites. Chill until it begins to set, then add nuts and cherries. Line a mold with macaroons and pour in the custard. Chill thoroughly and serve with whipped cream. Serves 12.

MRS. ROBERTSON G. MORROW

PLUM PUDDING (OLD ENGLISH)

2 loaves of bread
1 lb. beef suet
1 lb. currants
1 lb. seedless raisins
½ lb. citron
1 lb. sugar

1 c. flour
8 eggs, beaten separately
1 t. cinnamon
1 t. ground cloves
1 t. salt
1 t. grated nutmeg

Dredge currants, raisins and citron (cut in thin strips) in flour and more flour if needed. Grind bread, cut suet in small pieces. Beat yolks together. Add sugar, then all other ingredients. Fold in egg whites last. Make bags out of domestic about 4 x 12 inches. Fill and tie ends with cord. Boil 4 hours. On day it is to be served boil 2-3 hours. Serve with Plum Pudding Sauce (p. 140).

MRS. FERD HECKLE, JR.

MOCK PLUM PUDDING

1 c. raw grated carrots
1 c. raisins
1 c. broken pecans
2 t. lemon rind, grated
1¼ t. flour
½ c. butter

¾ c. brown sugar
1 egg
1½ t. baking powder
½ t. cinnamon
½ t. salt
½ t. nutmeg

Put carrots, raisins, nuts and lemon rind in large mixing bowl. Sift flour, baking powder, nutmeg, cinnamon, and salt over these ingredients and mix well. Cream sugar and butter together; add egg and beat well. Mix this well with floured carrots, etc. Put in covered mold and steam in dutch oven for 2 hours. Serve with hard sauce (p. 157). Serves 8 generously.

This is perfectly delicious and even those who don't like carrots rave over it.

MRS. DONNELL McCORMACK

PEARS ROMANOFF

6 pears (not too ripe)
¾ c. sugar
1 c. XX cream
¾ c. water
Pinch of salt

½ thinly sliced lemon
½ or whole thinly sliced
orange with peel
6 grated macaroons
(optional)

Pare, core and halve pears. Make syrup of sugar and water with pinch of salt. Pour over pears and simmer until tender. Remove pears to serving dish. Add sliced orange and lemon to syrup and cook until slices of fruit are tender and syrup thick. Pour this over pears and chill. Cover this with whipped cream. Sprinkle grated macaroons over the top just before serving. Serves 6.

MISS FRANCES C. CHURCH

PEARS IN CRABAPPLE JELLY

4 winter pears (preferably
thin, tall kind)
½ glass water

¾ glass crabapple jelly
(currant or blackberry)
Powdered mace

Rinse pears under cold water and dry, but do not peel or remove stems. Set in a shallow baking pan and pour over them a sauce made by melting over the fire the jelly and water. Sprinkle lightly with powdered mace and set in a preheated oven of 350°. Cook until tender (test with a straw) about ¾ hour basting them frequently with the jelly. When done, the pears should be brown and glazed; the jelly thick. Turn off oven and leave them in it. They are best eaten warm. If you yearn for a sauce, try half-melted vanilla ice cream or half-frozen XX cream. Serves 4.

MRS. HUBERT K. REESE

FRIED BANANAS

3 bananas
1 egg, beaten

Crushed corn flakes

Slice bananas, dip in beaten egg and then in crushed corn flakes. Fry in deep fat and drain on absorbent paper. Serves 4 to 6.

BANANAS MONICO

6 bananas
Brown sugar
4 T. butter

½ c. lime or lemon juice
½ c. dark Jamaica rum

Peel and roll the fruit in brown sugar, and place in a baking dish. Dot with butter, pour juice and rum over it and bake in a 350° oven, basting frequently, until bananas are soft but not mushy. Serves 6.

MRS. HUBERT K. REESE

CHOCOLATE ICE BOX CAKE

½ c. butter
1 c. powdered sugar
4 egg yolks
2 squares unsweetened
   chocolate

4 egg whites
1 t. vanilla
½ pt. XX cream
1 sponge cake or 2 doz.
   lady fingers

Cream butter well, beat in sugar; then beat in egg yolks, 1 at a time. Melt chocolate over hot water and add slowly to egg, sugar and butter mixture. Add vanilla. Beat egg whites until stiff, then gently fold into mixture. Line a mold with strips of cake or lady fingers, then put alternately a layer of filling and a layer of cake, making the top layer of the cake or lady fingers. (Removal of the cake to the serving platter is made easier if the mold is first lined with wax paper, leaving ends sticking out around the edge.) Chill until firm. Unmold and cover with whipped cream and grated chocolate. Serves 6-8.

MRS. GEORGE S. MILES

PINEAPPLE ICE BOX CAKE

½ lb. vanilla wafers
1½ c. confectioners sugar
½ c. butter or margarine
2 eggs

1 small can crushed pineapple
½ pt. XX cream
1 c. nutmeats

Crush wafers very fine. Butter a square cake pan and line the bottom with ½ of the crushed wafers. Cream butter and sugar. Gradually add beaten eggs. Beat until smooth. Pour this mixture over the crushed wafers. Whip the cream and add drained pineapple and chopped nuts to it. Pour over the egg mixture. Top with the remaining crushed wafers. Let stand in refrigerator several hours (preferably overnight). Cut into squares. Serves 12.

MRS. MAURICE EDWIN STANLEY

LEMON ICE BOX CAKE

¾ c. sugar
¼ t. salt
1 T. flour
3 eggs, separated
¼ c. lemon juice

Grated rind of 1 lemon
1 c. milk
1 T. butter
½ pt. XX cream
1½ doz. lady fingers

Mix sugar, salt and flour. Add egg yolks and beat well. Add lemon juice and rind, then milk and melted butter. Cook over a slow fire in a double boiler until thickened. Add beaten whites, blending gently. Cool and fold in whipped cream. Pour over lady fingers or stale cake in a bowl and chill in refrigerator. Serves 6.

MRS. DANIEL N. COPP

FRESH PEACH MOUSSE

1 c. fresh peaches, thinly
   sliced
14 marshmallows

⅜ c. water
1½ c. XX cream, whipped

Melt the marshmallows with water in a double boiler. Cool, and when slightly stiff, add peaches which should be ripe, well-flavored and chilled. Mix well and fold in whipped cream carefully. Chill. Serves 4.

CHOCOLATE MOUSSE

½ lb. dark, sweet chocolate   5 eggs, separated
5 T. water   2 t. rum

Melt chocolate in water. Carefully mix with well-beaten egg yolks and rum. Beat egg whites until they are stiff, and gently fold them into the chocolate mixture. Pour into individual molds and chill for at least 4 hours. Serve with whipped cream. Serves 6 to 8. For a large party, double this recipe and add 1 envelope plain gelatin softened in ¼ cup of cold water and dissolved over hot water. Pour into a large melon mold.

This is simple, foolproof, and very good, not too rich. Pretty, too!

MRS. RICHARD LEATHERMAN, ROBINSONVILLE, MISS.

EGGNOG MOUSSE

1½ T. gelatin   ¼ c. whiskey
½ c. cold milk   ½ pt. XX cream, whipped
3 eggs, separated   6 lady fingers
½ c. sugar   Maraschino cherries

Soften gelatin in cold milk, dissolve over hot water. Beat egg yolks until light, add sugar and beat until sugar is thoroughly dissolved. Add whiskey, then gelatin and milk and mix well. Fold in whipped cream. Beat egg whites stiff and fold into mixture. Pour into loaf pan or mold. When it begins to set, press in 6 lady fingers crosswise. Chill thoroughly. To serve, unmold and decorate with cherries. Serves 6.

MRS. FLORA MIMS

CHOCOLATE BLANC MANGE

5 egg yolks   5 squares bitter chocolate
1 c. sugar, more if desired   Pinch of salt
4 T. flour   1 t. vanilla
5 c. milk

Cream yolks and sugar. Add flour and milk. Melt chocolate and add to first mixture. Cook in double boiler until thick. Add vanilla, salt and chill. Pour into sherbet glasses and chill. Serve with whipped cream. Serves 14.

MRS. FERD HECKLE, JR.

BAKED ALASKA

Sponge cake (p. 175)   10 T. sugar
1 pt. vanilla ice cream   5 egg whites

Place sponge cake on heavy brown paper. Place cream in center of cake. Make a stiff meringue of egg whites and sugar. Cover cake and cream with thin layer of meringue. Sprinkle entire surface with granulated sugar. Run in 600° oven about 5 minutes to brown meringue quickly. Cream will not melt as paper, cake and meringue serve as insulation. But this must be made quickly and served immediately. Serves 10-12.

MRS. EMMETT R. HALL

CREME A RHUM

1¼ c. sugar
6 egg yolks
1 envelope gelatin
Pinch of salt
1 c. orange juice

½ c. white wine
¼ c. cold water
¼ c. lemon juice
3-4 T. rum
⅔ c. cream, whipped

Combine in a double boiler the sugar and the fruit juices, egg yolks, wine and rum. Place over heat and beat continuously with an egg beater until foamy and thickened. Remove from the heat, and add the gelatin which has been softened in the cold water. Cool until it is syrupy. Fold in the whipped cream. Pour into a well oiled quart mold, and chill for at least 3 hours. Serve with a small dish of whipped cream. Serves 6.

This has a light, rather tart taste that is excellent after a heavy meal, or as a summer dessert. Whole fresh strawberries are an attractive garnish.

MRS. RICHARD LEATHERMAN, ROBINSONVILLE, MISS.

BAVARIAN CREAM

1 envelope gelatin
1¼ c. cold milk
½ c. sugar
⅛ t. salt

2 egg yolks, slightly beaten
½ t. vanilla
2 egg whites, stiffly beaten
1½ c. XX cream, whipped

Soften gelatin in cold milk in top of double boiler. Add sugar and salt and place over boiling water, stirring until dissolved. Slowly pour hot mixture over egg yolks. Return to double boiler and cook over hot, not boiling, water, stirring constantly, until mixture coats spoon. Remove from heat and add vanilla. Chill until mixture is slightly thicker than the consistency of unbeaten egg whites. Fold in stiffly beaten egg whites and whipped cream. Pour into mold and chill until firm. Unmold and serve with fresh sweetened raspberries or strawberries. Frozen berries will do, but this is a spring dessert, a running-mate of fresh berries. Serves 8.

MRS. DANIEL N. COPP

MAPLE BAVARIAN CREAM

1 envelope plain gelatin
¼ c. cold water
1 c. maple syrup
3 egg yolks

Pinch of salt
1½ c. XX cream, whipped
1 c. broken nut meats

Soften gelatin in cold water. Heat syrup to boiling and pour gradually over beaten eggs. Beat well and heat in double boiler until slightly thickened. Add softened gelatin and stir until dissolved. Beat a little and place in refrigerator to cool, then fold in 1 cup of the whipped cream and the nutmeats. Pour into mold and set in refrigerator to become firm. Serve with the remaining ½ cup of cream, whipped and sweetened with a tablespoon of sugar. Serves 6 generously.

MRS. CHARLES M. KORTRECHT, COLLIERVILLE, TENN.

PEPPERMINT BAVARIAN CREAM

1½ T. plain gelatin
2 c. milk
¼ lb. peppermint stick candy

½ t. salt
½ pt. XX cream, whipped

Soften gelatin in ¼ cup of the cold milk. Heat the rest of the milk in the top of a double boiler with the candy which has been crushed. When candy is melted, add gelatin and salt and stir until thoroughly dissolved. Cool quickly. When mixture begins to thicken, beat until light. Fold in whipped cream. Turn into large or small molds. Chill. Serve with Chocolate Sauce (p. 138) and chopped nuts. Serves 10.

MRS. GEORGE W. HUMPHREYS

POT DE CREME

1 lb. New York Maillard's
   chocolate (sweet)

2 c. warm milk
6 egg yolks

Melt chocolate in milk. Boil until thick and smooth. Beat egg yolks until thick and lemon colored. Pour over chocolate mixture. Stir well. Strain through cheesecloth. Pour into individual molds and chill. If Maillard's chocolate is not available, use ¾ pound of German Sweet Chocolate (3 cakes). Serves 8.

MRS. HENRY LOEB, JR.

CREME BRULEE

4 egg yolks, well beaten
Brown or maple sugar

1 pt. X cream

Scald cream in double boiler. Remove from fire and pour slowly into beaten yolks, beating constantly. Return to fire, stir and cook 5 minutes in double boiler. Place in greased baking dish and chill thoroughly. Cover this custard with ⅓-inch layer brown or maple sugar. Place baking dish in pan of ice water under broiler (leave oven door open) to form crust and caramelize sugar. Chill again. Baked or canned pears may be served with it. This recipe may be made one day and caramelized the next. Serves 4 to 6.

MRS. DUNBAR ABSTON, GERMANTOWN, TENN.

PEAR BRULEE

8 egg yolks
1 c. sugar
⅛ t. salt
Juice of lemon
1 c. sherry wine

2 T. brandy
1 c. XX cream, whipped
2 large cans Bartlett pears
½ c. brandy

Beat egg yolks, sugar, salt and lemon juice until light. Cook over boiling water stirring constantly until thick, adding sherry and 2 tablespoons brandy slowly. Cool and fold in whipped cream. Chill. Heat pears in their syrup, then drain. Place pears in serving dish. Pour ½ cup brandy over them and take to the table flaming. Serve with chilled sauce. Serves 16.

MRS. J. PERVIS MILNOR, JR.

SCHAUM TORTE

2 c. sugar, sifted
6 egg whites
1 T. vinegar

Pinch cream of tartar
1 T. vanilla, optional

Beat egg whites with wire whisk until foamy and add cream of tartar. Continue beating until stiff and gradually add sugar, beating constantly. Continue beating until sugar is thoroughly dissolved. Add vanilla and vinegar just before last of sugar is added. Put in Schaum Torte pan (a spring-form pan). Put in cold oven. Set oven at 250° and bake until delicately brown, 1 to 1½ hours. To make individual shells for fruit or ice cream, form little nests with the uncooked mixture on greased brown paper. Serves 6 to 8.

MRS. FERD HECKLE, JR.

ALMOND TORTE

7 eggs, separated
1 c. sugar
4 stale lady fingers (8 halves) toasted and pulverized

2 t. lemon juice
Grated rind of ½ lemon
½ lb. unblanched almonds, put through meat grinder

Cream yolks of eggs with sugar until very light; add lady fingers, almonds, lemon juice and rind, and lastly fold in well-beaten whites. Bake in two 9-inch round pans (with prong attached to remove cake) in 325°-350° oven for 15 to 20 minutes or until medium brown. Layers are apt to fall a bit when removed from the oven, but that is all right. Cool thoroughly. To serve, ice with whipped cream between the layers and on top. Strawberries over the top add greatly to this dessert. Serves 12 to 14.

MRS. GEORGE P. PHILLIPS

CHOCOLATE BLACK WALNUT TORTE

½ c. chocolate cookie crumbs
½ c. chopped black walnuts
1 envelope plain gelatin
¼ c. cold water
1 pkg. semisweet chocolate

½ c. sugar
¼ t. salt
½ c. milk
3 eggs, separated
1 c. XX cream, whipped

Combine the crumbs and the nuts. Rinse out a spring-form pan with cold water. Line with wax paper, and cover the bottom of the pan with the crumb mixture, reserving some for the top. Soften the gelatin in cold water. Cook chocolate, ¼ cup of the sugar, salt and milk in a double boiler until it is well blended, and very hot. Beat egg yolks, and add the hot mixture, stirring constantly. Return to the double boiler, and cook until thickened, stirring constantly. Remove from heat, add gelatin and stir until it is dissolved. Chill until thickened. Beat egg whites, gradually add remaining ¼ cup of sugar and fold into the chocolate mixture. Fold in whipped cream and turn into pan. Top with remaining crumb mixture and chill until firm. Unmold to serve. Serves 6-8.

MRS. WILLIAM A. LEATHERMAN, ROBINSONVILLE, MISS.

LABUNSKI TORTE

6 c. ground pecans
12 eggs, separated

3 c. granulated sugar
1 T. vanilla

Beat sugar and egg yolks together until light; add ground pecans gradually, blending well. Beat whites separately and fold in with vanilla. Grease and flour round 8-inch cake pans well, leaving an extra coating of flour on bottom to avoid sticking. Put about 3 large kitchen spoonfuls in each layer pan (this recipe makes 6 layers). Bake in 350° oven for 25 minutes.

INSIDE FILLING

2 sticks butter
3 c. powdered sugar

$\frac{3}{4}$ c. cocoa
1 t. vanilla (optional)

Cream butter and sugar and add cocoa, blending well. Add vanilla if desired. This may be varied, according to taste, as to amount of cocoa used. Spread between cake layers after they have cooked and cooled.

OUTSIDE FROSTING

4 squares chocolate
1 T. cold water

$\frac{1}{2}$ c. sugar
$\frac{1}{2}$ stick butter

Combine chocolate, sugar and butter and bring slowly to a boil over low heat. Let simmer for about 5 minutes. Remove from fire and add tablespoon of cold water. Beat thoroughly until it thickens. If it doesn't thicken at first, return to the stove and simmer again. Add additional tablespoon of cold water and beat, being sure to always beat slowly. Any other chocolate icing may be substituted, if preferred. Serves 16.

This is simply delicious but deadly rich. Don't attempt to make it unless you are willing to go to a good deal of trouble and the better part of a day to prepare it. It is, however, more than worth the effort.

Mrs. George S. Miles

CRISP CHOCOLATE MERINGUE

3 egg whites
$\frac{3}{4}$ c. sugar
$\frac{1}{2}$ t. vanilla

$\frac{1}{2}$ c. chopped pecans
1 pkg. chocolate snaps, rolled
1 t. baking powder

Beat egg whites stiff, gradually adding sugar a little at a time. Add vanilla. Mix rolled snaps with baking powder. Add nuts. Fold this mixture into egg whites. Pile into greased pyrex pie plate and bake 325° about 40 minutes. When cool, cut in pie shaped wedges and serve with whipped cream, flavored with almond extract, or serve with ice cream. Serves 6.

Mrs. James W. Moore

CHOCOLATE NUT TORTE

5 eggs
2¼ c. sugar
1 T. butter
1¼ c. milk, scalded

2½ c. cake flour
⅛ t. salt
2½ t. baking powder
1 t. vanilla

Beat eggs until light. Gradually add 1 cup sugar and continue beating. Add remaining sugar and beat until light-colored and fluffy. Combine butter and hot milk; gradually add to egg mixture. Sift dry ingredients, add to egg mixture, then add vanilla. Mix well. Bake in 2 wax-paper-lined 9-inch layer pans in 350° oven for 30 minutes. Cool. Slice layers in half.

FILLING AND FROSTING

2 c. milk
¼ c. granulated sugar
½ c. enriched flour
½ c. cocoa
⅓ c. cold milk

¾ c. butter
1 c. confectioners' sugar
2 t. vanilla
1½ c. chopped California
  walnuts

Heat 2 cups milk in double boiler. Combine granulated sugar, flour, cocoa, and ⅓ cup cold milk. Add to hot milk and cook over hot water until thickened, about 20 minutes, stirring constantly. Remove from heat; cover and cool to room temperature. Thoroughly cream butter and confectioners' sugar. Add to cooked, cooled mixture. Add vanilla and beat until smooth. Spread between layers and on top and sides of torte. Cover sides of torte with chopped walnuts and make starlike design with them on top of torte. Serves 12 to 14.

Mrs. George S. Miles

MERINGUE LAYER TORTE

MERINGUE:

4 egg whites
1½ c. sugar

⅓ c. finely ground almonds

Whip egg whites until stiff and add gradually toward the last the sugar and almonds. Cut out four rounds of paper about 8 inches in diameter. Spread each round of paper with meringue and bake on baking sheet in 250° oven for about 20-30 minutes or until meringue is dry. Turn off oven, prop open oven door and leave meringue layers for about 15 minutes. Remove and turn layers over.

FILLING:

2 egg whites
½ c. sugar
2 T. sweet cocoa

1 c. butter
¼ lb. sweet chocolate

In top of double boiler, over hot, but not boiling, water beat egg whites until foamy. Beat in gradually sugar, cocoa, softened butter and melted chocolate. Beat well and remove from heat. When filling is firm, spread it on 3 meringue layers and put them together with fourth layer on top. Make a lattice work of 1 inch wide strips of paper on top of cake and dust heavily with powdered sugar. This cake should set for 24 hours. Serves 6.

GATEAU MALOKOFF

1 lb. glacéed mixed nuts with   Vanilla to taste
    caramelized sugar (no   ¾ lb. sweet butter
    peanuts)   ½ c. powdered sugar
5 T. powdered sugar   1 t. vanilla
7 egg yolks   Lady fingers
1 qt. milk

Put glacéed nuts (these are available at fancy grocers and you need the very best kind that has plenty of caramelized sugar on them) through meat grinder, using medium knife. Sift nuts through flour sifter and regrind part that won't sift through. Repeat this process, until the whole is reduced to a uniform fine powdered mixture. Make a quart of thick custard in the usual way, using the egg yolks, 5 tablespoons of sugar and the milk. When it has cooled, flavor it with vanilla and proceed to cream sweet butter until very creamy, then add the powdered sugar gradually. Then little by little incorporate the powdered nuts. Stir in vanilla and 6 tablespoons of cold custard. This will soften mixture to right consistency. Line 3-quart pyrex dish with lady fingers, placing two, cut in two, to form a cross on the bottom of the dish. Add nut and butter mixture carefully. Place waxed paper over it and cover dish with a plate, putting in ice box overnight. Turn out on round platter and pour cold custard around it and serve, accompanied by a bowl containing rest of custard. Serves 12.

This is the ultimate in fancy desserts and very easy to make. It is rich and creamy and extremely good. It must be made the day before using, and is therefore an ideal party dessert.

Mrs. Hubert K. Reese

TRIFLE

1 qt. boiled custard   Bourbon whiskey
    (p. 168)   Raspberry jam
2½ doz. lady fingers or   ⅔ c. chopped pecans
    macaroons   1½ c. XX cream, whipped

Make custard the day before dessert is to be used, so that it can be put together early in the morning and can set during the day. Thicken custard slightly so that it will be less runny. Using lady fingers split in two, dip half of them in bourbon. Put layer of lady fingers (½ plain and ½ dipped) and a layer of custard in a fairly deep bowl. Dot custard with jam and sprinkle broken pecans over it (save some pecans for top). Repeat these layers, then place lady fingers all around side of bowl so they will show when whipped cream is put on top. Top with whipped cream, sprinkle with chopped nuts and chill thoroughly. If it is convenient, put bowl in freezing compartment for an hour or two before serving. Serves 8 to 10.

Mrs. Daniel N. Copp

ALMOND MACAROON MOLD

3 doz. macaroons
Bourbon whiskey

½ pt. XX cream, whipped
2 qts. almond toffee ice cream

Line mold or silver bowl with macaroons. Pour in bowl and on macaroons as much whiskey as macaroons will absorb. Put bowl in refrigerator to chill. Whip cream stiff, flavoring highly with whiskey. Put ice cream in bowl of macaroons, spread whipped cream on top, and sprinkle crumbled macaroons over all. May be packed in mold and put in freezer if desired. Serves 8.

This is a delicious, quick, no-cooking dessert.

MRS. H. DUNCAN TAYLOR

CHOCOLATE SOUFFLE

2 T. butter
2 T. flour
¾ c. milk
½ c. sugar

3 eggs, separated
1½ squares chocolate, melted
1 t. vanilla

Melt butter, add flour, pour milk in gradually, stirring constantly. Add sugar. Melt chocolate over hot water and stir until smooth. Add to first mixture, then add beaten yolks and vanilla. Let cool, then fold in stiffly beaten egg whites. Put in buttered baking dish and set in pan of hot water and bake for 1 hour at 325°. Serves 6.

MRS. MILLARD M. BOSWORTH

CASHEW NUT SOUFFLE

1 c. rich milk
6 macaroons
6 lady fingers
3 eggs, separated

½ c. sugar
1 t. salt
1 t. vanilla
1 c. finely ground cashew nuts

Scald milk and then soak macaroons and lady fingers in it until milk is well absorbed. Arrange around side of buttered baking mold. Pour over them any remaining milk. Separate eggs and beat yolks well with ½ cup of sugar. Add salt, vanilla and nuts. Beat whites until stiff and fold into the mixture. Turn whole mixture into mold. Set in pan of hot water in moderate oven (350°) to bake until firm and well browned. Serve with sweetened whipped cream, flavored with vanilla. Serves 6-8.

MRS. GEORGE S. MILES

CREAM CHEESE SOUFFLE

6 oz. (2 pkg.) cream cheese
¾ c. thick sour cream
2 T. honey

Pinch of salt
3 egg yolks
4 egg whites

Soften cream cheese, add sour cream and beat until smooth. Stir in honey, salt and beaten egg yolks. Fold in stiffly beaten egg whites, and turn into a buttered baking dish. Bake in 350° oven for 35 minutes. Serve immediately with sweetened whipped cream and sliced, sweetened strawberries or raspberries. Serves 6.

CORN FLAKE RING WITH ICE CREAM BALLS

1½ c. brown sugar
2 T. white Karo syrup
½ c. milk

¼ c. butter
2 c. corn flakes
Vanilla ice cream

Mix brown sugar with corn syrup, milk and butter; mix well and cook until ball forms in cold water (just a soft ball). Place corn flakes in large mixing bowl and pour the hot syrup over and mix lightly. Pack lightly in greased ring mold. Cool, but do not put in refrigerator. Leave out and cover with wax paper until ready to serve. When ready to serve turn out on large platter. Place ice cream balls all around and in center of ring mold. Serve with Butterscotch Sauce (p. 138). Serves 12 to 14.

MRS. A. ARTHUR HALLE, CORDOVA, TENN.

CHOCOLATE ROLL

5 eggs, separated
1 c. confectioners' sugar

3 T. cocoa
½ pt. XX cream, whipped

Beat egg yolks until creamy. Add sugar and cocoa slowly. Fold in stiffly beaten egg whites. Line a 12x15-inch pan with wax paper. Pour mixture into pan and bake in moderate oven (350°) for about 25 minutes. When done turn out on a towel that has been well sprinkled with powdered sugar. Place damp cloth over top. When perfectly cool, spread top with whipped cream and roll like a jelly roll. Serve with Aunt Marj's Chocolate Sauce (p. 138). Serves 6.

MRS. D. HARBERT ANTHONY

BOILED CUSTARD

2 c. scalded milk
3 egg yolks
¼ c. sugar

Few grains salt
½ t. vanilla

Scald milk. Beat eggs slightly, add sugar and salt. Stir milk in gradually. Place in double boiler, stirring constantly until mixture thickens and coats spoon. Cool and add vanilla. If custard separates or becomes lumpy, put pan in cold water at once and beat with rotary beater until smooth again. This is a thin custard. If thicker custard is desired, add 2 tablespoons cornstarch dissolved in a little cold milk. It is also permissible to use 2 whole eggs.

MRS. A. ARTHUR HALLE, CORDOVA, TENN.

THIN DESSERT PANCAKES

2 eggs, beaten well
1 c. flour
¾ c. milk

¼ t. salt
1 t. baking powder
3 T. melted butter

Combine ingredients and beat until very smooth. Fry on greased griddle. Spread with jelly while hot. Roll in powdered sugar, fasten with toothpick and serve. Serves 4.

MRS. HENRY H. HAIZLIP

ENGLISH TOFFEE SQUARES

16 vanilla wafers,
(1 c. rolled)
3 eggs, separated
1 c. chopped nuts

1 c. powdered sugar
¼ lb. butter
1½ squares bitter chocolate
½ t. vanilla

Roll vanilla wafers into crumbs and mix together with chopped nuts. Using half of the mixture, cover the bottom of a buttered 9 x 9-inch pan. Cream butter and sugar, add beaten egg yolks, melted chocolate and vanilla. Fold in beaten whites. Pour over wafers and spread remaining crumbs on top. Put in refrigerator overnight. Cut in squares and serve with whipped cream. Serves 6.

Simple to make and can be done ahead. I've never served it that someone hasn't asked for the recipe.

MRS. PAUL E. SCHROEDER

GRANDMOTHER ALLEN'S CHARLOTTE RUSSE

1½ doz. lady fingers
2 envelopes plain gelatin
½ c. cold water
2 c. milk

6 egg yolks
1 c. sugar
Vanilla to taste
2 c. XX cream, whipped

Line angel cake pan or mold with lady fingers. Soften gelatin in cold water. Scald milk, beat yolks and sugar well, then stir into milk. Cook until it begins to thicken. Just before removing from fire, add gelatin and stir until well dissolved. Add vanilla and set aside. When thoroughly cool, fold in whipped cream and place in mold lined with lady fingers. Chill. To serve, unmold on cake plate and slice like cake. Serves 8.
VARIATION: 2 squares melted bitter chocolate may be added to hot custard.

This is delicious!

MRS. GEORGE P. PHILLIPS

DOROTHY'S DESSERT

18 lady fingers
30 almond macaroons
1 c. butter
1½ c. powdered sugar

5 eggs
½ lb. blanched almonds,
ground
2 - 3 T. sherry

Line bottom of mold with wax paper. Place lady fingers around mold. Lay macaroons close together on bottom, flat side down. Fill spaces with broken lady fingers. Cream butter and sugar, add 2 whole eggs, one at a time, beating well after each addition. Add 3 well beaten egg yolks, beat again. Add almonds and sherry. Fold in stiffly beaten whites of three eggs. Turn half of mixture in mold, cover with macaroons, put in the remaining half of mixture and top with macaroon crumbs. Chill 30 hours. Unmold onto serving dish.

Superb party dessert. Very rich. Easy and quick to prepare. Serves 8 generously and 12 adequately.

MRS. A. ARTHUR HALLE, CORDOVA, TENN.

FROZEN DESSERTS

LEMON BISQUE (ICE CREAM)

6 T. lemon juice
1½ T. grated lemon rind
2 c. sugar

1 qt. XX cream
Pinch of salt

Mix lemon juice, rind and sugar. Add salt to cream and whip until thick. Chill, stir in lemon juice and sugar. Freeze. Yield: 1½ quarts.

LOTUS ICE CREAM

Juice of 4 lemons
1 T. lemon rind, grated
2 c. sugar
Boiling water

3 eggs
1 pt. milk
1 qt. XX cream

Add lemon juice and grated peel to 1 cup of the sugar and add enough boiling water to cover. Stir until sugar is dissolved. Make a custard by cooking eggs and remaining sugar in top of double boiler over boiling water, stirring constantly as you add the milk, which has been scalded. Cook until smooth and thick. Cool and combine with lemon mixture, then add cream. Freeze in old-fashioned freezer. Yield: about 2 quarts.

MRS. GEORGE A. COORS

LIME CREME FREEZE

1 pkg. lime-flavored gelatin
1 c. boiling water
½ c. sugar
2 c. milk

1 c. light cream
¼ c. lemon juice
1 t. grated lemon peel
¼ t. salt

Dissolve gelatin in boiling water. Cool slightly. Add remaining ingredients and mix thoroughly. Freeze until firm. Turn into chilled bowl and beat with rotary beater until fluffy and smooth, but not melted. Freeze until firm. Serves 8.

MRS. JOHN MCDONOUGH

MONTEGO BAY ICE

3 c. sugar
3 c. boiling water
½ c. lime juice

1 egg white
½ c. rum
Drop of green coloring

Dissolve sugar in boiling water and cool. Add lime juice, rum and coloring; freeze to a mush. Add the stiffly beaten egg white and continue freezing until hard. Pack in a mold in ice and salt for 4 hours. Serves 8.

MRS. HUBERT K. REESE

THREE ICES

Juice of 3 oranges
3 bananas
Juice of 3 lemons

1 c. sugar
2 c. water

Mash bananas, add juice of oranges and lemons. Make a syrup of the sugar and water. Cool and mix with the fruit mixture and freeze. Serves 8.

ICE BOX PARFAIT

1½ c. coffee
26 marshmallows

1 t. vanilla
1½ c. XX cream

Pour coffee over cut up marshmallows and melt in a double boiler. Cool thoroughly and add vanilla. Whip cream and fold into above mixture. Put in freezer and freeze. Serves 6.

Mrs. McKay Van Vleet

RASPBERRY PARFAIT

½ pt. XX cream
1 can condensed milk (not evaporated)

½ c. top milk or light cream
1 c. strained raspberries

Whip the cream until it is about half stiff, then add condensed milk and fruit juice. Rinse out milk can with top milk before adding to raspberry mixture. Place in freezing compartment for 1 hour. Then beat well in freezing pan and return to freezing compartment. Raspberry jam, fresh strawberries or peaches may be substituted for the raspberries. Serves 6.

Mrs. McKay Van Vleet

MOCHA ICE BOX LOAF

6 t. instant coffee
¼ c. boiling water
½ c. sugar
½ c. cold water
½ c. butter or oleo
4 egg yolks

¼ c. chopped toasted blanched almonds
1¼ c. confectioners sugar
1 t. almond extract
½ lb. lady fingers

Dissolve coffee in boiling water. Add sugar. Stir until dissolved. Add cold water. Pour into shallow dish or pie pan to cool. Work fat until creamy. Beat in egg yolks and sugar alternately until smooth. Add almond extract and 2 T. coffee mixture. Dip lady fingers in coffee mixture lightly, quickly. Line up first layer on plate. Spread with filling. Repeat with more layers, more filling. Frost top and sides with remaining filling. Sprinkle with almonds. Chill 3 to 4 hours. Serves 6.

Mrs. F. Pearson Allen, Jr.

LEMON MILK SHERBET

4 c. milk   Juice of 3 lemons
1½ c. sugar   ¼ t. grated lemon rind

Mix all ingredients and freeze in a crank freezer. Serves 8.

This is a perfect summer dessert. Alone, it's cool and very light. For company, serve it in a ring of honeydew melon, garnished with fresh mint, and fresh cherries, on your coolest plates.

MRS. WILLIAM A. LEATHERMAN, ROBINSONVILLE, MISS.

CUSTARD ICE CREAM

1 qt. milk, scalded   1 T. vanilla
6 eggs   1½ qts. X cream
2 c. sugar   1 pt. XX cream

Beat eggs until thick, add sugar, then gradually add scalded milk, stirring constantly. Place in sauce pan or double boiler and cook over low heat, stirring constantly, until mixture coats spoon. Add vanilla and cream, cool and freeze in ice cream freezer. Yield: 1 gallon.

VARIATIONS: This is a good basic recipe for any flavor ice cream, the amount of sugar being varied according to individual taste and flavor used. For CARAMEL ICE CREAM, caramelize 2 cups of sugar and add to hot mixture, stirring until sugar is well dissolved. For PEPPERMINT ICE CREAM, crush 6 or 8 5-cent packages of peppermint stick candy and add to cooled custard just before freezing. For COFFEE ICE CREAM add one cup very strong coffee (more if desired) to cooled mixture just before freezing. Fresh fruit of any type desired may be used, amount varying according to taste.

MRS. JAMES K. DOBBS, JR.

CANTALOUPE FRAPPE

4 cantaloupes   4 T. lemon juice
1 c. sugar   ½ c. port wine
1½ c. water

Scoop out the pulp from 4 ripe cantaloupes and rub as much as possible of it through a coarse sieve. This should give you about 2 cups of pulpy juice. Boil the sugar moistened with the water for 5 minutes, and when it has cooled add it to the cantaloupe. Then add lemon juice and the port. Freeze in the usual manner until stiff, remove dasher and pack. When ready to serve fill centers of 8 cantaloupe halves which have previously been chilled. Just before serving trickle a few drops of cognac over each and serve at once. Serves 8.

MRS. HUBERT K. REESE

ORANGE SHERBET

1 c. sugar
1 c. water
½ c. lemon juice

½ c. orange juice
1 pt. ginger ale
1 can (small) crushed pineapple

Boil sugar and water together to make a syrup. When cool, add lemon juice, orange juice, ginger ale and pineapple. Freeze in ice cream freezer or refrigerator. If latter is used, whip with a fork several times while freezing. Serves 8.

MRS. JAMES W. WRAPE, COLLIERVILLE, TENN.

BISCUIT TORTONI

2 cups macaroons, crushed fine
1 cup sugar
1 pt. X cream

1 pt. XX cream
½ c. brandy
½ c. white port

Soak macaroon crumbs in X cream about 1 hour. Add to this the sugar, brandy, white port and fold in the whipped XX cream. Pour this mixture into paper ramekins. The recipe will fill about 24 cup cake size ramekins. Freeze.

JOSIE OLIVER, CATERESS

MOCHA ICE CREAM

4 eggs, separated
¾ c. sugar
1 t. cornstarch

1 lb. sweet chocolate
1 c. strong hot coffee
1 pt. XX cream

Mix cornstarch, sugar and coffee; stir into well beaten yolks. Melt chocolate in double boiler, add coffee mixture. Cook slowly until smooth, stirring constantly. Cool, fold in beaten egg whites and cream. Freeze. Serves 8 to 10.

MRS. A. ARTHUR HALLE, CORDOVA, TENN.

CHOCOLATE ICE CREAM

1 square bitter chocolate
15 marshmallows

½ pt. XX cream, whipped
1 c. milk

Melt chocolate and marshmallows. Add milk, cool and add whipped cream. Freeze in tray. Serves 6 to 8.

MR. A. ARTHUR HALLE, CORDOVA, TENN.

DATE MARSHMALLOW ICE CREAM

16 marshmallows
1 c. milk
Dash of salt

1 c. XX cream, whipped
⅓ c. nuts, chopped
½ c. dates, cut fine

Cut marshmallows in quarters with scissors and melt in milk over hot water. Add salt and let cool. Chill in tray of automatic refrigerator until thick. Fold into whipped cream with nuts and dates. Freeze 2 hours or more until firm. Serves 4 to 6.

Mrs. Hubert K. Reese

FROZEN EGGNOG

1 pt. cream, whipped
1 box vanilla wafers (small)
1 c. chopped nuts

2 eggs
½ c. sugar
6 T. rum

Separate eggs. Beat yolks, add sugar. Add rum slowly, then fold in beaten egg whites. Fold in whipped cream and add nuts last. Roll out wafers. Spread mold or refrigerator drawer with melted butter then pat crumbs over it. Pour in eggnog over this. Cover with more crumbs. Can be made the day before serving. Serves 6 to 8.

Mrs. Edward W. Cook

FRESH STRAWBERRY ICE CREAM

1 qt. milk
1 pt. XX cream, whipped
½ c. sugar
3 egg yolks
3 T. flour

2 to 3 T. water
2 T. vanilla
1 qt. sugared strawberries,
mashed

Mix flour and sugar, add water, then egg yolks well beaten. Beat well and add to hot milk. Cook until thick as mayonnaise. Cool, add vanilla, cream and berries. Freeze. Serves 6 to 8.

Mrs. Charles L. Piplar

WATERMELON ICE

½ large melon
Juice of 4 oranges
Juice of 3 lemons

1 c. sugar
1 egg white

Scrape meat from melon, extract juice. Add lemon and orange juice and sugar. Stir thoroughly and freeze. When slightly frozen add stiffly beaten white of egg and finish freezing. Serve in melon rind that has been neatly trimmed. Garnish with white grapes. Serves 6 to 8.

Mrs. Everett R. Cook, Germantown, Tenn.

CAKES

PLAIN CAKE

2¼ c. sifted cake flour
2½ t. baking powder
½ t. salt
½ c. butter (1 stick)

1½ c. sugar
2 eggs
1 c. milk
1 t. vanilla

Sift flour, baking powder and salt together. Cream butter and sugar together until light and fluffy. Add eggs and beat well. Add flour, alternately with milk, beating well after each addition. Add vanilla. Bake in two greased 9-inch layer cake pans 25 minutes at 375° or until top of cake is light brown and cake leaves sides of pans.

MRS. JAMES K. DOBBS, JR.

POUND CAKE

½ lb. butter
1¾ c. sugar
5 eggs

2 c. flour, sifted
1 t. vanilla
Pinch of salt

Cream butter and sugar thoroughly. Add eggs, one at a time, beating well after each addition. Add salt, then flour gradually, beating well. Add vanilla and bake in greased loaf pan at 325° for 55 minutes or until cake leaves sides of pan. This may be eaten plain or served with Lemon Sauce (p. 139).

MRS. JAMES K. DOBBS, JR.

SPONGE CAKE

9 egg yolks
1½ c. sifted sugar
¾ c. boiling water
2¼ c. sifted flour

½ t. salt
3 t. baking powder
1½ t. vanilla

Beat yolks until light and add sugar. Beat more and add water. Sift flour, salt and baking powder and fold into egg mixture. Add vanilla. Bake 45 minutes to 1 hour in 300-350° oven in an ungreased 9-inch tube pan. Remove pan from oven and invert until cake is entirely cold, then run a knife around the sides and bottom (if you have that kind of pan). Remove cake from pan and trim off any hard edges. Ice as desired or sprinkle with powdered sugar. Fine for using up yolks after making an angel food cake.

MRS. ADELE ORGILL

ONE EGG CAKE

2 c. sifted cake flour
2 t. baking powder
½ t. salt
⅓ c. butter

1 c. sugar
1 egg
¾ c. milk
1 t. vanilla

Sift flour once, then measure. Add baking powder and salt and sift three times. Cream butter, add sugar gradually and cream until light. Add egg and beat well. Add flour alternately with milk in small amounts beating after each addition. Add vanilla, and bake in greased 8-inch square pan in 350° oven 35 to 40 minutes. Good with Fudge Frosting (p. 186).

MRS. ARCHIBALD McCLURE

APPLESAUCE CAKE

½ c. shortening
1 c. sugar
1 c. unsweetened apple sauce
1 egg, well beaten
2 c. pastry flour
1 t. cinnamon
½ t. nutmeg

¼ t. ground cloves
Dash of salt
1 t. soda, dissolved in a
little hot water
1 c. raisins
1 c. nutmeats

Cream shortening, add sugar, applesauce, beaten egg. Sift a little flour over the raisins and nuts, then sift remaining flour with dry seasonings and fold into applesauce mixture. Blend in soda and water, then fold in raisins and nuts. Bake in greased 8-inch square pan at 350° for about 40 minutes. Cut in squares and serve sprinkled with powdered sugar.

MRS. STILES R. FIFIELD

BANANA CAKE

1 c. shortening
1½ c. sugar
2 eggs, beaten
1 c. mashed banana
1 c. pecans, broken
2 c. sifted flour

1 t. soda
1 t. baking powder
½ t. salt
¾ c. sour milk
1 t. vanilla

Cream sugar and shortening, add eggs and mix well. Add banana pulp and pecans. Sift dry ingredients and add to banana mixture alternately with sour milk. Add vanilla and bake in greased 8x12½-inch pan or in 2 layer cake pans. Bake 30 minutes in 350° oven. Ice with Caramel Icing (p. 187).

MRS. L. C. B. YOUNG, OSCEOLA, ARK.

COCONUT DELIGHT

1 large un-iced angel
food cake
1 qt. XX cream
1 whole fresh coconut, grated

2 t. sugar
2 t. vanilla
Small jar maraschino cherries

Preparation of this cake must be started the day or night before it is to be served. On the first day, roll off with a knife the brown part of un-iced cake. With two forks, gently tear the cake into pieces the size of walnuts. Whip a little more than half the XX cream until fluffy but not stiff (still runny). Add 1 teaspoon sugar and 1 teaspoon vanilla. Fold in the cake pieces with fork until all the cream is taken up. Place in a round bottom bowl, cover with a plate and let stand in the refrigerator overnight. Grate coconut and place on absorbent paper in cool place, so that it will be dry when ready for use. Next day, turn out soaked cake mixture onto the platter from which it can be served. Whip the balance of the cream until stiff, adding 1 teaspoon sugar and 1 teaspoon vanilla. Using a spatula, spread all the whipped cream over the mound of cake. Sprinkle the grated coconut over the entire rounded surface of the mound. Drain the juice from the cherries and pat them with a clean towel so there will be no moisture on them. Dot them over the coconut. Return to refrigerator until ready to serve. Serves 16.

MRS. JOSEPH L. TAGG

JAM CAKE

1 c. butter	3 c. flour, sifted
2 c. sugar	1 t. cinnamon
6 eggs, separated	1 t. allspice
1 c. buttermilk	1 t. cloves, ground
2 t. soda	1½ c. jam

Cream butter, add sugar, then add egg yolks and cream again. Dissolve soda in buttermilk. Sift flour with spices and add it to egg yolk mixture a cup at a time, beating well. Add buttermilk, jam, then fold in stiffly beaten egg whites. Bake in three 8-inch round pans in a preheated oven at 350° for 45 minutes to 1 hour. Spread with Marshmallow Icing (p. 185).

MISS SADIE EILBOTT

PINEAPPLE CAKE

6 eggs, separated	½ c. nuts
1 c. sugar	1 medium-sized can crushed
1 c. Zwieback crumbs	pineapple, drained
1 T. baking powder	1 c. XX cream, whipped

Beat egg yolks and sugar together. Add Zwieback, baking powder and nuts; then fold in stiffly beaten egg whites. Bake in greased 9-inch cake pan at 375° for 30 minutes or until done. When slightly cooled, remove from pan, pour the pineapple over it and serve warm or cold, topped with whipped cream. Serves 6 to 8.

MRS. HENRY LOEB, JR.

DEVIL'S FOOD CAKE

2 c. sifted cake flour	2 eggs, or 3 egg yolks,
1 t. soda	unbeaten
¼ t. salt	2 or 3 squares chocolate
½ c. butter	1 c. sour milk
1¼ c. sugar	1 t. vanilla

Sift flour once, measure, add soda and salt and sift together 3 times. Cream butter thoroughly, add sugar gradually and cream until light and fluffy. Add eggs one at a time, beating well after each addition. Melt chocolate and blend into egg mixture. Add flour alternately with milk, a small amount at a time, beating after each addition until smooth. Add vanilla. Bake 25 to 30 minutes in two 9-inch cake pans at 350-375°. Cool and frost with White Icing (p. 186).

MOIST COCONUT in cans is a valuable item to have on the shelf. Use it for topping cake icings; garnishing fruit salads or desserts; making homemade candies; in custard and cream pies; as a frosting for squares of bread dipped in sweetened condensed milk, then in coconut—and then toasted.

CHOCOLATE CAKE

½ c. cocoa
½ c. hot water
1 stick butter
2 c. sugar
2 eggs

1 c. buttermilk
1 t. baking soda
2 c. flour
½ t. salt
1 t. vanilla

Dissolve cocoa in hot water and let cool. Cream butter and sugar, add eggs. Dissolve soda in buttermilk. Add flour and milk alternately, beating well after each addition. Add chocolate, vanilla and salt. Pour into 2 greased 8 x 8-inch cake pans and bake in 350° oven about 30 minutes. Ice with Fudge Frosting (p. 186), or Fluffy White Icing (p. 185).

MRS. JAMES K. DOBBS, JR.

SIREN'S CHOCOLATE CAKE

2 eggs
2 c. buttermilk
2 t. vanilla
2½ c. flour
½ t. salt

2 c. sugar
2 t. soda
4 squares bitter chocolate
1 stick butter, or margarine

Beat eggs with buttermilk and add vanilla. Sift dry ingredients and add to egg mixture, then add butter and chocolate which have been melted together in double boiler. Beat thoroughly. Pour into 2 greased 9-inch cake pans and bake about 30 minutes at 350°. Frost with:

SIREN'S CHOCOLATE ICING:

1 lb. XXXX sugar
½ c. evaporated milk
2 t. vanilla

4 squares bitter chocolate
1 stick butter, or margarine

Add milk and vanilla to sifted sugar. Melt chocolate and butter together and add to first mixture. If icing is not thick enough to spread nicely, add more sifted powdered sugar.

Strong men melt, weak men feel like Atlas when confronted with this.

MRS. ARMOUR C. BOWEN, JR.

CHOCOLATE UPSIDE DOWN CAKE

1 c. flour
¾ c. sugar
1½ T. cocoa
2 t. baking powder
¾ t. salt
½ c. milk

2 T. melted butter
1 t. vanilla
½ c. brown sugar
½ c. white sugar
1 c. hot water
2 T. cocoa

Sift first 5 ingredients together, add milk, butter and vanilla. Pour into a greased 8-inch square pan. Make a thin syrup by boiling remaining ingredients for 5 minutes. Pour over batter and bake 40 minutes at 350°. While baking, syrup sinks to the bottom, thickening. Serve warm, upside down, with whipped cream. Serves 4 to 6.

MRS. CHARLES M. KORTRECHT, COLLIERVILLE, TENN.

CHOCOLATE CHIFFON CAKE

2½ c. sugar	4 T. cocoa
1 c. butter	1 c. buttermilk
3 c. sifted cake flour	5 t. strong coffee
1 t. soda	2 t. vanilla
Dash of salt	5 egg whites

Cream butter and sugar. Sift dry ingredients together and add alternately with milk to butter and sugar. Add coffee and vanilla. Last, fold in stiffly beaten egg whites. Bake in wax paper lined 8-inch round pans at 350° for about 35 minutes. Cool thoroughly before icing.

ICING:

½ c. butter (1 stick)	1 box powdered sugar, sifted
2 T. cocoa	2 t. vanilla
3 T. coffee	1 egg yolk, beaten well

Mix all ingredients well and beat until creamy. Spread on layers.

CHOCOLATE ANGEL FOOD CAKE

1¼ c. egg whites (about 1 doz.)	¼ c. cocoa
1 t. cream of tartar	1½ c. sugar
1 c. flour	1 pinch salt
	1 t. vanilla

Sift flour and cocoa together 3 times, and measure 1¼ cups. Beat whites until bowl may be inverted, adding cream of tartar when half beaten. Add sugar, salt and vanilla. Fold in flour. Place in cold oven, set temperature at 300° and bake for 20 minutes. Change temperature to 350° and cook 40 minutes. Turn pan upside down to cool. Remove cake when pan is cold. Ice with Fluffy White Icing (p. 185). White Angel Food Cake is made the same way, omitting cocoa.

Mrs. Adele Orgill

BITTERSWEET CAKE

1 Chocolate Angel Food Cake (recipe above)	½ t. cream of tartar
2 c. XX cream, whipped stiff	5 T. cold water
2 unbeaten egg whites	1 t. vanilla
1½ c. sugar	3 sq. unsweetened chocolate, melted

Split cooled cake in half and spread whipped cream between halves, also filling hole in center. Place in double boiler the egg whites, sugar, water and cream of tartar. Beat constantly over rapidly boiling water for 7 minutes. Remove from stove and add vanilla. Continue beating until of the proper consistency to spread. (For this cake this icing should be slightly softer than when used on other cakes.) Spread over cake and allow to set. Melt chocolate and spread over cake. Put in refrigerator until ready to serve. The cake may be made the day before using, but it is best to fill and ice it just previous to using. Serves 8 generously.

Mrs. George S. Miles

ORANGE CAKE

1 pkg. dates, chopped	4 eggs, separated
1 c. pecans, chopped	1⅓ c. buttermilk
4 c. sifted flour	1 t. soda
1 c. shortening	2 T. grated orange peel
2 c. sugar	

Dredge nuts and dates in small amount of flour. Cream shortening and gradually add sugar, then beaten egg yolks. Sift in ¼ of the flour while beating. Add remaining flour in thirds alternately with milk in which soda has been dissolved. Fold in dates, nuts and orange peel. Then fold in stiffly beaten egg whites. Bake in large greased angel food cake pan for 1½ hours. Start at 325°, then, when it has cooked about half the time, if it seems too fast, turn oven to 300°.

TOPPING:

2 c. sugar	2 T. grated orange peel
1 c. orange juice	

Mix before starting cake, stirring occasionally so the sugar will dissolve. Do not cook. After cake is removed from stove, while hot, puncture with old fashioned ice pick. Pour topping into puncture holes. Let cake stay in pan until topping soaks in. Serves 15 to 20.

MRS. CLARENCE HINANT, BROOKPORT, ILL.

WILLIE'S FRESH ORANGE CHIFFON CAKE

2¼ c. sifted cake flour	Juice of 2 oranges and enough
1½ c. sugar	water to make ¾ c.
¼ t. salt	2 T. grated orange peel
3 t. baking powder	1 c. egg whites (7-8 eggs)
½ c. salad oil	½ t. cream of tartar
5 unbeaten egg yolks	

Sift flour, measure lightly into cup, then sift again with sugar, salt and baking powder. Make well in center and slowly add oil, blending well. Add yolks, one at a time, stirring until well mixed. Add orange juice and peel and beat with spoon until mixture is smooth. Beat whites with cream of tartar until stiff. Pour yolk mixture into beaten whites and gently blend together. Bake in ungreased 9-inch tube pan in preheated 325° oven, for 50-60 minutes. Follow cooling directions of Sponge Cake (p. 175). Frost with Orange Cream Icing (see below).

ORANGE CREAM ICING:

½ c. butter	½ c. orange juice
4 t. flour	3½ c. powdered sugar, sifted
Pinch of salt	4 T. grated orange peel

Soften butter and blend with flour and salt. Add orange juice and peel. Stir in sugar gradually, beating until smooth.

MRS. ROBERT SMITHWICK

LUSCIOUS MOCHA CAKE

5 egg yolks	Pinch of salt
7 egg whites	1 c. granulated sugar, sifted
¼ t. cream tartar	1 t. orange flavoring
1 c. flour, sifted	½ pt. XX cream, whipped

Separate eggs. Set oven at 300°. Place wax paper in bottom of a stem cake pan. Sift flour 5 times. Beat egg whites until moderately stiff, sift cream of tartar into whites and continue beating until very stiff. Beat in sugar, sifting it in gently. Beat yolks until lemon colored, add salt, fold in whites, add flavoring. Gently fold flour in, sifting a little at a time, never beating. Bake 60 to 70 minutes at 300°. Leave in inverted pan to cool. Split in 2 layers and fill with whipped cream. Spread with mocha icing.

MOCHA ICING:

½ stick butter
½ lb. powdered sugar, sifted
1 T. dry cocoa
2 T. very strong coffee
⅔ c. chopped toasted nuts

Cream butter thoroughly. Add cocoa, then add alternately sifted sugar and the coffee until mixture is proper consistency to spread. Ice top and sides of cake. Cover top and sides with nuts. Chill until serving time.

MRS. WILLIAM D. GALBREATH

SUNSHINE CAKE

4 egg yolks	1 c. flour, sifted
Pinch of salt	1¼ c. sugar
8 egg whites	1 t. vanilla
½ t. cream of tartar	

Beat yolks and salt until light and lemon colored. Add sugar. Beat whites until foamy and add cream of tartar. Finish beating until stiff, but not dry. Sift flour once, fold yolks into whites, then fold in flour and add flavoring. Bake in 9-inch tube pan at 325° for 35 minutes. This may be iced with Chocolate Icing (p. 186) or with Fluffy White Icing (p. 185) or sprinkled with powdered sugar.

MRS. TANNEN HOLLENBERG

WHIPPED CREAM CAKE

½ pt. XX cream, whipped	¼ t. salt
1 c. sugar	2 t. baking powder
2 eggs, separated	1 t. vanilla
1½ c. cake flour	

Whip cream until thickened but not stiff enough to hold peak. Beat egg yolks, add sugar and vanilla and fold in cream. Add flour, salt and baking powder, sifted together. Mix only until smooth, then fold in stiffly beaten egg whites. Bake in a greased tube pan for 30 minutes at 350°. Cool and ice with Chocolate Icing (p. 186), or Never-Fail Creamy Caramel Icing (p. 187), or Fudge Frosting (p. 186).

CHEESE CAKE

CRUST:

1 9-oz. bag vanilla wafers	1 stick butter, melted
1 t. cinnamon	¼ c. sugar

Roll vanilla wafers, combine all but ½ cup of the crumbs with cinnamon, sugar and melted butter. Press into spring form cake pan.

FILLING:

4 eggs	1 t. lemon juice
1 c. sugar	2 lbs. cream cheese
⅛ t. salt	

Beat eggs, then add sugar slowly and beat until thick and lemon colored. Add salt and lemon juice and combine with cream cheese, continuing to beat well. Pour over crust and bake 25 minutes at 375°. Spread with topping (see below), and sprinkle with the remaining ½ cup vanilla wafer crumbs. Return to oven and bake 10 to 15 minutes at 475°

TOPPING:

1 pt. sour cream	4 T. sugar
1 t. vanilla	

Mix well and spread over cream cheese filling. Serves 12.

Mrs. William Leigh Smith

FROZEN CHEESE CAKE

½ box Zweiback	Juice of 1 lemon
3 T. butter	Rind of 1 lemon, grated
2 T. sugar	2 t. vanilla
3 egg yolks	1 lb. cream cheese
1 c. sugar	3 egg whites, stiffly beaten
½ pt. XX cream, whipped	

Roll Zweiback into crumbs and mix with butter and 2 tablespoons sugar. Line a 9-inch pyrex baking dish with this, reserving a little of the mixture to sprinkle over the top of the cake. Beat the egg yolks with 1 cup of sugar until light and fluffy. Add whipped cream, lemon juice, lemon rind, vanilla and softened cream cheese. Mix well, then fold in egg whites and pour mixture into baking dish. Sprinkle edge of cake with reserved crumb mixture and garnish top with maraschino cherries. Place in freezing compartment of refrigerator. (If freezing compartment will not accommodate pyrex dish, follow crumb crust procedure using refrigerator tray instead.) This cake may be tinted any color. For Christmas, use green coloring and red cherries. It may be made the day before using. Serves 6 to 8.

Mrs. Henry Loeb, Jr.

FRESH PINEAPPLE is the only fruit that cannot be used in gelatin preparations. There is a substance in the fresh pineapple that dissolves gelatin; cooking the pineapple destroys this substance and cooked or canned pineapple may be used with good results.

SPICE CAKE

2 c. light brown sugar
½ c. butter
2 eggs, beaten
2 c. sifted flour
¼ t. salt
1 t. baking powder

1 t. cinnamon
½ t. cloves, ground
½ t. nutmeg
1 t. cocoa
1 c. sour cream
1 t. vanilla

Cream butter and sugar, add beaten eggs. Sift all dry ingredients together, and add alternately with the sour cream, beating well after each addition. Add vanilla. Pour batter into 2 greased 9-inch cake pans. Bake in 375° oven about 25 minutes.

Mrs. James K. Dobbs, Jr.

MOTHER'S GINGERBREAD

½ c. shortening
½ c. butter
1 c. sugar
2 c. sifted flour
1 t. soda
1 t. powdered ginger

1 t. baking powder
1 t. cinnamon
2 eggs, beaten
1 c. molasses
1 c. boiling water

Cream shortening and butter, add sugar gradually while creaming. Sift dry ingredients. Add eggs, then sifted dry ingredients, then molasses and water to butter and sugar mixture. Beat with rotary beater to mix thoroughly and pour into well-greased oblong cake pans and bake at 350° for 30-40 minutes. Serve with Vanilla Sauce (p. 137). Serves 16 to 18.

Mrs. Edward H. Crump

CHRISTMAS FRUIT CAKE

1 c. currants
3 c. seedless raisins
½ c. candied orange peel, cut fine
½ c. candied lemon peel, cut fine
1½ c. citron, cut fine
1 c. candied cherry halves
1 c. candied pineapple, diced
1 c. shelled pecan halves
1 c. blanched almonds, cut lengthwise

2 c. sifted, enriched all-purpose flour
1 c. butter
1 c. brown sugar, packed
6 eggs, separated
1 t. nutmeg
1½ t. cinnamon
1¼ t. ground cloves
½ t. baking soda
¼ c. orange juice
¼ c. lemon juice
¼ c. bourbon whiskey

Thoroughly grease 9 or 10-inch tube pan or 2 loaf pans. Cut heavy waxed paper to fit bottom and sides of pan. Lightly grease paper. Aluminum foil may be used without greasing. Thoroughly mix first 9 ingredients with 1 cup of the flour until all particles are flour-coated. Heat oven to 300°. Cream butter with sugar until light and fluffy. Add egg yolks, one at a time, beating well after each addition. Sift remaining flour (1 cup) with spices and soda. Add alternately with juices and bourbon to egg mixture. When thoroughly mixed, stir into fruit mixture. Beat egg whites until stiff and fold into cake mixture. Turn into a pan and bake at 300° for 2 hours and 20 minutes. Put a whiskey-soaked cheese cloth around cake when cooled, then wrap it in aluminum foil to keep it moist. Keep in covered crock or tin box.

Mrs. George S. Miles

FRUIT CAKE

1 lb. butter
1 lb. sugar (2 c.)
10 eggs
2 wine glasses whiskey
1 t. ground cloves
1 t. cinnamon
1 t. allspice
1 t. nutmeg
1 lb. flour (4 c.)

1 lb. crystallized pineapple
1 lb. crystallized cherries
¼ lb. crystallized orange peel
¼ lb. crystallized lemon peel
½ lb. citron
1 lb. raisins
1 lb. currants
1 lb. pecans
1 lb. almonds

Cream butter and sugar together. Add the beaten egg yolks, then the whiskey. Sift the dry ingredients together and add to the fruit and nuts which have been cut in pieces. Add this to the butter mixture. Mix thoroughly, then add stiffly beaten egg whites. Pour into pans lined with 3 layers of greased brown paper (bottom and sides). Bake in 275° oven about 3 hours. This makes 3 large cakes.

Mrs. James K. Dobbs, Jr.

EASY FRUIT CAKE

1 lb. dates
1 lb. pecans
1 c. flour
½ t. salt
1 c. sugar

4 eggs, beaten
½ lb. candied cherries
½ lb. candied pineapple
2 t. vanilla

Cut dates in half, leave nutmeats whole. Sift flour and salt together and add to dates and nuts. Sift sugar into beaten eggs, then add dates and nuts. Add cherries, pineapple and vanilla last. Pour into 3 small loaf pans which have been lined with wax paper or well-greased brown paper. Bake in 325° oven for 1½ hours, having a flat pan of water in bottom of the oven. Yield: 3 small loaves.

Mrs. Frank M. Norfleet

NUT CAKE

½ lb. butter (2 sticks)
1 lb. sugar (2 c.)
1 lb. flour (4 c.)
2 t. cinnamon
2 t. nutmeg
6 eggs, separated

1 qt. pecans (4 c.) chopped
2 lbs. seedless raisins
2 t. soda (dissolved in
a little water)
1 wine glass bourbon whiskey

Cream butter and sugar. Sift flour and spices together. Beat egg yolks and whites separately and mix yolks with butter and sugar. Add flour and spices to raisins and nuts, then to yolk mixture, alternating with whiskey and soda. Then fold in stiffly beaten egg whites. Pour into greased loaf pans and bake 3½ to 4 hours in 250° oven. Yield: approximately 4 loaves.

Mrs. Dudley S. Weaver

CAKE ICINGS

FLUFFY WHITE ICING

2 egg whites
$\frac{3}{4}$ c. sugar
$\frac{1}{3}$ c. light corn syrup
2 T. water

$\frac{1}{4}$ t. cream of tartar
$\frac{1}{4}$ t. salt
1 t. vanilla

Combine first 6 ingredients in top of double boiler. Place over rapidly boiling water, beating with electric or rotary beater until mixture stands in peaks. Remove from heat and add vanilla. Continue beating until thick enough to spread. Bakers chocolate, grated over the top is attractive, or tinted or toasted coconut.

Variations:

HARVEST MOON: Substitute 1$\frac{1}{2}$ cups brown sugar, packed, for granulated sugar.

MARSHMALLOW: Add 1 cup of cut up marshmallows to frosting after removing from boiling water.

LADY BALTIMORE: To $\frac{2}{3}$ of completed frosting, add $\frac{1}{3}$ cup chopped raisins, $\frac{1}{3}$ cup chopped dried figs, 6 tablespoons chopped walnuts. This will fill 2 8-inch layers. Spread top and sides of cake with remaining frosting. If desired, sprinkle with chopped candied cherries.

TWO FRUIT: Substitute 6 tablespoons orange juice and 1$\frac{1}{2}$ teaspoons lemon juice for water. When frosting is completed, fold in $\frac{1}{2}$ teaspoon grated orange rind.

FOUR MINUTE: Halve each ingredient in Fluffy White Icing, using 1$\frac{1}{2}$ teaspoons light corn syrup. Make as directed, cooking about 4 minutes or until mixture holds a peak. Fills and frosts tops and sides of 2 8-inch layers.

WHITE ICING (UNCOOKED)

6 T. butter
2 T. cream

3 c. sifted powdered sugar
1 t. vanilla

Melt butter in saucepan, add cream, sugar and vanilla. Beat well. Place over hot water 5 minutes (this overcomes raw sugar taste). Cool and beat until it will spread. Thin with cream or thicken with more powdered sugar.

MARSHMALLOW ICING

2$\frac{1}{3}$ c. sugar
7 T. water
9 marshmallows

1$\frac{1}{2}$ t. vanilla
3 egg whites, beaten stiff

Put sugar and water in pan, stir until sugar is dissolved, then bring to boiling point. Cook until syrup spins a long thread. Remove from stove, add marshmallows and vanilla and beat until smooth. Pour mixture gradually over stiffly beaten egg whites, beating constantly until stiff enough to stand in peaks.

WHITE ICING

4 egg whites	1 c. cold water
3 c. sugar	1 t. vanilla

Combine sugar and water, and cook until it forms a soft ball in cold water when dropped from a spoon. Don't cook too long. Then pour this over the stiffly beaten egg whites. Add vanilla. Beat until it is the right consistency for spreading.

MRS. ROBERTSON G. MORROW

CHOCOLATE ICING

3 c. powdered sugar, sifted	Pinch of salt
2 T. butter	2 sq. bitter chocolate
1 egg	1 t. vanilla
3 T. cream	

Melt chocolate and butter over very low flame. Remove from fire, add salt, egg and cream and beat thoroughly. Add sugar and vanilla. Beat again. Place over hot water 5 minutes. Cool, then beat until right consistency to spread. If too thin, add powdered sugar. If too thick, add cream.

EASY CHOCOLATE ICING

1 pkg. semi-sweet chocolate bits	$2\frac{1}{4}$ c. sifted powdered sugar
3 T. butter	$\frac{1}{4}$ t. salt
$\frac{1}{3}$ c. hot milk	$\frac{1}{2}$ t. vanilla

Melt chocolate and butter over hot water. Stir hot milk into salt and sugar. Add vanilla, then chocolate mixture, and beat until smooth. This will frost two layers.

MRS. JAMES K. DOBBS, JR.

FUDGE FROSTING

3 c. sugar	$\frac{1}{4}$ t. salt
1 c. milk	4 T. butter
2 sq. bitter chocolate	1 t. vanilla
1 T. white corn syrup	

Cook gently sugar, salt, milk, grated chocolate and corn syrup, stirring constantly until mixture begins to boil. Boil gently, without stirring, until mixture forms soft ball in cold water. Remove from fire, add butter and vanilla, but don't stir. When lukewarm, beat until right consistency to spread on cake. This will frost three layers.

MRS. JAMES K. DOBBS, JR.

LIGHT CHOCOLATE ICING

2 c. sugar
½ c. milk
1 t. vanilla

3 sq. bitter chocolate
(4 sq. for darker icing)
2 well beaten eggs

Combine sugar, chocolate, milk, and eggs in double boiler. Stir constantly until sugar melts, then cook over blaze, still stirring, until it boils up. Take from fire, beat until thick, add vanilla and ice cake.

MRS. WILLIAM D. GALBREATH

THICK CHOCOLATE ICING

2 t. gelatin
3 T. cold water
¼ c. boiling water

¾ c. sugar
6 sq. bitter chocolate

Grate chocolate and set aside. Soften gelatin in cold water, add to boiling water and continue cooking 1 minute, stirring constantly. Remove from heat. Combine sugar and chocolate and add hot gelatin. Beat until cool and thick.

MRS. CHARLES M. KORTRECHT, COLLIERVILLE, TENN.

FILLING FOR ANGEL FOOD CAKE

1 T. gelatin
¼ c. cold water
¼ c. pineapple and cherry
juice
1 c. sugar
1 pt. whipped cream

½ lb. blanched, chopped
almonds
¼ c. crushed pineapple
¼ c. chopped maraschino
cherries

Soften gelatin in water. Combine juices and sugar and boil until sugar dissolves. Pour this into gelatin and beat until cold. Add the whipped cream, almonds, pineapple and cherries. Spread this over an Angel Food Cake and let set in the refrigerator.

MRS. D. HARBERT ANTHONY

NEVER-FAIL CREAMY CARAMEL ICING

2½ c. sugar
1 slightly beaten egg
1 stick of butter

¾ c. milk
1 t. vanilla

Melt ½ cup of sugar in iron skillet slowly, until brown and runny. Mix egg, butter, remaining sugar, and milk in a saucepan and cook over a low flame until butter melts. Turn the heat up to medium and add the browned sugar. Cook until it reaches the soft ball stage or until mixture leaves sides of pan. This takes about 10 minutes. Remove from fire, let cool slightly, and add vanilla. Beat until right consistency to spread. If it gets too thick add a little cream. This will ice a 2 layer cake.

MRS. PHIL THORNTON, JR., TUTWILER, MISS.

PIES

PIE CRUST

2 c. sifted flour   1 t. salt
⅔ c. shortening   4 to 6 T. ice water

Add ½ of shortening to flour and salt and cut it in with pastry blender until fine and looks like meal. Add remaining shortening and cut into flour coarsely to look like giant peas. Sprinkle minimum amount of water over it and blend in lightly with a fork. Use more water if necessary—but only enough to gather dough together. Let stand covered a few minutes to make it easy to roll out. Roll on lightly floured cloth-covered board with lightly floured cloth-covered rolling pin. Keep dough circular, don't bear down heavily. Work swiftly and lightly or it will be tough. If dough breaks at outer edges, pinch it together. Avoid stretching pastry in pan. Trim with knife or scissors. Brush pastry with 1 tablespoon melted butter. Set in refrigerator and chill thoroughly for flakiness. For shiny top crust, brush with milk. Makes sufficient amount for 1 9-inch pie or 6 3¾-inch tart shells. Bake in a very hot oven (425°) until brown.

MRS. FERD HECKLE, JR.

CORN FLAKE PIE CRUST

¼ c. sugar   ⅓ c. melted butter
1 c. fine corn flake crumbs   9-in. pie pan

Mix sugar and crumbs, blend in butter, press into pan and chill.

MERINGUE

3 egg whites   6 T. sugar
¼ t. cream of tartar

Beat egg whites until frothy, add cream of tartar and continue beating until stiff enough to hold a point. Gradually beat in sugar and continue beating until mixture is stiff and glossy.

CHERRY PIE

1 No. 2 can red pitted   ½ c. sugar
    cherries   2½ T. flour
1 9-in. unbaked pie shell
    (see above)

Drain cherries, mix with sugar and flour. Put into 9-inch unbaked pie shell. Bake 10 minutes at 450°. Reduce heat to 350° and bake 25 minutes longer, or until brown. Top with sweetened whipped cream.

SHARKIE PIE

1 c. blackberry jam   2 oz. bourbon whiskey
½ c. sugar   1 unbaked 9-in. pie shell
3 eggs beaten together   (see above)
⅓ stick butter   ½ pt. XX cream, whipped
1 t. vanilla

Mix first 6 ingredients thoroughly and pour into shell. Bake in 375° oven for 25 minutes and serve cool with whipped cream.

MRS. J. SPENCER SPEED

SCOTCH APPLE PIE

3 large tart apples
½ c. white sugar
Juice of 1 lemon

1 stick butter
1 c. brown sugar
1 c. flour

Peel and slice apples into pie pan. Cover with white sugar and lemon juice. Cream butter with brown sugar and work in flour. Crumble this over the apples and bake 25 minutes in a 300° oven.

MRS. EDWIN B. PHILLIPS

GARDEN OF EDEN APPLE PIE

PASTRY:

½ c. shortening
2 c. flour
¾ t. salt
6 to 8 T. cold water

1 c. grated New York cheese
or ½ c. American and
½ c. Cheddar cheese

Cut shortening into sifted flour and salt until mixture resembles peas in size. Mix cheese in lightly with fork. Add enough water to hold together. Roll lightly, brush bottom crust with melted fat to prevent soaking. Fill and cover top with pastry. Slash top to allow steam to escape.

FILLING:

5 or 6 large tart apples
¾ c. sugar
2 T. flour
⅛ t. salt

1 t. cinnamon
1 t. nutmeg (optional)
2 T. butter (or more)

Pare, core and slice apples. Lay slices in pie plate lined with cheese pastry. Mix sugar, flour, salt, cinnamon and nutmeg. Sprinkle over each layer, dot with butter and cover with crust. Press edges together and slash top. Bake in 9-inch pie pan in 450° oven for 10 minutes or until edges are brown. Reduce oven to 350° and bake about 30 minutes longer.

LEMON MERINGUE PIE

5 eggs (save 3 whites for
  meringue)
¾ c. sugar
5 T. water
Juice of 1½ lemons

Grated rind of 1 lemon
½ stick butter
1 9-inch baked pie shell
  (p. 188)

Beat eggs until light and add sugar gradually, beating constantly. Add water, lemon juice and rind. Put in double boiler over hot water. Add butter and cook until thick. Put mixture in shell, cover with meringue (p. 188) and bake in 300° oven, 15 to 20 minutes.

MISSES STELLA AND IRENE JOHNSON

FROZEN LEMON PIE

3 egg yolks
1 c. sugar
4 T. lemon juice

3 egg whites
½ pt. XX cream
Vanilla wafers, crumbled

Beat egg yolks well. Gradually add sugar beating constantly. Add lemon juice and cook in double boiler about 7 minutes, stirring constantly. Cool thoroughly, then fold in stiffly beaten egg whites and whipped cream. Butter refrigerator tray or mold and cover bottom and sides with vanilla wafer crumbs. Fill with lemon mixture and sprinkle more wafer crumbs on top. Freeze without stirring. It should be in refrigerator about 24 hours, as it freezes slowly. Serves 8.

MRS. WALTER LANE SMITH

HIGH LEMON PIE

4 beaten egg yolks
½ c. sugar
⅓ c. lemon juice
3 T. orange juice
½ t. salt
1 T. (1 envelope) plain
   gelatin

¼ c. cold water
½ t. grated lemon rind
½ t. grated orange rind
¼ c. sugar
4 stiffly beaten egg whites
1 9-in. baked pie shell
   (p. 188)

Combine egg yolks, ½ c. sugar, fruit juices, and salt. Cook in double boiler until thick, stirring constantly. Add gelatin which has been softened in cold water. Stir until gelatin dissolves. Add fruit rinds and cool until partially set. Gradually add ¼ c. sugar to egg whites while beating them until glossy and sugar is dissovled. Fold into cooked mixture, pour into shell and chill until firm. Top with whipped cream. Serves 6 to 8.

MRS. JOHN MCDONOUGH

ANGEL PIE

MERINGUE SHELL:

3 egg whites
⅛ t. cream of tartar
Pinch of salt

¾ c. sifted sugar
¾ c. finely chopped pecans
1 t. vanilla

Beat egg whites until foamy. Add cream of tartar and salt. Beat until whites will stand in peaks. Add sugar gradually and beat very stiff. Fold in pecans and vanilla. Turn into buttered 9-inch pyrex plate, building up the sides above the edge of the plate. Bake at 225° for 50 minutes. Cool.

FILLING:

4 oz. sweet chocolate
3 T. strong coffee

1 t. vanilla
1 c. XX cream

Melt chocolate with coffee in saucepan over low flame. Cool and stir in vanilla. Whip cream, fold into chocolate, pour into meringue. Chill. Put heaping tablespoon vanilla ice cream on top of each serving. Serves 6.

MRS. H. DUNCAN TAYLOR

MACAROON PIE

14 saltine crackers, rolled
  fine (count each square
  as one)
12 dates, cut fine
½ c. pecans, cut fine

1 c. sugar
3 egg whites
¼ t. salt
1 generous t. almond extract

Mix all ingredients but egg whites. Fold in beaten whites. Bake in buttered 9-inch pie pan for 45 minutes in 300° oven. Serve with whipped cream, flavored with sherry and powdered sugar to taste.

MRS. HERBERT HOOD, JR.

FRESH STRAWBERRY PIE

¾ c. sugar
1 T. cornstarch
1 c. water

¼ t. salt
1 qt. strawberries
1 9-in. baked pie shell

Wash, drain and stem the strawberries. Place the berries in the bottom of the baked pie shell. Slowly cook the sugar, cornstarch, water and salt until glossy. Pour this hot mixture over the strawberries and place in the refrigerator until cold. Just before serving, cover with whipped cream.

MRS. JOHN MAURY, JR.

CHOCOLATE CHIFFON PIE

4 squares bitter chocolate
½ c. water
1 T. (1 envelope) plain
  gelatin
¼ c. cold water

1 c. sugar
4 eggs, separated
1 t. vanilla
1 9-in. baked pie shell
  (p. 188)

Melt chocolate in ½ cup water. Soften gelatin in ¼ cup cold water then add it to the chocolate and stir until gelatin is dissolved. Mix ½ cup sugar with egg yolks, add to chocolate mixture, then add vanilla. Beat egg whites stiff with ½ c. sugar, fold into chocolate (cooled thoroughly). Pour into shell and chill at least two hours. Cover with whipped cream and grate bitter chocolate over cream.

MRS. H. DUNCAN TAYLOR

EGG CUSTARD PIE

2 eggs
1½ c. sugar
½ c. butter

1¼ T. flour
½ c. cream
½ t. vanilla

Beat yolks—add sugar and beat until very light—add softened butter, flour and cream. Beat well—fold in stiffly beaten egg whites—pour into unbaked pastry—9 inch—Bake in 450° oven for 15 minutes, then turn down to 325° for additional 30 minutes.

MRS. JAMES E. SHANNON

CHOCOLATE CREAM PIE

2½ c. milk
2½ squares unsweetened
   chocolate
1 c. sugar
4 T. flour
1 t. salt

4 egg yolks
2 T. butter
1 t. vanilla
½ pt. XX cream
9-in. baked pie shell (p. 188)

Scald milk with chocolate in top of double boiler. Mix sugar, flour and salt and add gradually to egg yolks which have been beaten until they are fluffy and light. Mix well. Pour small amount of scalded milk mixture over egg-sugar mixture and beat well. Gradually add rest of milk mixture. Return to double boiler and cook over medium flame until custard is quite thick. Remove from stove and add butter and vanilla. Cool and chill in refrigerator for several hours. When ready to serve, put filling in baked pie shell and cover with whipped cream.

MRS. GEORGE S. MILES

COCONUT CREAM PIE

3 egg yolks
⅓ c. sugar
¼ t. salt
2½ T. cornstarch
1 T. melted butter

2 c. scalded milk
1 c. grated coconut
1 t. vanilla or rum
¼ t. nutmeg
9-in baked pie shell (p. 188)

Beat egg yolks. Beat in sugar, salt, cornstarch and butter gradually. Pour in milk and blend. Cook over boiling water, stirring constantly until thick. Add coconut and cool. Add flavoring and nutmeg and pour into shell. Cover with meringue (p. 188) and bake 15 to 20 minutes in 300° oven. VARIATION: 2 or 3 sliced bananas may be substituted for coconut.

CINNAMON RUSK PIE

CRUST:

½ c. butter
½ c. sugar

1⅔ c. Holland Rusk crumbs
   (rolled fine)

Cream butter and sugar, blend in crumbs and line 9-inch pie pan with the mixture. Chill.

FILLING:

4 egg yolks
½ c. sugar
Pinch salt
1 T. flour

2 c. scalded milk
1 t. vanilla
1 t. cinnamon

Beat yolks slightly, add sugar, salt and flour and blend well. Add this gradually to scalded milk while stirring. Cook over hot water until it is like soft custard (about 8 to 12 minutes) stirring constantly. Cool slightly, then add vanilla. Pour into Rusk shell, top with meringue (p. 188). Sprinkle with additional Rusk crumbs mixed with cinnamon. Bake 20 minutes at 350°. Chill at least 5 hours.

MRS. CAREY G. BRINGLE

LEMON CHESS PIE

4 egg yolks
1 whole egg
1 cup sugar
1 tablespoon corn meal

1 tablespoon cream
Grating from peel of
    one lemon
1 heaping T. butter

Beat egg yolks and whole egg until light—add sugar gradually and continue beating. Add corn meal and blend thoroughly. Add cream and butter, mixing well and finally the grated lemon peel. Bake in 350° oven for about 45 minutes. This recipe makes 8 tarts or a 9 inch pie.

CHEWY CHESS PIE

1 c. brown sugar
½ c. white sugar
1 t. flour
1 t. vanilla

½ c. melted butter
2 T. milk
2 eggs, unbeaten

Mix white and brown sugar and flour. Break eggs into mixture, add milk and vanilla. Add melted butter. Bake in unbaked pie shell in 350 degree oven for about 40 minutes. When it cools, the pie falls and is rich and chewy. The recipe may be used for tarts, one T. in each uncooked tart shell. This is simple, delicious and rich.

Mrs. Vaughan Dow

MAPLE PECAN CHESS PIE

1 c. maple or brown sugar
2 T. butter
2 eggs, beaten
2 T. flour
Pinch salt

1 c. maple syrup
1½ c. pecans, chopped coarse
9-in. unbaked pie shell or 8
    small unbaked tart shells
    (p. 188)

Cream butter and sugar. Add eggs, flour, salt and syrup. Add pecans and mix well. Pour into unbaked pie shell. Bake 5 minutes at 400°. Reduce heat to 375° and bake until mixture sets (should be firm to touch in center), 30 to 40 minutes. Serve plain or topped with whipped cream flavored with vanilla.

Mrs. J. E. Williams, Jr.

SOUTHERN PECAN PIE

1½ c. dark molasses or
    sorghum
1 c. sugar
4 eggs
4 T. butter

1 t. vanilla
1½ c. pecans, chopped
1 9-in. pie shell baked just
    5 minutes (p. 188)

Cook sugar and syrup 5 minutes. Beat eggs and slowly add syrup. Add butter, vanilla and nuts. Pour into partially baked shell. Cook 45 minutes at 350°. As pie cools it will become firm.

Mrs. William A. Leatherman, Robinsonville, Miss.

RUM PIE

CRUST:

1½ c. fine gingersnap crumbs   8 T. soft butter

Mix crumbs and butter and line 9-inch pie pan with the mixture. Chill.

FILLING:

1 T. (1 envelope) plain   1 scant c. sugar
  gelatin   1 pt. XX cream
½ c. cold water   ¼ to ½ c. dark rum (to taste)
6 egg yolks

Soften gelatin in cold water and dissolve over hot water. Beat egg yolks until light, add sugar gradually, beating continually. Add gelatin, stirring briskly. Fold in stiffly whipped cream and add rum while gradually stirring. Cool until it begins to set and pour into crust. Chill 6-8 hours. Sprinkle top generously with shaved bittersweet chocolate curls or fine chopped pistachio nuts, garnish with whipped cream and serve cold.

A rich dessert, and delicious, for those who like a very sweet filling. Keeps well in deep freeze.

MRS. C. D. SMITH, II

BLACK BOTTOM PIE

CRUST:

20 ginger snaps, crumbed   5 T. melted butter

Roll gingersnaps, add butter, mix well. Pat evenly in deep pie pan. Bake 10 minutes at 250°.

FILLING:

1 T. gelatin   4 T. bourbon or rum
4 T. cold water   4 egg whites
2 c. milk   ¼ t. cream of tartar
½ c. sugar   3 T. confectioners sugar
1 T. corn starch   1 c. XX cream
4 egg yolks   Dash vanilla
1½ sq. bitter chocolate   ½ sq. grated bittersweet
1 t. vanilla   chocolate

Soak gelatin in cold water. Scald milk. Combine ½ cup sugar and corn starch. Make custard with milk, sugar, egg yolks and corn starch. Cook over hot water until custard coats spoon—about 20 minutes. Remove from heat, take out 1 cup of custard. Add melted chocolate. Beat well with egg beater; when cool add teaspoon of vanilla. Pour into crust. While remaining custard is still hot, blend in gelatin and cool, but do not allow to stiffen. Add whiskey. Make stiff meringue by beating egg whites until frothy; add cream of tartar, beat until stiff. Fold in meringue and dash of vanilla while custard is still soft. As soon as chocolate custard has begun to set, cover with fluffy custard and chill until firm. When ready to serve, spread with whipped cream sweetened with confectioners sugar. Sprinkle with grated bitter chocolate.

MRS. W. JETER EASON

CORONATION BUTTERSCOTCH PIE

1¼ c. brown sugar
⅓ c. flour
½ t. salt

2 c. hot milk
3 egg yolks
2 t. butter

Mix sugar, flour, salt and milk together in double boiler and cook until thickened. Just before removing from fire add egg yolks and butter. Let stand while making pastry (p. 188). Divide pastry and place on 3 round sheets the same size. Bake in 350° oven until brown. Place one pastry on platter, cover with ⅓ of filling. Repeat twice. Cover with meringue (p. 188) and brown in 300° oven for 15 to 30 minutes. Or ice with whipped cream and set in refrigerator.

MRS. PHIL THORNTON, JR., TUTWILER, MISS.

CHEESE PIE

Have all ingredients at room temperature.

CRUST:

14 graham crackers, crumbed
¼ lb. melted butter (1 stick)

Salt and sugar to taste

Crush graham crackers and mix well with butter. Add salt and sugar and line 9-inch pie plate.

FILLING:

4 3-oz. pkgs. cream cheese
½ c. sugar

2 eggs

Mash cream cheese with sugar. Add eggs and beat only until well mixed. Pour into crust and bake 15 minutes in 350° oven.

TOPPING:

½ pt. sour cream

2 T. sugar

Mix sour cream with sugar. Spread carefully over the pie and cook 5 more minutes. Chill and serve.

MR. A. ARTHUR HALLE, CORDOVA, TENN.

WILLIE'S SWEET POTATO PIE

1½ c. cooked sweet potatoes
(about 3 medium-sized)
½ c. sweet milk
2 eggs, separated
1 c. sugar

Nutmeg and cinnamon to
taste
Grape jelly
9-in. unbaked pie shell
(p. 188)

Cream potatoes with milk, beat in egg yolks and sugar. Add nutmeg and cinnamon and pour into shell. Cook until set in 375° oven. Then cover top with thin layer of grape jelly. Cover with meringue (p. 188) made with egg whites and bake in 300° oven, 15 or 20 minutes.

MRS. ROBERT SMITHWICK

PUMPKIN PIE

1 c. sugar	3 egg yolks
1¼ t. cinnamon	1½ c. pumpkin (canned)
⅛ t. ground cloves	¾ c. milk
¼ t. ground ginger	3 egg whites
¼ t. nutmeg	9-in. unbaked pie shell
1 t. salt	(p. 188)

Mix sugar, spices, salt together. Add beaten egg yolks to pumpkin. Mix with spices and milk. Fold in stiffly beaten egg whites and pour into pie shell. Bake for 10 minutes at 450°. Reduce heat to 375° and bake until filling is firm. Test with silver knife. If knife comes out clean, pie is done.

Mrs. Jesse E. Cook

CHERRY JUBILEE PIE

PIE SHELL:

2 egg whites	½ c. sugar
⅛ t. cream of tartar	½ t. vanilla
Dash of salt	1 c. shredded cocoanut

Add salt and cream of tartar to unbeaten whites. Beat until they form soft peaks. Add sugar, 2 T. at a time, beating well after each addition until well blended. Continue beating until very stiff peaks form. Fold in vanilla and cocoanut. Spread mixture on bottom and sides of greased and floured 9" pie pan. (Very important to grease and flour well.) Bake at 325 degrees about 30 minutes or until shell feels firm and dry. Cool.

SAUCE:

1 1 lb. 14 oz. can pitted black sweet cherries	¼ c. sugar
1 T. cornstarch	1 T. butter or oleo
Dash of salt	2 t. lemon juice

Drain cherries and save juice. Mix together in saucepan the cornstarch, salt, and sugar. Add 1 c. cherry juice and mix well. Cook and stir over medium heat until mixture comes to a boil, then simmer 3 minutes. Remove from heat and add 1 T. butter or oleo and lemon juice. Cool. Add cherries.

For serving, fill shell with strawberry ice cream, cut into pie shaped pieces and serve with sauce. May also be made in individual tarts with sauce already on tart. Saves cutting and extra serving.

Mrs. F. Pearson Allen, Jr.

MARMALADE TARTS

½ lb. cream cheese	1 T. orange juice
½ c. sugar	1 T. grated orange rind
¼ c. butter	Unbaked pie crust (p. 188)
2 egg yolks	Orange marmalade
¼ t. nutmeg	

Line 8 tart shells with pastry. Combine cheese, sugar, butter, egg yolks, nutmeg, juice and rind, and put into shells. Bake at 450° for 10 minutes. Reduce heat to 350° until pastry is golden and filling is firm. Invert tarts to cool. Serve them inverted, the shells iced with a thin coat of marmalade.

Mrs. H. Duncan Taylor

Cookies and Candy

Nostalgia —

> The aroma of hot ginger oozing out of grandma's oven —
>
> The great adventure of the first bite into a candied apple —
>
> The powdered sugar mustache that lingers after the cookie is gone — um-m-m-m — with just a tinge of saltiness to make it exciting —
>
> The smooth, round, caramel-covered marshmallows in the pink box that were your first grown-up Valentine —
>
> Simple little teacakes that spell magic by their special shapes and colors —
>
> The sense of contentment and fulfillment that comes with a spicy cake a-baking in the oven —
>
> A taffy pull for the children, or an evening fudge-making for the grown-ups —
>
> All these take mighty little doing, but make for a lot of pleasant living.

— 1952

See Table of Equivalents (p. 240) for sugar and cream references.

APRICOT STRAWS

1 lb. dried apricots   1 c. granulated sugar

These must be prepared a day in advance. Pour warm water over apricots and let stand for just 5 minutes. Drain and put in top of double boiler (have water in bottom already boiling) and steam for 5 minutes. Remove from stove and spread on a large pastry board. Remove skins and flatten each apricot with palm of hand. Cut into small strips with scissors. Roll in granulated sugar and let stand in cool place until straws stiffen.

Dainty and delicious for teas and bridge parties.

Mrs. Walter P. Armstrong

BUTTER CHEWS

¾ c. butter   1 c. chopped nuts
3 T. sugar   ¾ c. shredded coconut
1½ c. flour   3 egg whites
3 egg yolks   Powdered sugar
2½ c. brown sugar

Cream butter and sugar. Beat well and blend thoroughly with flour. Pour into greased, oblong cake pan and bake in 375° oven for 15 minutes, or until delicately browned. Remove from oven and set aside. Next, add brown sugar to well beaten egg yolks and blend in well. Add nuts and coconut and fold in stiffly beaten egg whites. Pour this over the baked mixture and return to oven for 25 or 30 minutes. Cut into squares and dust with powdered sugar. Cooking time: about 1 hour. Yield: about 16 squares.

Miss Gloria McPhillips

MINT PUFFS

1½ c. granulated sugar   1 egg white
2 T. light corn syrup   10 drops peppermint extract
¼ c. water   5 drops green coloring

Combine sugar, syrup and water; stir until sugar dissolves. Cook until the mixture reaches the soft ball stage (234°). Beat the egg white until stiff; pour cooked mixture over it slowly. Beat; halfway through the beating add flavoring and coloring a drop at a time. Beat until it holds its shape when dropped from spoon. Swirl candy from teaspoon, leaving a twist at the top of each drop. If they are not quite stiff enough, add powdered sugar until they are the right consistency.

These dainty, airy puffs keep for days. Ideal for teas and parties.

Mrs. Wallace Jorgenson, Aberdeen, Miss.

TO MELT CHOCOLATE: grease pan in which it is to be melted and place over boiling water.

CARAMEL FUDGE

5 c. sugar
2 c. cream
½ c. milk
½ stick of butter

1 t. vanilla
1 c. nuts
2 c. marshmallows

Put 4 cups of the sugar, the cream and butter on a slow fire. While this is cooking, put the remaining cup of sugar in a skillet and let it caramelize over a slow fire. When the first mixture comes to a boil, add the burnt sugar and milk. Cook until it reaches the soft ball stage (be sure to cook long enough). Let cool then add vanilla. Beat until thick, add nuts and cut up marshmallows. Pour into a buttered dish. Cut when cool into about 3 dozen pieces.

Mrs. Hal B. Howard

FOOLPROOF FUDGE

¼ c. Karo
½ c. X cream
2 c. sugar
2 heaping T. cocoa

Pinch of salt
½ stick of butter
1 t. vanilla
1 c. broken pecans

Mix cocoa, sugar and salt together. Add cream and Karo. Bring to a rolling boil and boil rapidly for 2 minutes. Remove from fire and add butter. When cool, add vanilla and beat well. When thick, beat in pecans and pour onto buttered platter to harden.

Mrs. George A. Coors

DATE KISSES

3 egg whites
1 c. sugar
1 c. chopped dates

1 c. broken pecans
½ t. vanilla

Beat egg whites until stiff. Add sugar slowly, beating constantly. Add vanilla, dates and nuts. Drop batter from teaspoon into floured hands and roll lightly. Place on a greased cookie sheet or on wax paper. Bake in 325° oven until lightly browned.

Mrs. George A. Coors

LUCY'S DIVINITY

2 c. sugar
½ c. water
⅓ c. Karo

2 egg whites
1 t. vanilla
1½ c. pecans

Cook sugar, water and Karo until it reaches the soft ball stage. Beat eggs until stiff and dry. Pour the cooked syrup over the whites and beat and beat! Add pecans and vanilla. Dip out by the spoonful onto greased platter.

Mrs. Malcolm G. Barboro

PEANUT BRITTLE

1 c. sugar
1 c. peanuts

2 t. butter
Pinch of soda

Cook sugar in an iron skillet, stirring constantly until it forms a syrup. Remove from stove and stir in peanuts that have been heated. Add butter and soda. Pour onto greased cookie sheet to cool.

MRS. FERD HECKLE, JR.

PRALINES

1 lb. light brown sugar
7 or 8 T. water

1 c. (or more) pecans
½ stick of butter

Let sugar and water boil hard, then add pecans. Cook until mixture reaches soft ball stage. Add butter and remove from fire. Beat until creamy, but of consistency that will spread. Drop by spoonfuls onto buttered cookie sheet and let harden. Make certain there are sufficient nuts in each spoonful.

MRS. GEORGE A. COORS

CANDIED PECANS

2 c. shelled pecan halves
1 c. sugar

4 T. water
1 t. salt

Mix sugar, water and salt in deep skillet or pan and cook until the simple syrup "hairs" when tested in cold water. Remove from heat and add pecans. Stir until they are completely coated.

VARIATION: A teaspoon of cinnamon added to syrup is delicious.

MR. W. GORTON BERRY

MY GRANDMOTHER'S ORANGE PECANS

Juice of 1 large orange
Rind of 1 large orange

1 c. sugar
1 qt. pecan halves

Let orange juice, grated rind and sugar come to a good quick boil. Add pecans a few at a time. Stir thoroughly. Cook until all syrup is absorbed, stirring constantly. Remove from fire and continue stirring until each pecan is alone. Turn onto wax paper to harden.

MRS. GEORGE A. COORS

CANDY MAKING is affected by the weather. It is impossible to make good hard candies in a moist, hot atmosphere. They become sticky, then sugary. It is advisable to take this into consideration when making all candies and to cook them to 2° higher than in dry, cold weather.

COOKIES

BLACK WALNUT STRIPS

⅞ c. butter (almost 2 sticks)
5 T. white sugar
2 c. flour

1 t. vanilla
1 T. water
1 c. chopped black walnuts

Cream butter and sugar, add flour, work in vanilla, water and, finally, the chopped nuts. Shape into fingers. Bake in 350° oven 20 minutes. Remove from oven and roll in powdered sugar. Makes approximately 4 dozen small rolls.

MRS. CHARLES B. DUDLEY, JR.

BUTTER COOKIES

½ lb. butter
4 T. sugar
3½ c. flour
Pinch of salt

Jelly, nuts or cinnamon and
  sugar
Powdered sugar

Cream butter and add sugar, salt and sifted flour. Roll out and cut. Dent and fill with tart jelly, or an almond or pecan or cinnamon and sugar. Bake in 350° oven for 20 minutes. Dust with powdered sugar. Yield: about 50 small cookies.

MRS. WILLIAM A. LEATHERMAN, ROBINSONVILLE, MISS.

BUTTERNUT COOKIES

1 c. brown sugar
1 stick of butter
1 egg

1 c. flour
½ c. nuts
1 t. vanilla

Cream butter and sugar. Add egg, sifted flour, nuts and vanilla. Drop from spoon onto greased cookie sheet and bake in 350° oven for about 10 minutes. Yield: about 24 small cookies.

MRS. ARTHUR B. BIRGE

BUTTERSCOTCH BROWNIES

1 stick of butter
1 lb. brown sugar (dark)
2 eggs
Pinch of salt

1½ c. flour
2 t. baking powder
1 c. nuts
1 t. vanilla

Melt sugar and butter in iron skillet. Cool. Add well beaten eggs to sugar mixture, then beat in flour and baking powder. Add salt, vanilla and nuts. Pour in a greased, shallow pan and bake in 350° oven for 45 minutes to 1 hour. Cool and cut into squares.

MRS. ADELE ORGILL

NUT MEATS will come out whole: soak in salt water overnight before cracking.

BROWNIES I

1 c. sugar	$\frac{1}{2}$ t. vanilla
1 egg, unbeaten	$\frac{1}{2}$ c. flour
$\frac{1}{2}$ stick of butter	$\frac{1}{2}$ t. baking soda
2 sq. chocolate,	$\frac{1}{2}$ t. salt
melted	$\frac{1}{2}$ c. chopped walnuts

First, sift together flour, soda and salt. Then mix all ingredients in order listed. Put in greased, square 8-inch pan and bake in 350° oven for 20 minutes; 10 minutes on low rack and 10 on high rack.

MRS. PUTNAM LIVINGSTON, SCARSDALE, N. Y.

BROWNIES II

1 pkg. chocolate bits	$\frac{1}{2}$ t. baking powder
$\frac{1}{3}$ c. butter	$\frac{1}{4}$ t. salt
2 eggs	1 t. vanilla
$\frac{1}{2}$ c. sugar	1 c. chopped pecans
$\frac{1}{2}$ c. flour	

Melt chocolate and butter over hot water. Beat eggs and sugar until thick then add sifted flour, baking powder and salt. Add the chocolate mixture to this along with vanilla and pecans. Pour into well greased, 8-inch square pan and bake in 375° oven for about 25 minutes. Makes 16 brownies.

MRS. JAMES K. DOBBS, JR.

FUDGE CAKE

2 sticks of butter	1 c. flour
2 c. sugar	1 t. vanilla
4 eggs	2 c. chopped pecans
4 sq. bitter chocolate	

Melt chocolate and butter in double boiler. Beat eggs and sugar together then combine with sifted flour. Blend well. Stir in nuts and, lastly, the chocolate mixture and vanilla. Pour into a greased and floured oblong cake pan and bake for 45 minutes in a 275° oven. Yield: about 20 squares.

MRS. ERNEST M. BARBER

EASY BROWNIES

1 can Eagle Brand milk	1 6-oz. pkg. chocolate bits
18 graham cracker squares	Dash of salt

Roll graham crackers until fine, then mix with remaining ingredients. Pour into 8-inch square pan that has been greased and floured and bake 30 minutes in 350° oven. Cut in squares while still warm and remove from pan. Yield: 20-25 squares. (Nuts may be added, if desired.)

MRS. WILLIAM H. MORSE

OATMEAL LACE COOKIES

½ c. flour
½ c. granulated sugar
2 T. heavy cream
½ c. melted butter

¼ t. baking powder
½ c. rolled oats
2 T. light corn syrup
1 T. vanilla

Sift flour, baking powder and sugar together in a bowl. Add to this mixture rolled oats, heavy cream, corn syrup, melted butter and vanilla. Drop by small spoonsful on cookie tin, leaving space for cookies to spread as they bake. Bake at 375° for 6-8 minutes or until golden brown. Cool slightly and lift from cookie tin with spatula. Let harden on paper towel until crisp.

MRS. EDWARD M. COBB

WILLIE'S DOUGHNUTS

1 c. sugar
2 T. melted shortening
2 eggs
1 c. milk
½ t. salt

3 t. baking powder
½ t. cinnamon
½ t. nutmeg
3 c. flour
Powdered sugar

Beat eggs until light then add milk and shortening. Pour this into sifted flour, baking powder, salt, nutmeg and cinnamon. Work into a light firm dough. (More flour may be added.) Cut with doughnut cutter and fry in deep fat. Brown on one side, turn only once. Cool and roll in powdered sugar. Yield: about 2 dozen doughnuts.

Plan to eat these the day they are made.

FRENCH TOAST FINGERS

¼ c. flour
1 egg
½ c. milk

6 slices dry bread
Deep fat

Make smooth batter of flour, egg and milk. Trim crusts from bread and cut diagonally. Dip bread into batter. Fry in deep fat heated to 365° F. for 2-3 minutes, or until golden brown. (Temperature of fat is right when an inch cube of bread browns in 60 seconds.) Drain on absorbent paper. Sprinkle toast with cinnamon and powdered sugar and serve at once. For pan-fried French toast, dip bread in batter and fry in hot fat about ¼ inch deep in heavy skillet. Fry about 3 minutes on each side. Serves 6.

This is delicious. It will serve six, but not adequately if you love it as we do.

MRS. JOHN McDONOUGH

LEMON ICE BOX COOKIES

1 c. shortening ($\frac{1}{2}$ oleo,   2 T. lemon juice
  $\frac{1}{2}$ shortening)   1 T. grated lemon rind
1 c. sugar ($\frac{1}{2}$ brown, $\frac{1}{2}$ white) $\frac{1}{4}$ t. soda
2 c. sifted flour $\frac{1}{4}$ t. salt
1 egg $\frac{1}{2}$ c. chopped nuts

Cream shortening and sugar well. Add egg and lemon juice, then the dry ingredients. Put dough in refrigerator until it is cool, then make into a long roll in floured wax paper. Return to refrigerator. When it is thoroughly chilled slice into thin cookies and bake in a 400° oven for 10 minutes.

VARIATIONS:

1) Substitute 1 cup of coconut for lemon juice and rind.
2) Substitute 2 squares of melted and cooled chocolate and $\frac{1}{2}$ teaspoon vanilla for lemon juice and rind.
3) Omit lemon juice and rind and add $\frac{1}{2}$ cup of chopped nuts and $\frac{1}{2}$ teaspoon of vanilla.
4) Reduce sugar to $\frac{2}{3}$ cup and add 6 teaspoons of marmalade.
5) Omit lemon juice and rind and add $\frac{1}{2}$ cup of finely chopped dates and $\frac{1}{2}$ teaspoon of vanilla.

This dough may be kept in the refrigerator for a week or more.

MRS. M. AMES SAUNDERS

MOLASSES LACE COOKIES

$\frac{3}{4}$ c. granulated sugar $1\frac{1}{2}$ c. sifted flour
$\frac{1}{2}$ c. dark molasses $1\frac{1}{2}$ t. baking powder
$\frac{1}{2}$ c. water $1\frac{1}{4}$ t. cinnamon
$\frac{3}{4}$ c. butter or margarine   1 c. chopped pecans

Combine sugar, molasses, water and butter in a saucepan and heat until they come to a boil. Remove from heat and stir until butter melts. Sift flour with baking powder and cinnamon then add to first mixture gradually, blending well. Fold in nut meats. Drop by teaspoonsful, about 3 inches apart, onto greased cookie sheet. Bake in 325° oven 12 to 15 minutes. Let cool a minute and remove with spatula before cookies harden. Place them on wax paper to cool. Yield: about 4 dozen cookies.

NUT TEA CAKES

$\frac{3}{4}$ c. sugar   Pinch of salt
$\frac{1}{2}$ c. butter   Cinnamon and spices to taste
2 eggs   1 cup shredded pecans
1 c. flour

Cream the butter and sugar then mix in all the remaining ingredients. Drop by teaspoonsful onto a greased cookie sheet. Spread with a knife to even them up. Bake in 300° oven for about 20 minutes. Yield: 30 cookies.

GERMAN COOKIES

6 eggs
4 c. brown sugar
2 c. flour
1 stick of butter
1 c. chopped nuts

1 t. vanilla
2 level t. baking powder
1 c. powdered sugar
½ c. cream (approx.)

Put eggs and sugar in a double boiler and cook until they form a light custard. Sift flour and baking powder together and beat into custard tablespoon by tablespoon. Add vanilla. Grease a pan with a little butter then cut up the remaining butter into chips over bottom of pan. Sprinkle the nuts over the butter and pour the batter evenly over the nuts. Bake in a 300° oven for 25 minutes. Add enough cream to powdered sugar to make the icing. Spread it over the cookies in the pan while they are still hot. Cool before cutting. Yield: 4 dozen cookies.

Mrs. Thomas R. Price

HARD TACK

1 c. sugar
¾ c. sifted flour
1 t. baking powder
½ t. salt

1 c. dates, chopped
1 c. nuts, chopped
2 eggs

Mix and sift dry ingredients. Add dates and nuts, mixing with hands. Add slightly beaten eggs. Spread mixture in greased 8-inch square pan. Bake 25-30 minutes at 350°. When cool, cut in strips and roll in powdered sugar.

Mrs. William H. Morse

SUGAR COOKIES

2 sticks of butter, or
1 of butter, 1 of oleo
1 c. sugar
1 egg
1½ c. cake flour

½ t. salt (scant)
½ t. vanilla
Coconut or cinnamon, sugar
and grated orange peel

Cream butter and sugar and add unbeaten egg. Beat well and add flour, sifted with salt, gradually. Blend well. Add vanilla. Drop by teaspoonful onto lightly greased cookie sheet. Press with fork prongs and sprinkle with lightly toasted coconut, or cinnamon and sugar, or grated orange peel. Bake in a 375° oven for 12 to 15 minutes, or until lightly browned. Let them harden for a few minutes, then remove from the pan with a spatula. Yield: about 4 dozen cookies.

Mrs. C. P. Stewart, W. Hartford, Conn.

SPICE COOKIES

1 c. sugar
⅔ c. shortening
1 t. soda dissolved in a
little hot water
1 c. nuts, put thru meat
grinder

2 full c. flour
2 eggs
1 t. cloves
2 c. dates, put thru
meat grinder
1 t. cinnamon

Mix all ingredients together. Drop in very small quantities on cookie pan with plenty of space between. Bake 10 minutes in 400° oven. Makes about 90 cookies if small. They keep indefinitely.

PEANUT BUTTER COOKIES

⅔ c. butter or oleo
1 c. brown sugar
1 c. white sugar
1 c. peanut butter

2 eggs
2 c. flour before sifting
1½ t. soda
½ t. salt

Cream butter and sugar. Mix in eggs and peanut butter. Sift soda and salt with flour, then add to sugar mixture. Make into balls the size of marbles and place on cookie sheet. Mash each one flat with fork. Bake in 350° oven for 10-20 minutes. Yield: about 6 dozen cookies.

Mrs. Merrill Parrish Hudson

PECAN COOKIES I

1 stick of butter or oleo
2 T. granulated sugar
1 t. vanilla
1 c. ground pecans

1 c. cake flour
1 t. salt
Powdered sugar

Cream butter and sugar and work in remaining ingredients. Make into balls the size of large marbles and place on cookie sheet. Bake about 45 minutes in 300° oven. Roll in powdered sugar while warm, or you may wait for them to cool. Yield: 3 dozen cookies.

Mrs. Charles W. Montgomery

PECAN COOKIES II

½ lb. butter
1 c. sugar
1 egg

2 c. flour
½ t. cinnamon
1 lb. pecan halves

Cream butter and sugar then add egg yolk, flour and cinnamon. Spread out very thin on a large, greased pan and smear egg white over the top. Then, place a layer of pecans over top and bake in 350° oven until golden brown. Cut in squares while still hot, making certain there is a pecan on each cookie. Yield: 30 cookies.

Mrs. J. N. Beley

PECAN SQUARES

3 c. coarsely chopped pecans
3 c. brown sugar
2 c. cake flour

1 t. baking powder
6 egg whites

Beat egg whites until stiff and mix all ingredients together. Bake in square pan in 350° oven for 25 minutes. **Do not over bake.** Cool and cut into squares. Yield: about 24 squares.

Amounts may be cut down in proportion.

Mrs. Daniel N. Copp

SCOTCH SHORTBREAD

3½ c. self rising flour
½ c. rice flour
¾ lb. butter

1 t. lard
½ c. sugar

Sift, then mix together all the dry ingredients, except the sugar, and set aside. Leave butter at room temperature until quite soft. Add sugar to butter and knead with hands until it is the consistency of putty. Now add flour, handful by handful, keeping the butter and sugar mixture as consistently firm as possible. Knead continually. Do this until all flour has been added and mixture is in a firm lump. Sprinkle baking board with a small amount of sugar. Divide mixture with knife into desired cookie sizes and place a piece in both hands to mold and soften. Then, place on board and shape with left hand (keeping the shape round) and knead with knuckles of right hand until ½ inch thick. "Frill" it with finger and thumb around edges and prick all over with a fork. Grease a cookie pan and line it with wax paper. Slide cakes onto paper and bake in preheated 350° oven for 20 minutes, until golden brown. Put on wire racks to cool and store in tins.

Ground rice may be used instead of rice flour. Serve with tea or sherry, or anytime a rich cookie is desired.

Mrs. Hugh Monteath, Jr.

MRS. SINGLETON'S SPICE COOKIES

1 c. granulated sugar
½ c. brown sugar
⅔ c. melted shortening
1 c. raisins
1 c. pecans
2 unbeaten eggs
1 t. baking soda

2 T. hot water
1 t. cinnamon
1 t. ground cloves
1 t. allspice
½ c. oatmeal
2½ c. flour

Dissolve the soda in the hot water, then combine all ingredients in order given. Mix together thoroughly. Drop by teaspoonful onto baking sheet. Bake in 350° oven for 15 minutes. Yield: 130 cookies.

Mrs. M. M. Jamieson

WHISKEY BALLS

2 lbs. vanilla wafers
1½ c. crushed pecans
1 c. XXXXXX sugar

½ c. white Karo
¾ c. bourbon whiskey
Powdered sugar

Roll and crush wafers until fine. Mix with sugar and Karo, then add whiskey and pecans. Roll into balls and roll in sifted powdered sugar. Delicious! Yield: about 4 dozen balls.

Adele Brake, Cateress

Preserves and Relishes

Breathes there a man with taste so nought
Who never in his life hath thought,
"These store-bought jams don't make the grade.
Where are the ones like Mother made?"

His query is answered here with pages that are laden with
gems of preserving artistry. Is his desire for the lowly blackberry,
borne in buckets by barefooted, "prick-fingered" hawkers, or
for the lofty Damson plum, ripened on its high throne?

Or does he dream of the muscadines he gathered in his youth,
while mosquitoes feasted upon the fetcher? Perhaps his reverie
sees the colorful strawberry, transformed in but a few minutes
to a sparkling jelly jewel.

Maybe he remembers the spiced pickles Mother made — the
relishes so tart that added zest to every meal. If you would have
his dreams come true, you'll find them all herein.

—1952

See Table of Equivalents (p. 240) for sugar and cream references.

BAKED CRANBERRY RELISH

1 qt. cranberries	1 t. cinnamon
2 c. sugar	½ c. chopped nuts

Wash and pick over a quart of cranberries. Put in a quart baking dish (earthenware or pyrex) with granulated sugar. Bake in a 275° oven until cranberries become juicy. Add a teaspoon cinnamon. Cover baking dish and bake 350° until berries look clear and are still whole. Cover the top of the cranberries with chopped nut meats and serve warm with meat. Serves 8 to 10.

Keeps for days in the ice box and may be served cold.

MRS. HUBERT K. REESE

FROZEN HORSERADISH RELISH

1 c. whipping cream	3 T. chopped chives
1 c. cottage cheese	½ c. horseradish
Cayenne	2 T. tarragon vinegar
Salt to taste	2 t. sugar

Mix together cream whipped stiff and the cottage cheese. Add cayenne, salt and chives. Mix horseradish with vinegar and sugar and fold into first mixture. Pour into refrigerator tray and freeze. Serve with fish or as a relish on salad plate. Serves 10.
Do not make day ahead as horseradish loses its flavor.

MRS. H. DUNCAN TAYLOR

WALNEY INDIA RELISH

1 pt. sweet red pepper	1 large cauliflower
1 pt. sweet green pepper	12 medium cucumbers
1 pt. white onions	¼ c. salt

Chop fine all ingredients or put through coarse blade meat chopper. Place in large enameled kettle or bowl and cover with salt. Let stand overnight. Drain and rinse well. Bring following to boil:

4 c. vinegar	½ t. red pepper
3½ c. sugar	1 t. turmeric
4 T. mustard seed	1 t. ginger
2 t. salt	Alum
2 t. celery seed	

Add vegetables to boiling mixture. Bring again to boil. Pack in sterile jars and seal. Put ¼ teaspoon powdered alum in each jar. Yield: 4 pints.

This is an original relish recipe named "Walney" for the lovely old house in Virginia where the donor lived at the time.

MRS. JOHN McDONOUGH

BRANDIED PEACHES

1 peck cling peaches   Brandy
4 lbs. sugar

Peel 1 peck uniform medium cling peaches. Keep covered with water as peeled so peaches won't darken. Remove from water, place in vessel and cover with sugar. Let stand for 30 minutes. Bring to a boil and cook 5 minutes. Place peaches in sterile jars. Drop jars gently on counter to settle peaches, add another peach or more to jar if necessary. Cover with syrup leaving space for ½ cup of brandy per jar. Let cool before brandy is added. Screw on tops. Yield: 6 quarts.

Mrs. Jack G. Gordon, III

CHIPPED GINGER PEAR

8 lbs. green pears   3 lemons
6 lbs. sugar   ¼ lb. preserved ginger

Peel, solid not soft, pears and chip off in small slices. Let pear, sugar and ginger stand together overnight. Slice whole lemons fine and add. Boil all together 30 minutes. Take out the fruit and boil syrup down until dark and thick (1 hour). Put fruit back in syrup and heat. Pour in sterile glasses and cover with paraffin. Yield: 6 quarts.

Mrs. Charles B. Dudley, Jr.

CONCORD GRAPE AND NUT JAM

3 lbs. ripe Concord grapes   1 c. sliced nuts
7 c. sugar   ½ bottle fruit pectin

Wash and drain grapes. Slit skins and save, simmer pulp 5 minutes. Press through sieve, removing seeds. Chop or grind skins and add to pulp. Add nuts. Add sugar and boil. Cook for 1 minute. Remove from heat and pour in pectin. As it jells pour into sterile jars. Cover with paraffin. Yield: 10 8-ounce jars.

Mrs. Jack Gates

STRAWBERRY PRESERVES

4 c. strawberries   3 c. sugar
1½ T. lemon juice

Boil berries and lemon juice 3 minutes. Add sugar, boil hard 6 minutes. Pour into shallow bowls (china or porcelain). Let stand 24 hours, turning thoroughly several times to allow air to get into preserves. Spoon into sterile jars. Cover with paraffin. Yield: 2 glasses.

This is a rich dark preserve.

Mrs. W. E. Lamb

DAMSON PLUM CONSERVE

2 qts. Damson plums
4½ c. sugar
1½ lemons

1½ oranges
3 c. seeded raisins
1½ c. chopped nuts

Wash Damson plums, cover with water and cook until tender. Remove seeds and chop. Measure 6 cups plum pulp. Add sugar, juice and grated rind of lemons and oranges, and raisins. Cook until thick and clear. Add nuts. Pour into sterile glasses. Cover with paraffin. Yield: 12 6-ounce glasses.

Delicious over vanilla ice cream.

MRS. JOHN F. BARBEE

FRUITS IN SEASON

1 qt. brandy
Sugar

Fruits in season

Place 1 quart brandy in a stone crock with a lid. Then as the fruits come into season put them into the crock with an equal amount of sugar. One quart of any fruit is usually enough. Omit any fruits with large seeds. Suggested fruits are: strawberries, cherries, apricots, peaches, pineapple. This is good served with meat or as a sauce over desserts.

The best part of this is that it can be dipped into at any time.

MRS. JAMES HARRISON, FERGUSON, MO.

ORANGE MARMALADE

4 oranges
1 lemon
1 pt. water to each lb. fruit

1½ lb. sugar to each lb. fruit
and juice

Wash fruit and cut into thinnest possible slices. Cover with cold water, using 1 pint water to each pound fruit. Set aside overnight in a china or enamel bowl. In morning bring to boiling point, cover kettle and cook very slowly until the skins are tender enough to be pierced easily with the head of a pin. When cold weigh again and add 1½ pounds sugar for each pound of fruit and juice. Cook until thick and transparent (about 20 minutes). Put in sterile glasses and seal when cold. Yield: 10 jelly glasses.

MRS. ERICH MERRILL

SPICY ORANGE SLICES

8 seedless oranges
4 c. sugar
1 c. vinegar

½ c. water
10 whole cloves
2 sticks cinnamon

Slice oranges about ½ inch thick; discard end pieces. Cover with water and simmer in covered pan until tender (1 hour). Drain. Boil all other ingredients 5 minutes. Add oranges and simmer until slices are well glazed (1 hour). Pack in small sterile jars; fill with syrup, cool and seal with paraffin. Serve with meat or poultry. Yield: 4 pints.

MRS. HOWARD S. JECK, JR.

PLUM JELLY

1 gal. medium ripe plums   1 c. sugar to each c. juice

Place fruit in kettle with water ½ way up on fruit and cook until tender (30 minutes). Strain in cloth bag while hot. Bring juice to boil, add 1 cup sugar to each cup juice for about 15 minutes. Test for jell by dropping a few drops in saucer and let cool. If not jelled cook 5 minutes longer. Skim while boiling. Pour in sterile glasses and let cool. Cover with paraffin. Yield: 16 glasses.

This same proportion, cup for cup, of sugar and fruit can be used for all jellies with these changes in first water cooking:

CRAB APPLE:

Cover quartered fruit with water for first cooking.

GRAPE:

2 pecks fruit, 2 quarts cold water. Cook until tender (10 minutes).

MRS. WILLIAM T. BRAUN

RAW CRANBERRY RELISH

2 c. cranberries   2 c. sugar
2 large oranges

Put washed cranberries through food chopper. Slice the oranges and put them through the chopper, peel and all. Stir sugar into mixture. Place in bowl in ice box to chill. Serve with fowl. Serves 8.

MRS. ADELE ORGILL

BREAD AND BUTTER PICKLES

8 c. thinly sliced cucumbers   4 green peppers
2 c. thinly sliced onions   2 t. celery seed
2 c. vinegar   2 t. turmeric
1 c. water   1½ sticks cinnamon
2 c. sugar   ¼ c. salt

Combine cucumbers and onions and sprinkle with salt. Set aside 1 hour. Put in sauce pan with vinegar, water, sugar, celery seed, turmeric, cinnamon and peppers finely chopped. Bring to a boil and cook 10 minutes. Place in sterile jars and seal. Yield: 2 quarts.

MRS. CHARLES L. PIPLAR

CANTALOUPE PICKLE

1 c. cubed cantaloupe   1 t. salt
1 c. sugar   1 T. whole allspice
1 c. vinegar

Use the hard part of 1 large or 2 small cantaloupes. Peel, cut in ½ inch cubes. Soak in a little vinegar overnight. For each cup of fruit put 1 cup of sugar and 1 cup of vinegar in a saucepan and boil thoroughly. Add fruit. Skim off foam. Boil hard for ten minutes with salt and allspice added. Cool and jar. Yield: 1 pint.

MRS. PEARL G. COOPER

CHILI SAUCE

24 ripe tomatoes
6 chopped green peppers
8 sliced onions
4 c. vinegar
8 T. sugar

6 T. salt
1 T. cinnamon
1 T. cloves
1 T. allspice
1 T. nutmeg

Boil all together until thick. Mash with potato masher to distribute flavor. Seal in sterile jars while hot. Yield: 6 pints.

MRS. HUBERT K. REESE

CORN CHOW CHOW

1 qt. green tomatoes (12)
5 lbs. cabbage
1 pt. little green butter beans, cooked
6 or 8 ears summer corn

4 large white onions
6 green peppers
2 red peppers
2 hot peppers (optional)
1 c. salt

Drop corn in salted boiling water 5 minutes. Slice off cob. Put everything except corn and beans in coarse grinder. Salt down all ingredients overnight with 1 cup salt. Next morning squeeze dry.

BRINE OR SYRUP:

1½ qt. vinegar
1 c. brown or white sugar
1 pkg. mustard seed
1 pkg. celery seed

1 T. turmeric
1 T. dry mustard
½ c. cold water
1 box pickling spices in bag

Boil 5 minutes. Put all vegetables except corn and beans into brine. Cook and stir over high flame 10 minutes, then add corn and beans. Place in sterile jars and cover chow chow with brine. Yield: 12-14 pints.

MRS. ROY M. GIBSON

DILL TOMATOES

Small green tomatoes
1 small bell pepper

1 stalk celery
1 garlic pod

Fill pint jars with tomatoes about size of marbles, combined with chopped pepper, celery and garlic.

DRESSING:

1 pt. vinegar
2 pts. water

½ cup salt
2 dill flowers

Combine and let come to a boil. Cook 5 minutes and pour over tomatoes. Seal. This must stand six weeks before serving. Yield: 6 pints.

Excellent as an hors d'oeuvres. Chill to serve.

MRS. EDWARD H. CRUMP

GARLIC PICKLE

25 large sour pickles	5 pods garlic
5 lbs. sugar	1 pt. tarragon vinegar
1 pkg. pickling spice	1 c. olive or salad oil

Cut pickles in ¼ inch slices and place in crock in layers. Cover alternately with sugar and spices. Add garlic. Let stand 3 days stirring occasionally with wooden spoon. Then add vinegar and oil, stirring thoroughly. Let stand 10 days, then jar. Yield: 10-12 pints.

Even a beginner can do it!

MRS. WILLIAM T. BRAUN

GREEN TOMATO PICKLE

1 gal. green tomatoes, sliced	½ doz. sliced green peppers
½ doz. sliced onions	

Let above soak overnight in salt water. Next morning squeeze dry.

1 T. ground black pepper	1 T. dry mustard
1 T. whole cloves	1 pt. brown sugar
1 T. powdered cinnamon	1 T. (scant) ground
1 T. white celery seed	horseradish
1 T. white mustard seed	Vinegar (enough to cover)
1 T. (scant) ground mace	

Put all in pot on stove and let come to boil. Seal in sterile jars while hot. Yield: 4 quarts.

As full of character as "Mother" Chandler.

MRS. WILLIAM H. CHANDLER

ICED TOMATO PICKLE

7 lbs. green tomatoes	3 c. slack lime

Cut tomatoes in thick slices and soak in 2 gallons water with slack lime for 12 hours. Wash off and soak in clear water for 3 hours. Drain.

SYRUP:

5 lbs. sugar	3 qts. vinegar
1 t. whole cloves	1 t. powdered ginger
1 t. allspice	1 t. celery seed

Let come to boil and pour over tomatoes. Let stand overnight. Cook 1 hour and seal in sterile jars while hot. Yield: 5 quarts.

MRS. DUDLEY S. WEAVER

SPICED PEACH PICKLE

1 qt. cider vinegar
4 c. sugar
2 pkg. allspice (in bag)

6 sticks cinnamon
9 firm clingstone peaches

Dissolve sugar in vinegar. Add allspice and boil 5 minutes. Drop in whole peeled peaches and boil until tender. Place 3 peaches in each quart mason jar with 2 sticks cinnamon. Seal while hot. Yield: 3 quarts.

For added flavor stick several cloves (with heads removed) in each peach.

MRS. W. E. LAMB

LOUISIANA PICKLED FIGS

3 qts. ripe figs
6 c. sugar
1 c. vinegar

2 T. broken cinnamon sticks
2 T. whole cloves

Cover figs with 2 quarts boiling water. Let stand 5 minutes and drain. Mix 1 cup water with vinegar and sugar in large sauce pan. Add spices in bag. Bring to boil and add figs. Boil 10 minutes. Let stand until next day (2nd day). Boil 10 minutes. Let stand until next day (3rd day). Boil 10 minutes. Remove spice bag and pack in sterile jars. Yield: 4 pints.

MRS. JACK GATES

OKRA PICKLE

Wash and trim okra and soak in ice water for 24 hours. The next day sterilize jars and in each jar place a clove of garlic, a clump of dill, and a strip of red pepper about ½ inch by two inches. Rinse off okra and pack in jars alternating the ends of the okra. (A strip of celery and carrot packed against outside of jar adds color.) Pour in hot solution until jar is full. Let jars stand for an hour or so, until solution stops bubbling. Refill jars to the brim again and screw cap on tightly.

SOLUTION:

1 qt. vinegar
2 qts. water

1 scant cup of salt
1 pea-sized piece of alum

Bring ingredients to a boil, stirring well, and keep at a slow boil for 10 to 15 minutes. Solution must be hot. Excess may be kept and used later, but always re-heat. If okra is scarce, other vegetables such as carrots, celery, cauliflower and beans may be substituted.

DR. C. BARTON ETTER

WATERMELON PICKLE

Trim off green skin and pink part of watermelons. Cut in pieces, wash and weigh. To each 7 pounds rind:

7 c. sugar
2 c. vinegar

½ t. oil of cinnamon
½ t. oil of cloves

Cover 7 pounds rind with cold water, cook until clear but not mushy. Drain. Place in crock. Boil other ingredients and pour over rind. Let stand overnight. Drain off syrup and heat again. Pour over rind. Let stand overnight (2nd night). Bring all together to a boil. Seal in sterile jars. Yield: 4 pints.

Oil of cinnamon and oil of cloves may be obtained at drug store.

MRS. JACK G. GORDON, III

"QUICK-UPS"

Magicians are made, not born. So, Mrs. Blackstone, bring a little Wizardry to your work. Try the magic of these helpful hints for every household chore, and enjoy added leisure hours and a boost to that now extinct little item — the Budget!

"PICK-UPS"

Parties are for pleasure, so "pick-up" your next with a dash of "can-chicanery." Your talents will be toasted and your suppers will be sung. These are as fast as sleight of hand, and can be prepared from a shelf of cans.

"HIC-UPS"

'Twas once said, "A loaf of bread,
A jug of wine and thou"
Is all you need your joy to speed.
'Twas no truer then than now.

— 1952

See Table of Equivalents (p. 240) for sugar and cream references.

'QUICK-UPS'

1. LAUNDRY LEGERDEMAIN:

You can stop lint from accumulating in your washing machine and clogging your laundry drain by wiring a tea strainer to the end of the drain hose on the machine. It's easily removed for cleaning.

You can fool the moths by adding one cup of moth balls to the last rinse water when you wash clothes prior to storing.

A folded band of cellophane placed between the leather sweat-band and the hat will prevent oil and perspiration from soaking through and staining the outside of the hat.

To remove spots from dark garments, a piece of old nylon stocking may be used for applying the cleaning fluid or tepid soap solution. Nylon leaves no lint.

For washing Baby's knitted suits and sweaters, baste them onto a bath towel while still dry. Wash as usual, squeeze out and hang the towel on the line to dry. This will keep their correct size and shape.

Candle wax drippings may be removed from wool and linen by placing brown wrapping paper over the wax spots and then pressing with a medium hot iron. The brown paper absorbs the wax completely.

For blue jeans with that faded look, try one package of dark blue dye dissolved in a little warm water then added to the hot water in the washing machine. This is enough to bring back the new look to three or four pairs of jeans. Let them wash for about forty minutes.

If you can't get around to ironing all the clothes that you have sprinkled, wrap the left-overs in waxed paper and place them in the refrigerator. This will keep them from souring or mildewing and will also give them a nice smooth finish when you iron them.

Dainty curtains and underwear may be laundered safely in your machine if put in a pillow case tied shut.

Trying to rub or wash soot from a felt or fabric hat only spreads the stain. To clean the spot, cover it with salt and remove with a stiff brush.

Portions of clothing which are scorched during ironing may be renewed quickly with a five-cent piece. Spread the fabric taut on the ironing board and rub the scorched area with the coin.

II. PARENTAL PRESTIDIGITATION:

A doubly or triply divided egg poacher is ideal for heating small portions of canned food for Baby. There is no danger of scorching and food can be kept at the proper temperature. Feed the baby right from the small containers.

Baby's new shoes are slippery, so try rubbing sand paper lightly over the soles. If sand paper isn't handy, rub the soles on your door step or brick wall.

For southern climates, "sockees" are more comfortable than bootees. Just sew a piece of pastel-colored seam binding at the back of Baby's sock just above the ankle and tie in front

For a playtoy "pick-up", attach a couple of Baby's toys to each end of a length of ribbon and tie the ribbon at the center to the stroller. The ribbon should be short enough to keep the toys off the ground.

An old clean white cotton glove with the finger tips cut off is an ideal solution to keeping a bandage on a youngster's injured hand.

School lunches make for a hectic morning. Why not make up a large batch of assorted sandwiches and label them? Put them in the freezer during one of the less busy hours of the day and have them handy for the rest of the week. Your youngster's lunch will be thawed by the noon bell.

When taking small children on a trip, fill a wide-mouthed screw-topped jar (a Chee-wee jar is perfect) half full of soapy water and put a wash cloth in it. Screw the top on tightly and keep it in the car, ready to wipe dirty or sticky hands and faces.

To keep your youngster (or husband) from pulling unevenly on his shoe-string and getting one end much longer than the other, tie a knot in the middle of each shoestring before putting them in the shoes.

III. HOUDINI IN THE HOUSE

If you drip candle wax over the kindling, your fire will get a quicker start, and it's a wonderful way to use up your old candle stubs.

In order to patch a screen, cut a piece from an old screen a little larger than the hole. Then ravel the edges until the patch is only a wire or two larger than the hole. Press the loose wires through the screen and bend the ends back.

When hanging pictures on a plaster wall, drive the nail through a scotch tape X at the center. This greatly reduces the possibility of the plaster cracking.

Tool box bedlam can be eliminated by nailing jar tops to the underside of a shelf and then screwing glass jars filled with nails, tacks, and washers into the tops. This saves shelf space and you can see what you have.

IV. CLEANING CAPERS:

White cotton gloves turned inside out or dime store gardening gloves make dusting venetian blinds and furniture a wonderfully easy job. Drop the gloves in the washing machine come wash day.

Cleaning the tines of your forks is tedious, but not if you stick the forks, tines down, into a jar of your favorite paste polish. Let them stand while polishing other pieces, and when the forks are removed, a minimum of rubbing is required.

Silver polish is wonderful for removing burned starch on the bottom of your electric iron. Disconnect the iron, allow it to cool and apply polish. Then wipe the iron with a slightly damp cloth and follow with a dry one.

Macaroni and spaghetti will not stick to the bottom of the kettle in which they are cooked, if the inside of the kettle is slightly greased before the water is put on to boil.

Foods which have burned or stuck to your casserole or baking dishes will be easy to remove if the dishes are soaked for a few minutes in warm water to which a tablespoon of baking soda has been added. Then wash as usual.

The bottoms of your barbecue pots and pans will stay bright if they are rubbed with a cake of soap before you use them over the open fire. The smoke stain will vanish, come wash-up time.

An old putty knife, attached to a stout cord hanging by the back door, serves as a useful reminder when muddy shoes approach your freshly mopped floor.
Adhesive tape wrapped over the top and about two inches down the sides of colored mops or broom handles will prevent them from streaking the walls and marking the furniture, should they fall or be knocked over. The handles of children's toys can have the same treatment.
A good brass polish may be made by mixing cooking soda and vinegar until it is a paste.
An orange stick is useful in removing salt corrosion spots on silver.
If you own a car-washing hose-brush, its uses may be multiplied by putting it to work cleaning porches, outside walls, screens and windows.
Don't try to scrape off paper which has become stuck to a polished table top. To be safe, moisten the paper with olive oil and then rub it off.
To restore the shine to aluminum utensils, add one teaspoon of cream of tartar per quart of water and boil the solution in your utensils for about twenty minutes.

V. CAGEY KITCHEN KEEPING:

Shallow pans or dishes containing a cupful of ammonia placed in the oven and broiler overnight will greatly speed the removal of grease and stains when wiped out in the morning. The fumes do a great loosening job.
In order to keep lard from spattering during frying, put a pinch of salt in it.
Come "Open Season", the de-feathering of birds is a foul job! It will help, though, to put some paraffin in boiling water, wait until it melts and then dip the birds up and down in the mixture. After they are well coated, wrap in several thicknesses of newspaper, let cool and strip down feathers. Old candle stubs are grand to use for this.
An old spice can (the kind with a sliding top) makes a good salt shaker for lunch and picnic boxes. It can't spill.
The layers of a cake will come out of their pans without sticking if you will set the hot pans on a damp cloth when they come out of the oven.
A large lump of charcoal placed in an open jar in your refrigerator will greatly reduce icebox odors.
When cooking something that requires frequent stirring, leave the spoon so that the handle is directly over the handle of the pan. You will save yourself many burns.
Weep no more, my lady! An unlighted kitchen match held between your teeth while working with onions will dissipate the onion fumes. It works!
A little butter on the lip of a cream pitcher will eliminate the usual drip when pouring.
Cheese mold can be kept to a minimum by wrapping the cheese and a couple of lumps of sugar in tin foil and placing it in a covered container.
Don't worry about getting your plate back when donating a cake to the church or club bazaar. Just substitute an old phonograph record neatly covered with waxed paper or aluminum foil. A paper lace doily may be added for dress-up.
Use up the end crusts of your bread by putting them on top of pots in which

you are cooking cauliflower, cabbage or greens. It will absorb cooking odors.

Save that manicure! Spare your nerves and nails from steel-wooling your stove's drip pans. Line each one instead with tin foil, cutting out holes for the gas eyes with a knife or your thumb nail, and press the outside edges under the outer edges of the drip pan. Don't forget to cut holes for pilot lights. This treatment should last about three weeks with just easy weekly wiping. Lining the inside of your frying pans likewise saves a world of scouring.

To remove onion odor from your hands, rub them with celery.

Defrost your refrigerator and deep freeze with your vacuum cleaner! No joke! Attach the hose to the blowing end of your tank vacuum instead of the suction end and leave off all cleaning attachments. After food has been removed, line the bottom of the box with newspaper to catch frost and drippings. Let the air blow on collected frost, holding hose in the left hand, while loosening sheets of frost with a wooden spatula or spoon held in the right hand. Frost drops off in sheets and is easy to remove from box by lifting out the newspaper.

Frozen foods may be quickly thawed by placing package in front of an electric fan.

VI. NEEDLE NECROMANCY:

For an inconspicuous mending job on sheer curtains, apply a bit of colorless nail polish and press the torn edges together with your fingers. The tear will be almost invisible.

For mending holes in gloves, try using a lipstick case with a rounded end as a darning egg.

When it is necessary to remove the needles from your knitting, slip the stitches onto a pipe cleaner. Then bend the ends back and the stitches won't slip off.

Buttons sewed on heavy garments with dental floss will save many a lost button on your youngster's clothes. This requires a needle with a larger eye.

If you are stuffing children's toys, it is a good idea to use old discarded nylon stockings instead of cotton. When the toys are washed they will dry quickly and the stuffing will not lump.

When stitching heavy material (or several thicknesses) so that the needle has a hard time going through on the sewing machine, rub soap along the seam before running it through the machine. This will save needles and speed sewing.

To replace elastic that has lost its snap, open the seam and pin the end of the old elastic to one end of the new. Grasp the free end of old elastic and pull. New elastic will slip into place as you pull out the old.

To wind your yarn into a ball, put the skein around a lamp shade to fit. Unscrew the fineal until the shade turns freely and winding the yarn will be easy.

A cylindrical lamp shade that has become shabby may be salvaged by the use of yarn in a shade to complement your color scheme. Wrap the yarn around the shade in the same way the protective cellophane is put on. Wrap until the entire shade is covered, inside and out.

VII. FOOD FOOLERY:

To make milk sour quickly, mix a half cup of evaporated milk with a half cup of water and a tablespoon of strained lemon juice.

Stale bread may be salvaged by slipping it into a paper bag, closed tightly, and placing it in a 350° oven, for ten or fifteen minutes. If the bread is very stale, sprinkle it lightly with warm water before putting it in the bag.

When fricasseeing chicken, try rolling the pieces in pancake mix before frying. It is an inexpensive substitute for a costly milk and egg batter.

In order to ripen fruit more quickly, "bury it" in your meal bin. This will usually work overnight with avocados and apples, for example.

Before boiling a cracked egg, rub table salt into the cracked portion. This will keep the egg white from seeping out.

In order to poach eggs without an egg rack or to soft boil an egg which cracks in the water, add a teaspoon of vinegar to the boiling water. This will hold the poached eggs together and will keep the soft boiled eggs in the shell.

You can have rich brown gravies in a jiffy! Just place two cups of sifted flour in a dry iron skillet, put over a medium flame and stir constantly until the flour turns a rich beige color. Store this in a jar in a dry place and use when making gravies. There will be no waiting for the flour to cook.

If you have a little wild rice left over from any recipe, try adding it to spinach.

One teaspoon of lemon juice to each quart of water may be used for boiling rice. This will keep it fluffy.

Add a tablespoon of fat to cooking water for spaghetti to keep it from boiling over.

Slit chicken livers with a sharp knife to prevent grease from spitting while frying.

Dredging chicken in flour placed in a paper bag saves a big clean-up job. This is also a good method for rolling bread and cracker crumbs with no mess.

Gravy made with cornstarch as a thickening agent instead of flour can be reheated many times without causing the grease to separate.

To crisp celery, wash and cut an Irish potato into six pieces and drop them into a container with the celery. Add ice and water and place it covered in the refrigerator. This will make your celery cracker crisp.

In making mayonnaise, oil should be chilled to prevent separation. Should it separate anyway while making, dip out one tablespoon of the mayonnaise mixture and put it in another mixing bowl with two or three tablespoons of coldest ice water. Beat well, and add original mixture to cold mixture, beating constantly. Continue until the contents of both bowls are together.

As soon as your tomatoes get home from market, drop them into hot water before storing in the refrigerator. They will not spoil as easily and will be ready for peeling when needed.

Ten uses for leftover ham: Chopped in hot potato salad, scrambled eggs, French omelet, muffin batter, Spanish rice, pinwheel biscuits, ham sticks or bits of macaroni and cheese casserole, scalloped potatoes, celery soup, split pea soup, corn chowder and tossed salads.

In baking dishes (tins for popovers, for example) olive oil will heat to a much higher degree than butter.

One-half cup of milk added to the water in which cauliflower is cooked will keep it from turning yellow.

If you find that your dinner hour will be later than you had planned on a night when you are having a soufflé, you may prolong the cooking time successfully by slowly lowering your oven temperature.

VIII. PAINT PRANKS:

On a long paint job, wrap your brush tightly in aluminum foil instead of cleaning it every day. Wrapped in such a way, it will stay soft for several days. Clean your brush thoroughly, however, before putting it away permanently.

If you must use your newly painted shelves before they have thoroughly dried, put wax paper on them instead of shelf paper. It will not stick to shelves or dishes.

Partially used paint cans should be sealed air tight. Replace the cover tightly, turn the can upside down momentarily, then right side up again. The paint inside acts as a self-sealer.

Before storing that partly-used can of paint, paint a thin line on the outside of it at the level of the leftover paint. This tells at a glance how much and what color paint you have without re-opening the can.

Often you need a paint sample for matching fabrics. Dip a white blotter in the paint and allow to dry thoroughly. This will serve as an accurate sample when shopping.

After painting your kitchen, add a top coat of buttermilk to the walls and ceiling and see how easy your next wall-washing job is.

When painting chair legs, place a jar cover upside down under each leg. This allows room for the brush and catches paint drippings.

Apply one or two thin coats of clear shellac to your art reproductions before framing them. They will then more closely approximate original paintings.

IX. GARDENING GIMMICKS:

African violet plant leaves have a tendency to die if the stems touch the edge of the pot. In order to prevent this, cut a slit in a lace paper doily, remove and discard the center and slip the doily under the leaves of the plant, collar fashion.

A small brass extension curtain rod is an excellent support for a tall plant. As the plant grows pull the rod out to the proper height.

Old nylon hose are fine for tying up dahlias, tomatoes, or anything needing support, as they do not cut tender stems.

"A Pair of Parties for Pennies"

WINTERTIME VEGETABLE SOUP PARTY

This is ideal as Sunday night fare for newlyweds, or for distribution to hungry relatives or bachelors.

Menu

Vegetable Soup

French bread—Marrow butter

Red wine

Dessert

Coffee

VEGETABLE SOUP:

1 large beef knuckle bone with lean meat	1 red pepper, chopped
3 4-in. shin bones for marrow	2 T. salt
1 lb. lean brisket (in 2-in. cubes)	1 T. pepper
	2 T. Worcestershire sauce
1 No. 2 can tomatoes	1 T. celery salt
1 8-oz. can tomato juice	1 t. crushed red pepper
4 large stalks celery, chopped	1 t. "Dash"
2 large onions, chopped	1 t. Tabasco
1 leek, chopped	2 bay leaves
1 No. 2 can okra and corn in tomato sauce	1 c. chopped parsley
	4 large carrots, diced
	1 7-oz. pkg. soup mix

Remove hard skins from meat cubes and wash. Sear meat cubes and knuckle bone in hot skillet until brown. Place in 3 gallon kettle with marrow bones. Cover with warm water until within 3½ inches of kettle top. Add all ingredients listed except carrots, parsley, soup mix and okra and corn in tomato sauce. Bring to a boil and simmer gently with top on for 3½ hours. Add carrots and parsley and continue to simmer for 20 minutes. Add can of okra and corn and package of soup mix. Simmer gently 15 minutes. Place kettle in cool place until orange-colored grease forms crust on top (about 4 to 10 hours, depending on temperature). Remove grease crust with wide cooking spatula. Remove bones and scrape out marrow into separate small bowl. Remove meat, fat, and gelatin from knuckle bone, cut up in small pieces and return to soup. Leave meat cubes whole in the soup and serve one to each portion. Keep soup in cool place until ready to serve. This will keep 3 to 4 days under refrigeration. Serve from a tureen. Serves 18.

MARROW BUTTER:

½ lb. butter	1 t. hot mustard
Marrow from bones	Garlic salt

Cream butter with marrow from bones. Add hot mustard. Butter slices of French bread (cut thick) and sprinkle each with garlic salt. Run loaves in 400° oven just before serving.

Mrs. Dore Fly

SUMMER "CORN HUSKER"

This is a buffet supper ideally suited to porch, terrace or yard.

Menu

Corn on the cob

Hearty green salad

Soft buttered rolls

Iced tea

Dessert

CORN ON THE COB:

Allow at least 2 ears per person. Shuck and clean the corn, then wrap each ear in some of the inner husk leaves, using elastic bands. Arrange on a tray until ready to cook. Wash remaining inner husk leaves and boil in huge kettle of salted water for 15 minutes. Remove leaves and save the water. Bring water back to slow boil by party time. Provide large waste basket on porch or terrace and sometime during cocktails, pass the tray of corn and ask each guest to "shuck" as many ears as he may want, explaining that this is the mainstay of the forthcoming meal. Corn husks go in the waste basket, of course. All this makes for informal fun. Drop corn into already boiling water and allow to cook 6 to 12 minutes until tender. Drain and serve in large preheated casserole with cover. Provide tongs for serving. Place casserole on tray or big platter and surround with jigger bottles (the kind used for coffee cream at drug stores) of salted, melted butter. Allow ¼ stick to a person.

While corn is cooking, add dressing to already prepared Hearty Green Salad, and toss well. Just before placing corn tray and salad on table, pop rolls in the oven and pour iced tea into already dressed glasses (ice, orange slice, mint sprig) which are arranged on tray with spoons and sugar bowl.

HEARTY GREEN SALAD:

2 large heads lettuce	½ c. minced parsley
½ lb. leaf lettuce	1 c. small cream cheese balls
4 peeled and quartered tomatoes	½ c. chopped cucumber
1 c. celery, chopped	2 c. diced baked or boiled ham
½ c. chopped spring onion tops	4 quartered hard-boiled eggs (for garnish)

DRESSING:

½ pt. mayonnaise	½ c. French dressing
2 T. "Mr. Mustard" mustard	3 big dashes garlic salt

Add mustard to mayonnaise and mix well. Add garlic salt to French dressing and mix well. Pour French dressing over salad and toss gently. Then add mayonnaise and toss thoroughly. Garnish with egg quarters. Serves 10.

Mrs. Dore Fly

"Surprise Them With Soup"

ARCTIC ASPARAGUS SOUP

1 can asparagus soup
1 can beef consommé
1½ c. milk

1 bay leaf
1 leek, sliced

Combine the ingredients, bring to a boil and let simmer for five minutes. Chill well and serve cold. Serves 4.

MR. A. ARTHUR HALLE, CORDOVA, TENN.

CLAM AND CHICKEN SOUP

1 can cream of chicken soup
1 can consommé

1 small can clams, minced
1 chopped onion

Combine in double boiler chicken soup, onion, consommé and the juice from the clams. Simmer for 20 minutes. Add clams last and simmer just long enough to heat. Serves 4.

MRS. DUNBAR ABSTON, GERMANTOWN, TENN.

CORN AND MUSHROOM SOUP

½ c. sliced onion
2 T. butter
2 slices bacon, chopped

1 can cream style corn
1 can mushroom soup
¼ t. curry powder

Sauté onion in butter until tender. Sauté bacon. Dilute mushroom soup with milk or water and add to the corn, sautéed onions, sautéed bacon and curry powder. Heat well and serve. If desired, bacon and curry powder may be omitted. Serves 4.

MRS. GEORGE G. EARLY

CRABMEAT BISQUE

1 can condensed pea soup
1 can condensed tomato soup
1½ pt. cream

½ lb. crabmeat
¾ c. chicken broth (optional)
1 wineglass sherry

Heat soups. When just under the boiling point, add cream, crabmeat and sherry. Serves 4.

MRS. LANDON ROGERS

CREAM GLACÉE

Add 1 cup of tomato juice to 3 cups of cream vichyssoise. Chill. Serves 4.

MR. A. ARTHUR HALLE, CORDOVA, TENN.

EASY SOUP

1 can tomato soup
1 can pea soup
1 pt. coffee cream
½ t. dry mustard

½ t. curry powder
Dash Worcestershire sauce
½ t. salt

Put all ingredients in a bowl and beat thoroughly. Serve hot or cold. Serves 6.

MRS. HUBERT K. REESE

QUICK GUMBO

1 pkg. noodle soup mix
3 c. water
2 c. leftover meat hash
1 t. B. V. paste

1 can mixed corn, okra, tomatoes
1 small can shrimp (optional)
½ c. leftover rice (optional)

Cook soup in water for 10 minutes. Add remaining ingredients and cook 5 minutes longer. Serves 8.

MRS. CARROL C. TURNER

CREAM OF PEA SOUP WITH MINT

Mince some mint leaves very fine and cook them in a little butter. Dilute and heat a can of cream of pea soup, and just before serving, stir in the mint. Serve with croutons. Serves 4.

MRS. HUBERT K. REESE

CURRIED PEA SOUP

1 can cream of pea soup
½ t. curry powder

1 carrot, grated
½ c. cream, whipped

Dilute soup with milk, add curry powder and heat. Garnish with grated carrot and whipped cream. Serves 4.

MRS. DUNBAR ABSTON, GERMANTOWN, TENN.

"Bake A Pick-Up"

VARIATIONS FOR FRENCH BREAD

Toast thick slices of the bread with garlic butter and while very hot, sprinkle generously with parmesan cheese. Serve at once. This may also be done with hard rolls which have been cut in half lengthwise.

MARMALADE MUFFINS

Place canned biscuits in ungreased muffin tins and press middle with thumb. Put pat of butter and spoonful of marmalade in indentation and bake at 450° for 12 to 15 minutes.

MRS. R. CARL DICKERSON, JR.

"Sunday Night Satisfiers"

BEEF CASSEROLE

4 T. butter	1 8-oz. can tomato sauce
1 clove garlic, chopped	2 4-oz. cans mushrooms
2 medium onions, chopped	2 1-lb. cans macaroni in
1½ lb. ground chuck beef	cheese sauce
2 t. salt	½ t. Tabasco

Melt butter and cook onions and garlic in it until tender. Add ground beef and brown, breaking it into small pieces as it cooks. Stir in the remaining ingredients, and heat well. This may be placed in a casserole and heated in 300° oven until serving time. Serves 8.

MRS. WALTER P. ARMSTRONG

VEAL MADEIRA

Cold sliced veal	1 c. fresh cream
Leftover gravy	¼ c. madeira wine
¼ pt. sour cream	

Heat all ingredients except veal in skillet and pour over meat, hot or cold.

QUICK CHICKEN CURRY RICE

1 to 2 c. cooked rice	1 can chicken and
Curry powder, to taste	rice soup

Add undiluted soup to the rice and sprinkle the entire surface lightly with curry powder. Stir and cook over a slow fire until rice absorbs liquid and is thoroughly moist.

MRS. CARROL C. TURNER

DE LUXE HAMBURGERS

3 lb. ground round steak	¾ bottle catsup
1 pt. unwhipped cream	8 hamburger buns

Add cream and catsup to roundsteak. Mold into large patties and fry or broil. Serve in buns. Serves 8.

MRS. ARTHUR B. BIRGE

MARSHALL FIELD SANDWICH

3 slices rye bread (without	1 slice ham
crust)	1 slice turkey
2 slices crisp bacon	1 hard-boiled egg, grated
1 slice tomato	2 T. catsup
¼ c. mayonnaise	

Place turkey and ham on first slice of bread and cover with second slice. Place bacon and tomato on second slice and cover with third. Make a dressing with mayonnaise and catsup and cover the sandwich generously. Sprinkle top with grated egg and sprig of parsley. Serves 1.

MRS. THOMAS R. PRICE

MOCK PIZZA PIE

4 English muffins, split and
buttered
8 slices tomato, ¼ in. thick

½ c. sharp cheese, grated
Chopped oregano

Place slice of tomato on buttered English muffin half. Sprinkle generously with grated cheese, then with a little oregano. Bake in 450° oven, or until the cheese melts and the "pie" is hot through. Serves 4 to 8.

MRS. JOHN McDONOUGH

MONTAUK SANDWICH

1 lb. cheddar cheese,
grated fine
1 t. baking powder
1 t. Worcestershire sauce
½ t. salt

6-12 slices bacon,
partially fried
1 egg, beaten
2 T. milk

Mix all ingredients, except bacon. Spread on bread which has been toasted on the other side. Top with 1 or 2 slices of bacon. Broil under hot flame for 3 minutes. Mixture may be kept in the refrigerator several days. Serves 6.

MRS. E. HARRISON HUMPHREYS

BAKED PORK CHOPS

Pork chops
Cornflakes, crushed

Salt and pepper to taste

Roll chops in crushed cornflakes, seasoned with salt and pepper. Coat fat edge also. Put in shallow pan, lightly greased, and bake in 325° oven for 60 minutes. Make sure the chops are well-coated with the cornflakes.

These are nice and juicy, crisp on the outside.

MRS. ARCHIBALD McCLURE

RICE, MUSHROOM AND TUNA CASSEROLE

¾ c. uncooked rice
½ c. wild uncooked rice
2 cans tuna fish

2 c. rich cream sauce
¾ c. sharp cheese (grated)
1 4-oz. can mushrooms

Cook rice, braise mushrooms in butter. Season cream sauce with a little red pepper, marjoram and chopped parsley. Mix all ingredients together and put in casserole. Sprinkle a little cheese on top. Cook for 30 minutes in 300° oven. Serves 6.

MRS. ERIC BABENDREER

SAUSAGE AND RICE CASSEROLE

1 lb. sausage (links or patties)
2 large onions, sliced
1 c. uncooked rice

2 T. bacon grease
1 c. water
1 medium can tomatoes

Melt bacon grease in skillet and brown onion, rice and sausage (cut each link in 3 pieces or make small patties out of sausage meat). Pour off excess grease. When browned, pour in casserole with tomatoes and water, salt and pepper to taste. Bake for 1 hour in 350° oven. Top may be sprinkled with grated cheese. Serves 6.

MRS. ARCHIBALD MCCLURE

CREAMED SPINACH

2 pkg. frozen chopped spinach
1 garlic pod
½ stick butter

1 can mushroom soup
Salt and pepper to taste

Cook spinach and drain thoroughly. Grate garlic, put in skillet with butter and let simmer 3 to 4 minutes. Add spinach and mix thoroughly. Add can of mushroom soup and mix together well. This may be put in a casserole, covered with bread crumbs and baked in 325° oven until thoroughly heated. Or it may be kept warm in top of double boiler, if covered, for several hours.

MRS. GEORGE S. MILES

"Good for Gourmets"

CAFE BRULOT

2 strips lemon rind
2 strips orange rind
4 whole cloves
3 sugar dots

4 whole allspice
1 small stick cinnamon
1½ c. brandy
3 c. strong coffee (hot)

Heat brandy in large ladle. Ignite and pour over all other ingredients except coffee, which have been placed in brulot bowl or chafing dish. Continue ladling until sugar is dissolved. Gradually add coffee, ladling the mixture until the flames fade. Use as after-dinner coffee. Makes 8 small cups or 4 portions.

MRS. GUS MORGAN

SPICED TEA

24 c. boiling water
1 t. ground cinnamon
1 t. cloves
Juice of 3 lemons

Juice of 6 oranges
1 to 2 c. sugar
5 t. orange pekoe tea

Put cinnamon and cloves into a bag of cloth. In another bag put tea. Allow bags to steep in boiling water 5 minutes. Remove bags and add lemon juice, orange juice and sugar. Serve hot or cold. Serves 40.

MRS. W. GORTON BERRY

DRIPPED COFFEE CREOLE

This is only for real coffee-lovers. A French drip coffee pot is a must! You can buy them almost anywhere in Southern Louisiana.

Have a pot of boiling water on the stove. Set the coffee pot in hot water. Put into the dripper 2 level tablespoons coffee to a cup, if you like it strong. Pour the boiling water over the grounds frequently, ½ cup at a time. **Never let the coffee boil.** A tablespoon of chocolate dissolved in a little of the coffee, then added to the rest, gives a very special flavor.

MRS. HAROLD L. MCGEORGE

"Delight Them with Dessert"

RUSSIAN BLACK CHERRIES

1 No. 2 can black cherries   2 T. rum or whiskey
1 small glass currant jelly   ½ c. sour cream

Pit cherries and drain well. Combine with beaten jelly and rum. Place in refrigerator and chill several hours. Serve with sour cream. Serves 4 to 6.

MRS. KEITH M. SPURRIER, JR.

CHOCOLATE ICE CREAM

1 pkg. chocolate "Frostee"   2 T. cocoa
8-10 marshmallows, chopped   or 2 T. chocolate syrup

Follow directions on package, only add the cocoa or syrup during first beating and the chopped marshmallows during last beating. Serves 6.

MRS. R. CARL DICKERSON, JR.

GRAPEFRUIT DELIGHT

Grapefruit segments   Green or white grapes
Brown sugar   Créme de Menthe

Melt brown sugar with juice of fruit. Pour this over cold grapefruit, and cover with cold Créme de Menthe.

MRS. DUNBAR ABSTON, GERMANTOWN, TENN.

MACAROON PEACHES

1 can Raggedy Ann peaches   2 T. brandy, sherry or Kirsch
6 to 8 macaroons, crushed   1 c. heavy cream, whipped

Mix brandy with crushed macaroons and fill peaches. Bake in 350° oven 10 minutes. Serve with whipped cream while hot. Serves 6 to 8.

MRS. DUNBAR ABSTON, GERMANTOWN, TENN.

HOT APPLESAUCE DESSERT

Add a handful of raisins to hot sweetened applesauce. Spread over hot croutons. Sprinkle with sugar and cinnamon and chopped nuts.

BANANA DUCK DINNER DESSERT

2 T. butter
4 bananas
2 T. brown sugar

Juice of ½ lime
⅛ c. brandy

Sauté bananas in butter with brown sugar and lime juice, pour brandy over all, then ignite. Cooking time about 15 minutes.

This is an elegant dessert to prepare after the main course, when nothing else vital is on your mind.

MRS. FRANK PIDGEON, JR.

SLICED PEARS IN ORANGE JUICE

6 to 8 large ripe pears
2 large glasses orange juice

2 T. powdered sugar
2 T. Curacao

Squeeze, strain and chill thoroughly the glasses of orange juice. Ten minutes before serving, peel, core and slice the pears in very thin slices. Then sprinkle with powdered sugar. Add Curacao to the orange juice and pour over the pears. Serve with hot cookies. Serves 8 to 10.

MRS. ELIZABETH DANTZLER GRAYSON, BILOXI, MISS.

QUICK SPICED PEACHES

1 large can of peaches
½ c. white corn syrup

½ c. vinegar
1 T. pickling spice

Add spice and vinegar to the syrup. Boil 10 minutes. Add peaches and simmer 5 more minutes. Chill and serve. Serves 6.

MISS FRANCES GIBSON

PARFAIT DESSERT

Vanilla ice cream
Maraschino Cherries

Creme de Menthe

Fill parfait glasses with vanilla ice cream. Pour over top of each 2 teaspoonful Creme de Menthe. Top with a cherry. This may be varied by using lemon ice instead of vanilla ice cream.

It is a quick and delicious party dessert.

MRS. LEO J. BUCHIGNANI

"Hi, there! What'll y'have?"

"ANDY BROWN"

⅓ cherry cordial or brandy (cordial preferred), ⅔ white rum, a pinch of lemon juice and a mite of pineapple juice, shaken together with plenty of ice.

The legal limit should be one and even then, for heaven sake, hold onto your hat!

"DAIQUIRI COCKTAIL"

1 jigger rum	½ t. Curacao
1 t. sugar	1 t. orange juice

Combine ingredients and shake well with ice.

MRS. GEORGE S. MILES

"SPECIAL DAIQUIRI COCKTAIL"

1 jigger rum	4 to 5 mint leaves
1 t. sugar	1 t. lime juice

Blend above, ice and shake well.

MRS. GEORGE S. MILES

"GIN JULEP"

1½ jiggers gin	½ jigger simple mint syrup

Fill glass with crushed ice, gin and simple mint syrup. Top with a sprig of mint and a cherry. Put glasses in deep freeze 1 hour before using.

SIMPLE MINT SYRUP: Boil 1 cup of sugar with 1 cup of water and 1 large handful of mint. Strain.

MRS. EMMETT R. HALL

"BLOODY MARY"

To make 1 pint, use ½ tomato juice and ½ vodka. Add juice of 1 lemon, 1 tablespoon Worcestershire sauce, pepper and lots of salt. Stir or shake with ice and strain.

"HOT-WEATHER HI-BALL"

⅔ red wine, ⅓ soda water, 1 teaspoon of lemon, ice.

"MAJOR BAILEY"

Use your regular recipe for Planters Punch, but substitute gin for whiskey. Use extra mint.

"SPECIAL COCKTAIL"

2 T. sugar (heaping)	1 T. Angostura bitters
1 bottle 7-Up (6 oz.)	⅓ qt. sweet vermouth

Combine above ingredients in a quart bottle and fill rest of the bottle with good whiskey. Chill. This mixture will keep indefinitely.

Caution: Go slowly!

MRS. LOVICK P. MILES, JR.

"SUMMER STINGER"

60% gin, 40% white or green Creme de Menthe. Add a large twist of lime or lemon peel. Shake or stir with ice and serve very cold.

"SWAMP WATER"

1 part lemon juice	1 part rum
2 parts orange juice	Maraschino cherry juice to
Powdered sugar to taste	taste
1 part bourbon	

Mix, chill, serve in cocktail glasses garnished with a cherry or orange slice.

Guaranteed to be better than it sounds, and the perfect answer for guests who don't enjoy the taste of whiskey.

MRS. FRANK M. NORFLEET

"Hello, Come In—"

CHAMPAGNE COCKTAIL

Juice of 3 lemons $\frac{2}{3}$ bottle sauterne
2 T. sugar   1 bottle champagne

Dissolve sugar in a few drops of water and add to lemon juice. To this add sauterne wine. Stir well. Just before serving pour in champagne. **Do not stir.** Serve immediately. Be sure to have a cherry and small twist of lemon in each glass.

MRS. EDWARD A. HALL

CHAMPAGNE PUNCH

2 bottles light sauterne (dry) $\frac{1}{3}$ bottle light brandy or rum
1 qt. charged water $\frac{1}{2}$ c. lime juice
3 T. sugar

Dissolve sugar in lime juice and add brandy. Add sauterne and stir. Put in bowl with ice and add charged water.

This is a good imitation champagne and if you don't boast too much, you can get away with it. To serve the "Ladies Aiders," leave out the brandy and use a large can of pineapple juice.

MISS FRANCES E. SHIELDS

"CAFE ROYALE"

2 qt. strong coffee   1 qt. vanilla ice cream
1 qt. rum

Mix all ingredients except ice cream, beat well, add ice cream in spoonfuls. *Very good . . . rather like eggnog and easy to make.*

MRS. JAMES A. HUSTON

"COFFEE-NOG"

1 qt. vanilla ice cream $1\frac{1}{2}$ c. whiskey
1 c. strong black coffee

Shake together in shaker until ice cream is melted.

MRS. PEARL G. COOPER

DR. FREDRICK'S COCKTAILS

16 oz. orange wine
8 oz. bourbon
1 oz. gin
1 oz. lime juice

1 oz. Italian vermouth
1 oz. grenadine or simple
syrup

Combine in shaker, shake, add ice. Serve immediately.

Mrs. M. M. Jamieson

MOCK LEMONADE

1 pt. bourbon
½ pt. water

Juice of 3 lemons
3 T. sugar

Combine and let stand in bowl in cool place. Slice lemon peels and add to mixture. Let stand for 24 hours. Remove peels, pour over ice and serve.

Mrs. M. M. Jamieson

EGGNOG SUPREME

1¼ c. sugar
¼ c. water
8 to 12 eggs

½ pt. rye or bourbon
½ pt. brandy
1 qt. heavy cream, whipped

Put 1 cup of the sugar and all the water in a pan and boil until it threads. Let this cool slightly and beat into stiffly beaten whites. Add rest of sugar to well beaten yolks and mix thoroughly. Beat whiskey gradually into yolks and sugar. Add whites gradually, beating between each addition. Fold in whipped cream. Put in ice box for 3 hours. This will keep several days.

Mrs. Pearl G. Cooper

HOLIDAY PUNCH

1 qt. rum
1 qt. tea

2 c. lemon juice
1 c. melted sugar

Mix above ingredients. Add 1 quart of mixture to 1 quart of soda water.

Mrs. Howard S. Jeck, Jr.

"How Do You Do?"

RUM PUNCH

3 qt. rum
5 qt. charged water
3 c. sugar

1 pt. lemon juice
1 pt. orange juice

Mix sugar in lemon and orange juice. Add rum, then charged water. Pour over ice in large bowl. Serve when chilled. Yield: 60 punch cups.

Mrs. Walter P. Armstrong

KENNY'S EGGNOG

2 qt. heavy cream
2 doz. eggs
1½ c. sugar

1 qt. bourbon (corn whiskey the best)

Separate eggs and beat yolks until creamy. Whip sugar into yolks. Beat whites until they stand in peaks, adding ½ cup of sugar, if desired. Beat yolks and whiskey together, add whites. Add cream last. Makes 2½ gallons.

Mrs. Everett R. Cook, Germantown, Tenn.

CLARET CUP PUNCH

4 qt. claret
1 qt. rum
Juice of 2 doz. lemons
Juice of 2 doz. oranges

Juice of 2 pineapples (or 2 cups)
1 qt. sparkling water

Mix ingredients together and pour over block of ice in punch bowl.

Mrs. George S. Miles

PARTY MILK PUNCH

⅔ qt. bourbon
⅓ qt. cognac
½ qt. rum

2 qt. milk
1 qt. coffee cream
10 T. sugar

Chill all liquid ingredients in refrigerator. Mix together and serve in chilled bowl buried in ice. Grate nutmeg over top of punch. This recipe makes more than a gallon or about 30 servings. For an individual serving, substitute the word "jigger" for "quart", and use 1 teaspoon of sugar.

Mrs. Dore Fly

WINE CHART

Name	When to Serve	Temperature	Characteristic
Sherry	Cocktails Soup Oysters	Room Temperature	Dry or Sweet. Pale to Brown.
Sauterne Rhine Wine Other White Wines	Fish Seafood Chicken or all thru meal	20° below room temperature	Dry to Sweet. Light in color.
Chablis	Fish Seafood Meat, light or dark	20° below room temperature	Light straw color. Fruity flavor.
Claret Burgundy (still) Chianti	Red meat Game Lamb Spaghetti Cheese	Room temperature	Dry. Red in color.
Sparkling Burgundy	Red meat Game Lamb Thru meal	Thoroughly chilled	Dry. Red in color.
Champagne	Dry—Thru meal Sweet— Desserts	Thoroughly chilled	Dry to slightly sweet. Pale amber.
Port	Nuts Cheese Fruit	Room temperature	Deep Red. Rich, heavy, sweet.
Madeira Muscatel	With dessert	Room temperature	Pale to dark. Sweet.
Tokay	Fruit or Dessert	Room temperature or slightly chilled.	Amber. Sweet.
Liqueurs Brandy	Coffee after Dessert	Room temperature unless frappé	Colors vary. Very sweet.

General Rules

1. White wines should be stored in the ice box prior to serving and served cold.

2. Red wines should be served at room temperature.

3. Burgundy and Claret should be uncorked and placed in the room in which they are to be served for several hours before serving.

4. When removing the cork, hold the bottle with a napkin to allow for the possibility of breaking the neck. Wipe rim of bottle carefully before serving.

5. When opening sparkling wines hold bottle at 45° angle. Do not let cork fly out of hand.

6. Glasses should never be filled more than 2/3 full.

7. White wines are served with fish.

8. Red wines are served with meat, salad and cheese.

9. Champagne is usually served with dessert, but it is perfectly proper to serve it with any course and at all times during the meal.

10. Care should be taken never to follow a sweet wine by a dry wine, or a heavy wine by a light wine.

11. Wine should please the eye so avoid use of colored glasses.

12. Any good, sound, simple wine may be served throughout the meal. This is probably the best rule of all to remember.

HERB CHART

	Basil	Bay	Chervil	Marjoram	Mint	Oregano
Appe-tizers	Tomato and vegetable juices, stuffed celery, fish, pot cheese	Tomato juice, aspic	Garnish, stuffed eggs	Cheese, stuffed mushrooms, liver or mushroom pate', butters	Fruit cup, juice, ices, jellies, melon balls, cheese rolls	Tomato, guacamole
Soups	Tomato, vegetable, mock turtle, minestrone	Stock, bouquet garni	Spinach, sorrel, vichyssoise	Clam broth, mock turtle, onion, spinach, mushroom	Cream of split or fresh pea	Tomato, bean, minestrone
Egg & Cheese	Aspic, rarebit, all type eggs, cream cheese, fines herbes		Fines herbes for egg dishes, cream cheese	All type eggs, fines herbes for ramekins	Cream or cottage cheese	Boiled eggs, Huevos Rancheros
Fish	Shrimp, sole, cooked fish, butter sauce for mackerel	Court-bouillon, broiled, baked, creamed or pickled fish, shish kebab	In melted butter for fish sauce	Broiled, baked or creamed fish, in melted butter for white fish	In fines herbes for mackerel	In fish stuffings
Meat	Chopped meat, sausage, liver, lamb, spaghetti stews	Stews, pot roast, tripe, marinade for shish-kebab, water for kidneys	Butter sauce with Madeira for cutlets, Bearnaise sauce for filet	Pork, veal, beef, lamb, pot-roast, meat balls, veal stew, ravioli	In all stews, in sauce with vinegar for lamb, veal	Meat loaf, chili, lamb, sausage, pork, veal scallopini
Poultry & Game	Venison, stuffing, sauces for wild duck, fricassees	Stews, in water for stewing chicken, pot pie, fricassees	In melted butter for sauce, chicken	In stuffings for all fowl, over roasting goose, creamed chicken		Marinades, stuffings, pheasant, guinea hen
Vege-tables	Eggplant, peas, potatoes, tomatoes, onions, beans, spaghetti, squash, spinach	Stewed tomatoes, carrots, potatoes, zucchini		Peas, tomatoes, beans, egg-plant, squash, asparagus, carrots, rice, mushrooms	Peas, carrots, potatoes, zucchini, spinach with nutmeg	Tomatoes, cabbage, lentils, broccoli
Salads	Green, fish, vegetable, tomato, celery, vinegar	Tomato aspic, fish	Alone in French dressing over greens	Green, chicken, in vinegar for asparagus	Fruit, green, cole slaw	Tomato aspic, fish
Sauces	Tomato, mustard paste, spaghetti, orange for game, butter for fish	Marinades, Espagnole, Champagne, spaghetti	Madeira, Bearnaise, in butter for fish, chicken vinaigrette	In lemon sauce, cream, brown and sour cream	Mint sauce, curry	Spaghetti, tomato, all paste sauces, Italian
Dessert & Bev-erage		Fruit cup, fruit drinks	Custards and creams		Fruit, ices, frostings, fruit drink, tea, juleps, rum or gin cocktails	

HERB CHART

	Rosemary	Saffron	Sage	Savory	Tarragon	Thyme
Appetizers	Fruit cup	Saffron butter	Pot cheese, cottage or cheddar	Tomato and vegetable juices, liver sausage	Tomato juice, fish, fruit cocktail, Ravigote butter	Aspic, tomato and vegetable juices, fish, cheese
Soup	Spinach, pea, turtle, tomato, chicken, bouquet garni	Bouillabaisse, fish, consomme, chicken	Fish chowder, cream soups	Lentil, split pea, consomme', vegetable, fish, bean	Chicken, tomato, consomme', turtle, mushroom	Onion, tomato, broth, chowder, oyster stew
Egg & Cheese	In fines herbes, omelette, scrambled eggs	Cream cheese, scrambled eggs	Cream, cottage or cheddar cheese	In fines herbes, deviled or scrambled eggs	Deviled eggs, all egg dishes, omelette	Eggs In fines herbes, tomato sauce, cottage cheese
Fish	Salmon stuffing	Halibut, sole	Stuffings, use sparingly with salt fish	Stuffed bass, broiled or baked fish	Frog legs, broiled fish, Lobster Thermidor, butter sauce	Bouillabaisse, broiled, fried or baked fish, lobster water
Meat	Beef, veal, with sage over pork roast, ham loaf, lamb	Veal	Pork roast, sausage, stews, meat loaf, skewered meat	Pork, veal, beef, with sage in sausage	Bearnaise sauce, veal, sweetbreads, Yorkshire pudding	Stuffed veal, mutton, stews, roast beef, pork, meat loaf, chopped meat
Poultry & Game	Bouquet garni for fricassees, capon-duck, rabbit, partridge	Arroz con pollo, curries, chicken	Stuffings for all fowl, goose, turkey, rabbit	Chicken fricassee, poultry stuffing	Any chicken dish, duck, squab	All fowl stuffings, venison, fricassees, rabbit
Vegetables	Spinach, peas, French fried potatoes	Risotto, rice, Spanish rice	Stewed tomatoes, string beans, onions, lima beans, eggplant	Beans, lentils, peas, savory rice, sauerkraut, tomatoes	Tomatoes, mushrooms, beets, greens, potatoes, peas	Rice, carrots, onions, peas, tomato, egg-plant, beets, potatoes
Salads	Fruit salads	Fish	Cream or cottage cheese	Stuffed tomato, green, string bean, salad dressings	Chicken, fish, aspic, green, alone with chervil	Tomato, vegetable, pickled beets, French dressing
Sauces	Cream sauce, spaghetti, jelly	Fish		Horse-radish, fish sauce, tomato sauce, meat gravy	Cream sauce, butter sauce, mustard, tartare, fish, verte	Creole, tomato, meat, fish, espagnole
Dessert & Beverage	Fruit compote, gin punch	Frostings, buns, cake	Sage tea	Stewed pears, pear compote		

Bouquet Garni   ½ t. each of dried basil, thyme, marjoram, savory, or other herbs . . . celery, parsley, etc.

2 parts of sweet marjoram, savory, thyme; 1 part basil; ½ part sage, bay, celery tops and dried lemon peel.

WEIGHTS, MEASURES and EQUIVALENTS

EQUIVALENTS

A	few grains	less than $\frac{1}{8}$ teaspoon
1	coffee spoon	$\frac{1}{4}$ teaspoon
3	teaspoons	1 tablespoon
2	tablespoons	1 fluid ounce
$1\frac{1}{2}$	ounce	1 jigger
$\frac{1}{2}$	jigger	1 pony
16	tablespoons	1 cup
1	cup	$\frac{1}{2}$ pint
2	pints	1 quart
4	cups	1 quart
4	quarts	1 gallon
8	quarts	1 peck
4	pecks	1 bushel
16	ounces	1 pound
X	cream	coffee cream
XX	cream	whipping cream

1	pound flour	3 cups
1	pound butter	2 cups
$\frac{1}{2}$	pound butter	2 sticks
1	stick butter	$\frac{1}{2}$ cup or 8 tablespoons
$\frac{1}{4}$	pound grated cheese	1 cup
1	pound cheese	$4\frac{1}{2}$ cups
1	pound brown sugar (1 box)	$2\frac{2}{3}$ cups
1	pound confectioners (1 box)	$2\frac{1}{2}$-3 cups (powdered or XXXX sugar)
1	pound granulated sugar	2 cups
1	pound lump sugar	55-70 lumps
1	pound seeded raisins	$2\frac{1}{2}$ cups
1	pound seedless raisins	3 cups
1	pound coffee	5 cups—yield 40-50 cups of coffee
1	pound rice	2 cups—yield 3-4 cups cooked rice
1	square chocolate	1 ounce or 3 tablespoons grated chocolate
$\frac{1}{2}$	pound marshmallows	16 marshmallows
1	pound crab meat	2 cups
1	pound pitted dates	2 cups
1	pound figs (chopped)	3 cups
1	pound nut meats (chopped)	4 cups
1	cup noodles	$1\frac{1}{2}$ cups when cooked
1	egg	$\frac{1}{4}$ cup
5	eggs	1 cup
9	eggs	1 pound
8-10	egg whites	1 cup
16	egg yolks	1 cup
1	lemon, average size	3 tablespoons juice, 3 tablespoons rind
1	orange	$\frac{1}{2}$ cup juice
4	medium tomatoes	1 pound
3	large bananas (skin on)	1 pound
2	quarts apples	3 pounds
4	medium potatoes	1 pound
1	pound peas, in pod	1 cup when shelled

12 quarts punch	96 punch glasses
1 gallon punch	serves 20
12 pound ham	serves 20
20 pound turkey (or chickens)	serves 20 generously
1 gallon ice cream	serves 30 if scoop is used
11 inch casserole	serves 8 amply
A 4 pound chicken	yields 4 cups diced chicken

SUBSTITUTIONS

1 sq. chocolate	$2\frac{2}{3}$ T. cocoa plus $\frac{1}{2}$ T. butter
1 T. cornstarch	2 T. flour (for thickening)
1 t. baking powder	$\frac{1}{4}$ t. soda and $\frac{1}{2}$ t. cream tartar
1 c. sugar	1 c. honey and $\frac{1}{2}$ t. soda (reduce liquid in recipe $\frac{1}{4}$ c.)
	1 c. maple syrup and $\frac{1}{4}$ t. soda (reduce liquid in recipe $\frac{1}{4}$ c.)
	1 c. molasses and $\frac{1}{2}$ t. soda (reduce liquid in recipe $\frac{1}{4}$ c.)
	$\frac{1}{2}$ c. maple syrup and $\frac{1}{4}$ c. corn syrup (reduce liquid in recipe $\frac{1}{4}$ c.)
1 c. molasses	1 c. honey
1 c. milk	$\frac{1}{2}$ c. evaporated milk and $\frac{1}{2}$ c. water.
	$\frac{1}{2}$ c. condensed milk and $\frac{1}{2}$ c. water (reduce sugar in recipe)
	4 T. powdered milk and 1 c. water.
1 c. butter	4/5 c. bacon fat (clarified) increase liquid in recipe $\frac{1}{4}$ c.
	$\frac{2}{3}$ c. chicken fat, clarified (increase liquid in recipe $\frac{1}{4}$ c.)
	$\frac{7}{8}$ c. cottonseed, corn, nut oil (solid or liquid)
	$\frac{7}{8}$ c. lard and salt
	$\frac{1}{2}$ c. suet and salt (increase liquid in recipe $\frac{1}{4}$ c.)
1 c. sour milk	1 c. sweet milk and 1 T. lemon juice or vinegar

SIZES OF CANS

No. 1	can	$1\frac{1}{2}$	cupfuls used for baked beans, meats, soups, fruits, veg.
No. 1	(tall)	2	cupfuls
No. 2	can	$2\frac{1}{2}$	cupfuls used for beans, peas, and corn
No. $2\frac{1}{2}$	can	$3\frac{1}{2}$	cupfuls used for tomatoes, spinach, beets, and pumpkin
No. 3	can	4	cupfuls
No. 10	can	1	gallon used for both fruits and vegetables
No. 5	can	7	cupfuls (almost $\frac{1}{2}$ gallon) used for fruit juice

OVEN TEMPERATURE CHART

	Degrees Fahrenheit
Slow oven	250°-325°
Moderate oven	325°-375°
Quick or hot oven	400°-450°
Very hot oven	450°-550°

TERMS USED IN COOKING

BLANCH—To immerse fruits or nuts in boiling water to remove skins, also to dip fruits and vegetables in boiling water in preparation for canning, freezing or drying.

BRAISE—To brown meat or vegetables in small quantity of hot fat, then to cook slowly in small amount of liquid.

CLARIFY—To clear a liquid, such as consommé, by adding slightly beaten egg white and egg shells. The beaten egg coagulates in the hot liquid and the particles which cause cloudiness adhere to it. The mixture is then strained.

COATS SPOON—When a mixture forms a thin even film on the spoon.

FOLD IN—To combine two ingredients or two combinations of ingredients by two motions, cutting vertically through the mixture and turning over and over by sliding the implement across the bottom of the mixing bowl with each turn.

FLAMBE—Sprinkled with brandy or a liqueur and ignited.

JULIENNE—Food cut in very thin strips.

LARD—To insert strips or pieces of fat into uncooked lean meat for added flavor and juiciness. Or slices of fat may be spread on top of uncooked lean meat or fish for the same purpose.

MACEDOINE—A mixture of fruits or vegetables.

MARINATE—To let foods stand in a marinade, usually an acid-oil mixture of oil and vinegar or wine, often flavored with spices and herbs.

MINCE—To cut with knife or scissors into very fine pieces.

PAN-BROIL—To cook uncovered on a hot surface, usually a skillet. The fat is poured off as it accumulates.

PAN FRY—To cook in a small amount of fat; synonymous with sauté.

PARBOIL—To boil until partially cooked.

PUREE—To force vegetables, fruits and other foods through a fine sieve to remove skins, seeds and so forth, and to produce a fine-textured substance.

RAGOUT—A thick, well-seasoned stew.

REDUCE—To evaporate some of the liquid in stock or sauce by boiling.

RENDER—To heat meat fat, cut in small pieces, until fat is separated from connective tissues.

SAUTE—To fry lightly in a small amount of hot fat, turning frequently.

SCALD—To heat a liquid to just below the boiling point. Milk has reached a scalding point when film forms on surface.

SCORE—To cut narrow grooves or gashes.

SEAR—To cook at a very high temperature for a short time in order quickly to form a brown crust on the outer surface of meat.

SIMMER—To cook in a liquid that is kept below the boiling point. Bubbles form slowly and break below the surface.

STOCK—A liquid in which vegetables or meat has been cooked.

INDEX

KEY TO ABBREVIATIONS USED

c.—cup(s)
t.—teaspoon(s)
T.—tablespoon(s)
pt.—pint(s)
qt.—quart(s)

gal.—gallon(s)
oz.—ounce(s)
lb.—pound(s)
pkg.—package(s)
min.—minute(s)

hr.—hour(s)
in.—inch(es)
diam.—diameter
doz.—dozen

RECIPES SHOWN ON COVER:

MEMPHIS JUNIOR LEAGUE PUBLICATIONS
2711 Union Ave., Extended
Memphis, Tennessee 38112

	Unit Price	Postage	TN Tax	TOTAL
Please send me:				
_____copies of **PARTY POTPOURRI**	$14.95	$2.00	$1.16	_____
_____copies of **THE MEMPHIS COOKBOOK**	9.95	1.75	.77	_____
_____copies of **A MAN'S TASTE**	7.95	1.75	.62	_____

Enclosed is my check or money order for $_____

Name _____

Address _____

City _____

Make checks payable to Memphis Junior League Publications.

· ·

MEMPHIS JUNIOR LEAGUE PUBLICATIONS
2711 Union Ave., Extended
Memphis, Tennessee 38112

	Unit Price	Postage	TN Tax	TOTAL
Please send me:				
_____copies of **PARTY POTPOURRI**	$14.95	$2.00	$1.16	_____
_____copies of **THE MEMPHIS COOKBOOK**	9.95	1.75	.77	_____
_____copies of **A MAN'S TASTE**	7.95	1.75	.62	_____

Enclosed is my check or money order for $_____

Name _____

Address _____

City _____

Make checks payable to Memphis Junior League Publications.

· ·

MEMPHIS JUNIOR LEAGUE PUBLICATIONS
2711 Union Ave., Extended
Memphis, Tennessee 38112

	Unit Price	Postage	TN Tax	TOTAL
Please send me:				
_____copies of **PARTY POTPOURRI**	$14.95	$2.00	$1.16	_____
_____copies of **THE MEMPHIS COOKBOOK**	9.95	1.75	.77	_____
_____copies of **A MAN'S TASTE**	7.95	1.75	.62	_____

Enclosed is my check or money order for $_____

Name _____

Address _____

City _____

Make checks payable to Memphis Junior League Publications.

FREE COPY AVAILABLE

Send names and addresses of stores in your area that may be interested in handling *MCB*. If any of the stores you suggest order, you will receive one free copy.

_____

_____

_____

_____

_____

_____

_____

FREE COPY AVAILABLE

Send names and addresses of stores in your area that may be interested in handling *MCB*. If any of the stores you suggest order, you will receive one free copy.

_____

_____

_____

_____

_____

_____

FREE COPY AVAILABLE

Send names and addresses of stores in your area that may be interested in handling *MCB*. If any of the stores you suggest order, you will receive one free copy.

_____

_____

_____

_____

_____

_____

MEMPHIS JUNIOR LEAGUE PUBLICATIONS
2711 Union Ave., Extended
Memphis, Tennessee 38112

	Unit Price	Postage	TN Tax	TOTAL
Please send me:				
_____copies of **PARTY POTPOURRI**	$14.95	$2.00	$1.16	_____
_____copies of **THE MEMPHIS COOKBOOK**	9.95	1.75	.77	_____
_____copies of **A MAN'S TASTE**	7.95	1.75	.62	_____

Enclosed is my check or money order for $_____

Name _____

Address _____

City _____

Make checks payable to Memphis Junior League Publications.

. . . .

MEMPHIS JUNIOR LEAGUE PUBLICATIONS
2711 Union Ave., Extended
Memphis, Tennessee 38112

	Unit Price	Postage	TN Tax	TOTAL
Please send me:				
_____copies of **PARTY POTPOURRI**	$14.95	$2.00	$1.16	_____
_____copies of **THE MEMPHIS COOKBOOK**	9.95	1.75	.77	_____
_____copies of **A MAN'S TASTE**	7.95	1.75	.62	_____

Enclosed is my check or money order for $_____

Name _____

Address _____

City _____

Make checks payable to Memphis Junior League Publications.

. . . .

MEMPHIS JUNIOR LEAGUE PUBLICATIONS
2711 Union Ave., Extended
Memphis, Tennessee 38112

	Unit Price	Postage	TN Tax	TOTAL
Please send me:				
_____copies of **PARTY POTPOURRI**	$14.95	$2.00	$1.16	_____
_____copies of **THE MEMPHIS COOKBOOK**	9.95	1.75	.77	_____
_____copies of **A MAN'S TASTE**	7.95	1.75	.62	_____

Enclosed is my check or money order for $_____

Name _____

Address _____

City _____

Make checks payable to Memphis Junior League Publications.

FREE COPY AVAILABLE

Send names and addresses of stores in your area that may be interested in handling *MCB.* If any of the stores you suggest order, you will receive one free copy.

_____

_____

_____

_____

_____

_____

FREE COPY AVAILABLE

Send names and addresses of stores in your area that may be interested in handling *MCB.* If any of the stores you suggest order, you will receive one free copy.

_____

_____

_____

_____

_____

_____

FREE COPY AVAILABLE

Send names and addresses of stores in your area that may be interested in handling *MCB.* If any of the stores you suggest order, you will receive one free copy.

_____

_____

_____

_____

_____

_____